Guerrilla Travel Tactics

Guerrilla Travel Tactics

Hundreds of Simple Strategies Guaranteed to Save Road Warriors Time and Money

JAY CONRAD LEVINSON

THEO BRANDT-SARIF

American Management Association

New York • Atlanta • Brussels • Chicago • Mexico City • San Francisco
Shanghai • Tokyo • Toronto • Washington, D.C.

Special discounts on bulk quantities of AMACOM books are available to corporations, professional associations, and other organizations. For details, contact Special Sales Department, AMACOM, a division of American Management Association, 1601 Broadway, New York, NY 10019.
Tel.: 212-903-8316. Fax: 212-903-8083.
Web site: www.amacombooks.org

Library of Congress Cataloging-in-Publication Data

Levinson, Jay Conrad.
Guerrilla travel tactics : hundreds of simple strategies guaranteed to save road warriors time and money / Jay Conrad Levinson, Theo Brandt-Sarif.
p. cm.
ISBN 0-8144-7170-6
1. Business travel. I. Brandt-Sarif, Theo. II. Title.

G156.5.B86L48 2004
910'.2'02—dc22

2003025986

Printing number

10 9 8 7 6 5 4 3 2 1

Contents

Preface

If you're a business traveler, what you don't know about travel can hurt you. In the pocketbook. On the road. At the airport. At the hotel. In large cities. In small towns. At home. In foreign countries. Yet, the pain of ignorance is felt by business travelers every single day and on every continent. I hear a resounding "ouch!" What makes the pain go away? Knowledge. Strategies. Information. Insights. Enlightenment. Just the kind of wisdom contained in this book.

Guerrilla travelers achieve conventional goals using unconventional means. This means you'll get where you need to . . . or where you've always wanted to visit, only now you'll learn new ways of getting there, ways that can save you scads of money, avoid inconvenience, prevent frustration. As one who has traveled the world extensively, I consider myself not only a road warrior, but one who has made all the mistakes possible, including several bordering on the impossible. I've overpaid on every one of the continents, failed to capitalize on a galaxy of bargains, truly been a poster child for unsophisticated, needlessly expensive travel on land, sea, and air. But I have learned from my mistakes, and with this book, you can too.

These aren't tactics reserved for the rich and famous, the connected and powerful. These are tactics available to any traveler at any time. These are tactics that can save you a whale of a lot of money—and I'm referring to the largest whale that ever prowled the ocean deep.

Guerrilla travel tactics involve the how-to's of travel, along with the where-to's, the when-to's, and even the why-to's. Did you know that the most efficient way of reaching hotel reservation departments is by fax? It's the truth. Did it ever dawn on you that strategies for obtaining the best values in coach-class airfares are very different from those for business or first class? Did you realize that just three mileage-earning credit and charge cards tower above all the rest when it comes to maximizing free travel?

I'm just barely scratching the surface when I disclose these money-saving gems to you, and I'm only referring to saving on hotel rates. There are mind-boggling tactics that can also help you save big money on car rentals and flights. There are eleven chapters devoted entirely to helping you save huge money on air travel. There are tips for getting the most from your online connection and using the Internet to save monster amounts of money. You'll learn which credit cards to use—and which not to use—when traveling. You'll be given the lowdown on nonrefundable airline tickets. Most of all, you'll be given the proper mindset to cut your travel costs drastically. And you'll learn the best strategies for obtaining value. Value is, after all, the name of the travel game.

The astute road warrior means business when he or she travels, but far too many are clueless when it comes to gaining the most for their travel dollar. Businesslike they are not when they leave the confines of their office for the airport. Information they gained when they first began in business has been replaced by more current information. If you're a road warrior—and if you're a true-blue guerrilla—you'll make it your business not only to learn these travel tactics, but to save a fortune by putting them to use. It's incredibly easy. In many cases, it's painfully obvious. But I guess it's not that obvious or there would be no need for this book. Instead, there is a crying need for this book. And as a guerrilla, you need only to breathe life into these tactics with your own travel.

At this point, I'm not certain whether to give you a hearty "Bon voyage!" or a wink and a high five for learning what savvy business travelers—but not the travel industry—want you to know. I'll tell you what: Here are my congratulations for being poised on the threshold of a whole new travel mentality . . . and here are my wishes for a delightfully frugal bon voyage!

Jay Conrad Levinson, Marin County, California

Acknowledgments

Theo Brandt-Sarif would like to thank:

My father and mother, who gave me the courage to explore new frontiers and instilled my passion to travel.

Jeff Herman, our agent, for his expert guidance.

Ellen Kadin, senior acquisitions editor at AMACOM, who has the patience of a saint.

Mike Sivilli, associate editor at AMACOM, for his excellent editing.

Susan Lerner and Jean Lynott, for their incredible research skills.

Patrick Lynott and Danielle Lerner, who did much of the groundwork for the appendixes.

Randy Gage, for his ongoing guidance on how this book should be.

Vicki McGown, the editor-in-chief, who made our writing come alive.

Philip Wolf, Internet visionary, who has taught me so much about online travel.

Tracie Grossman at United Airlines, who exemplifies outstanding customer service.

My inspiring children—Trevor, Justin, and Lauren—who transform my trips into magical experiences and memories of a lifetime.

And above all, to my wife and soul mate Deborah, who has stood by me like a rock.

Where not specified, any stories contained in this book may reflect the experiences of either author.

Since the travel industry is highly volatile, information provided in this book may change. The book is intended to be a guide to travel strategies rather than providing a detailed overview of every rule and regulation. Please be sure to verify information provided with the supplier or vendor concerned.

Guerrilla Travel Tactics

CHAPTER ONE

Fasten Your Seat Belts—We're About to Take Off

I'd like you to take a minute and remember your college days. Were you one of those people ready to try weird and wild things and considered it all a wonderful adventure? What about traveling—were you like so many college students who gamely set off for Europe, prepared to hitchhike for a month, fortified with few dollars but lots of optimism? Were you like me fifteen years ago—an MBA student huddled in a sleeping bag on the deck of a state ship, cruising through Alaska for just $200?

Now, switch gears, think again for a few more seconds, and imagine yourself on your dream trip—no expenses spared. Which way would you rather travel? If you want luxury at a fraction of its cost, read on.

Soon after I completed my MBA in 1986, I met and married the woman who is truly my soul mate. One of the things we have most in common is that we both love to travel. During the summer of 2000, we went on a *dream* trip with both our sons. This was no Chevy Chase/*National Lampoon* kind of vacation, but the luxury trip of a lifetime the whole family enjoyed. Many of my seminar participants, when they see our sixty-five–night, around-the-world itinerary, ask, "Will you adopt me?" "That's not necessary," I tell them, "if you just follow the strategies I give you." In this book, I reveal those same strategies so you, too, can not only travel in style, but get the most for your travel dollar.

What do you think it would cost to go around the world, living in luxury for two whole months and covering *all* travel *and* daily living expenses? Some of the highlights our family of four enjoyed:

Staying at the Singapore Ritz Carlton in a huge four-room suite, with all rooms—and the bathtub—overlooking the city of Singapore

Traveling *first class* across Japan on the bullet train, the fastest in the world, from Tokyo all the way south to Kyoto, and back

Flying British Airways business class roundtrip from Los Angeles to London and Nairobi

Cruising Alaska on a luxury Princess ship

Along the way we shopped in Singapore, laid on the gorgeous beaches of Bali, were humbled by Hiroshima, savored salad Niçoise in Paris, were thrilled by the magnificence of the French and Italian Rivieras, delighted in watching our children's faces when they hand-fed a giraffe in Kenya, marveled at the economic miracle of beautiful Ireland.

Most people would say at least $250 per person each day, maybe even $400 per day, which would be closer to the retail price. I'll tell you the answer. It cost us $84 per person, per day. Now, *remember*, this included ALL travel costs, meals, even the photos—let's not forget those Kodak moments.

In this book, you will learn the strategies that helped make this trip possible—the same strategies you can use to do what we did.

Why Do We Need to Save on Travel?

In today's business environment, we need to *make more* money, but it's just as important to find legitimate ways to spend it wisely. Nowhere is this more relevant than in travel, since airfares and hotel costs have been volatile over the past five years.

The tragedies of September 11 placed a short-term dampener on airfares. However, indirect costs to travelers have included restructuring of airlines by dramatically reducing capacity and decreasing availability of flights, the laying off of staff with a corresponding drop in customer service and morale, and attempts to tighten security with significant inconveniences. The travel experience has been made more arduous not only by airfares creeping up, but also by increases in penalties associated with nonrefundable tickets, by costly new rules for excess baggage, and by cutbacks in meal service. An emerging variable to factor in to the travel planning process is an inversion of the old paradigm, whereby the typical leisure traveler purchased travel far in advance, while the business traveler sought airline tickets and hotel accommodation at the last minute. Specifically, we are now seeing an increase in the leisure travelers planning trips at the last minute and business travelers purchasing tickets in advance. This adds another layer of complexity to how travel suppliers will price their product. Similarly, as hotel occupancy rates have edged up toward prior highs, hotel rates have moved in tandem. All of these changes challenge the patience and resilience of world travelers and road warriors alike. With this book, however, we promise to help you find your way through the maze that travel has become, confident that you know how to get the best service for your travel dollar.

According to American Express Travel Service's annual surveys of their business clients, travel and entertainment have been the second-largest controllable business expense after salaries. The Professional Sales Association indicates that entrepreneurs and sales professionals spend an average of fifty-seven nights away from home each year. Even Internet-focused companies acknowledge that truly understanding a client or closing a sale requires face-to-face communication.

So how can we help you survive the challenges of travel post–September 11? Through trial and error—and sometimes paying too much—we have learned how to travel in luxury for (much, much) less. We have invested decades researching, analyzing, and testing all the intricate rules and regulations, all the Web sites, all the books on the topic of travel savings. Obviously, we have spent huge amounts of time and money gathering this valuable information, all in one place, and refining it for ease of understanding. Before today, it has never been presented in one book geared exclusively to sophisticated world travelers and road warriors fed up with paying rising prices for air, hotels, and car rentals—all while being pressured to downgrade.

Won't Your Travel Agent Help You Utilize All These Strategies?

The first key principle of travel savings is that *you* are the sole person responsible for obtaining great values for your travel needs. Neither travel suppliers (airlines, hotels, and so on) nor travel agents have the responsibility for expending the time and energy to find exceptional values, or even informing you when they may know of better values. In fact, if anything, just the opposite holds true.

Suppliers in all industries inevitably seek to get the highest amount for a given product or service; airlines, hotels, and car rental companies are no different. It gets even worse when we consider travel agents: Agency commissions from airlines were cut back dramatically in 1997, thereby providing the impetus to charge service fees and scale back their efforts to find exceptional value for budget-conscious travelers. In 2002, airline companies reduced travel agent commissions to zero! Still, travel agents may have preferred override agreements with an airline, meaning they receive a special commission for booking in volume with a specific airline—a little secret they will not divulge to you, the traveler. However, the only two products that consistently provide travel agents with commissions of 10 percent or higher are packages/tours and cruises. Don't be surprised when travel agents try to steer your vacation plans toward these prepackaged arrangements.

Within these pages, we expose those secrets jealously guarded by travel insiders and industry suppliers. You won't learn about them from your travel agent—in fact, he will likely tell you that what we advise is impractical or even impossible. Don't believe it. We've done it and so can you.

Finally, are we completely pessimistic regarding the potential for travel agents assisting the world traveler or road warrior? Absolutely not! There are several instances where a travel agent with specific expertise or attention to excellence in service can be worth his or her weight in gold (and then some). . . .

Won't Saving Money Take Up Too Much of My Time?

The more money you want to save, the more time you will need to invest, especially as you acquire basic skills. It's just like learning how to select mutual funds or deliver a performance review. The more time you put in—especially when starting out—the more you will save.

We acknowledge that there are points in your career when you have more time than money, and points when you have more money than time. Many of the ideas you will learn from this book apply to anybody with an interest in basic cost management—regardless of your financial situation. It's like taking your vitamins and flossing your teeth. You may choose not to take advantage of *all* the skills you can learn, but just know that these powerful strategies are available to you. And we guarantee that as prudent world travelers and road warriors, each of you will find certain strategies in the following chapters that are perfect for your unique circumstances.

What Is "Value in Travel"?

Guerrilla travelers never pay full price for their airfares, hotels, or car rentals. Retail travel prices are outrageously high, and most times serve as little more than a standard to make the majority of customers feel good when they get a discount! But savvy world travelers and seasoned road warriors know the value of a dollar. Also, being much smarter than the average business traveler, whose company reimburses every travel expense, they are always on the prowl for *deep* discounts.

So who determines what value is? You do! Let's take an example. Which is a better value: $150 at a Hilton Hotel or $250 at a Four Season Hotel? There is no right answer since it is *you* who gets to decide. Value is ultimately a subjective matter that for some people simply means getting rock-bottom prices, while for others it may be obtaining lots of value-added services. The important point to remember is that the smart traveler knows what he wants and will do whatever it takes to achieve his goals.

While value is absolutely "in the eyes of the beholder," we can provide you with a benchmark. When the money comes out of our pockets—for business or leisure—it is unusual for us to pay more than $700 for a roundtrip airfare outside the United States or $500 roundtrip for domestic travel; $200 per day for a hotel room abroad or $120 for one in the United States; or $100 per day for an international car rental or $65 here at home. This holds true no matter where we travel, no matter what the circumstances.

Taking an Integrated Approach

One of the keys to slashing travel costs is to apply an integrated strategy, much like choosing a mix of stocks, bonds, and mutual funds to build your wealth. Specifically, by applying what resembles a portfolio of tactics, sophisticated world travelers and road warriors will choose from, and often combine, sale pricing, promotions, discount coupons, upgrade certificates, frequent flyer miles/hotel points, and Internet-only pricing to ensure rock-bottom prices with established brands.

Skill or Experience—Which Is Important for Guerrilla Travelers?

The answer is—both! This book will help you acquire the core set of skills it takes to be a world-class road warrior. As with any endeavor, guerrilla travel is a skill set that is refined by practice and experience. The more you travel, the better you will become at identifying savings opportunities. These skills feed upon themselves . . . the more you practice them, the better you will become. This book aims to teach you the basic skills, but experience can only be gained one way—by doing it!

Even though this book taps into the extensive collective experience of its co-authors, we could never cover every eventuality! Furthermore, so much of what constitutes "experience" is specific to each of our unique circumstances. This story illustrates the point.

I landed at New York's JFK airport late one winter evening just after midnight, right after a huge snowstorm. With treacherous road conditions, the line for taxicabs was outrageously long, and I realized it would take several hours before I'd be in a cab and on the road to my Manhattan hotel. Looking for alternatives, I asked around and found I could take a bus to the nearby train station, which would connect me to the subway into New York City. A bit more of hassle than a cab, but I decided I'd rather be moving toward my goal. I jumped on the next inner circle airport transport headed to the subway station. When the bus stopped to pick up riders at the next terminal, I noticed a line of taxis—with no customers! I jumped off the bus and into a cab, and was on my way into the city in less than one minute! I have never read about this strategy or heard anyone talk about it, but it has served me well several times since. At peak travel times,

I will not hesitate to go from one terminal to another in search of a short line for taxis. Experience is a great teacher.

The Critical Importance of Focus

Another key to being a guerrilla traveler is to focus on a few effective strategies that provide a huge "bang for the buck." Learn to do those things very well and keep duplicating these few strategies. For example, know every subtlety and minutia of your favorite airline's frequent flyer program.

Let's finish up with one more piece of advice regarding the critical importance of focus. The 80/20 rule applies for guerrilla travelers as much as it does for salespeople (or any other endeavor)—80 percent of the "profit" emanates from just 20 percent of the effort. In our final chapter, "The Last Word," we summarize the travel survival strategies we believe have the highest priority, the ones that will provide you with the biggest bang for the buck. You may even want to read the final chapter before you begin reviewing the body of content that makes up the bulk of this book.

Try Different Strategies Until You Find One That Works for You!

As we weave our way through a variety of ideas, it should be understood that no one strategy works every time, in every circumstance. In fact, the reason we illustrate so many different tips is because you never know which one will work. If a hotel is not offering one type of discount, ask about another. And even another. Be persistent. What we shall provide you with is a toolbox from which you can select the tool that best fits the job. Your task is to become adept at using those tools that consistently work well for your unique travel patterns and habits.

And diversify. For example, accumulate frequent flyer miles in as many programs as possible so that if one airline has no available award seats for the dates you want, you can try another. Remember, you can never be too rich, too beautiful, too thin—or have too many frequent flyer miles!

Are Some Strategies Likely to Be More Effective Than Others?

We've written this book to help you get the most information in the least amount of time. In each section, you will find that the first strategy is the most important one. Stated differently, everything you see is prioritized, so the first bullet point is the most important, with decreasing importance as you go down. We suggest you eventually try them all. But if you are going to implement just one or two strategies, start with those that we present first within each chapter. These few will give you the biggest payoff for the least investment of time.

In Summary

- Everybody can travel in luxury for (much, much) less. In this book, we shall reveal little-known money-saving strategies you can use to enjoy more upscale travel, but at unbelievably low prices.
- It doesn't matter whether you travel for business or leisure—we guarantee that if you implement the strategies you learn in this book, you will transform your travel budget and enhance your comfort!
- Spend time acquiring a few skills and keep replicating these skills to save tons of money over a prolonged period of time!
- Saving on travel is like managing a portfolio—you use a variety of different strategies to maximize your returns while minimizing the risk, depending on each unique circumstance.
- Stay focused: Using just a few "high-yield" strategies will save you boatloads of money, while conserving your precious time.

CHAPTER TWO

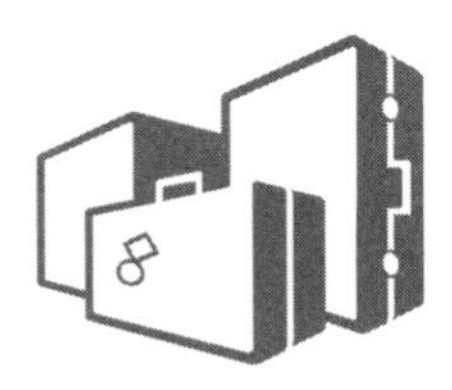

Airfare Savings—Part I

Saturday Night Fever and the Power of 7, 14, and 21

Two years ago, while making plans to attend the National Speakers Association's annual meeting, I diligently went to work, following the principles in this book to try and find a great airfare. My research paid off when I booked a terrific sale fare at the rock-bottom price of $252 for a Los Angeles to Philadelphia nonstop roundtrip ticket. Feeling pleased with myself—especially since I had a $100 discount coupon I could apply for additional savings, bringing the fare down to an unheard of $152—I stopped by a United office not far from my house the following day to pay for my ticket.

"With the discount coupon, your fare comes to $468," the agent told me.

"What?" I sputtered. "What happened to the $252 fare I was quoted yesterday?"

She gave me a sympathetic smile. "I'm sorry. Evidently there's been a fare increase since then. And I'm sure you know that your fare is never guaranteed until paid for."

Pay strict attention to ticketing deadlines given by the airlines and other travel companies. Know the rules and apply them correctly. If you don't, you may find yourself paying more for an airfare than you anticipated—or losing it altogether.

She was right—I did know that. Even though the airlines will typically hold a reservation for twenty-four hours (or until midnight the next day), the price is locked in only when purchased. That little slip-up of mine cost me $316 overnight!

Don't make the same costly mistake. If you are quoted a *really* good price, either when talking directly to the airlines, working with an agent, or booking online, act that same day, making sure payment is made before midnight. If you wait till the next day, you may find that the wonderful price has vanished.

The following key steps will help you understand what it takes to obtain spectacular values on major airlines, assuming you purchase your ticket at least seven to fourteen days prior to departure and will have a Saturday night stay in your destination. If you can't fulfill these two conditions, there are still some creative methods you can use to get good fares, as we will illustrate in the next chapters.

Why Advance-Purchase Airfares with Saturday Stayover Are the Cheapest

With computer programs that use historical information and forecasting models, airlines know the cost of operating a flight, as well as the percentage of seats that will likely be occupied at different fare levels. From these complex calculations, which attempt to optimize the balance between demand and supply at each price point, the airline can estimate how many fares to sell within each fare category or class. This practice is known in the industry as "yield management," which estimates the optimal balance between selling cheaper advance-purchase tickets and holding over just the right number of seats for last-minute travelers who will be willing to pay top dollar. As part of this concept, flight load is assessed regularly, meaning that demand falling below prediction may result in an increase in cheaper seats being offered, and *vice versa*.

How Airlines Account for Different Price Points Customers Are Prepared to Pay

We all know that different passengers assign very different values to the price they are willing to pay for a flight. For example, the consultant or marketing professional who has been called urgently to solve a problem or close a sale in a remote city will pay whatever it takes to travel, while the annual vacationer seeking a summer break with his family will pay only a fraction of that amount.

Using a hypothetical roundtrip flight from New York to Boston, the business traveler may readily pay $400, while the vacationer will not pay anything more than $150. Naturally, the business traveler would prefer to pay $150—even though she will be willing to pay a higher price, if need be. To differentiate between the two types of travelers, airlines impose restrictions to close off the lower fares to last-minute travelers—the two most important being:

1. Requirements for advance purchase (typically at least seven to twenty-one days before date of departure, which business travelers may not be able to do)

2. The need to stay over a weekend (which leisure travelers are happy to do, while business travelers prefer to be at home for their weekend!)

So What Does This Mean for You in Your Quest to Get the Lowest Fare?

What this all means for you, the traveler, is that an airline ticket price is determined by a vast array of variables, including class of service (coach, business, first) as well as fare category (including 3-, 7-, 14-, or 21-day advance purchase, whether you will stay in your destination over a Saturday night, low or high season, whether purchased direct from the airline or from a travel agent or consolidator, and so on). When overall demand is lower, airlines may start a sale to boost cash flow. Conversely, seats for flights departing at peak times (such as Monday morning and Friday afternoon) will typically be higher because these are preferred flight times for business travelers.

Buyer, Beware—What If You Need to Cancel or Change a Nonrefundable Fare?

Nonrefundable airfare means exactly that—you cannot get your money back. But that does not mean you cannot change your date and itinerary, as long as you know the rules (which you should clarify with the airline *before* paying for your ticket). Most major airlines permit a change, provided you call to cancel prior to the ticketed departure time (although some may not require you to do so). Failure to call and cancel the scheduled itinerary in a timely manner will result in 100 percent of the ticket value being lost. Some airlines may give you one year from date of purchase to use the value of your ticket toward another trip—while others may give you one year from the date of the ticketed departure date. Change fees are typically $100 per ticket for domestic travel, and $200 for international. Some airlines may have rules prohibiting an unused international ticket being applied to domestic travel.

When exchanging a nonrefundable ticket for domestic travel on a major airline for a new itinerary at a lower price, the airline will likely offer you a travel voucher for the remaining dollar value. However, certain international tickets may only be exchanged for another ticket having the same or higher price, meaning that you will lose money when exchanging for a ticket of lesser value. Low-cost airlines, on the other hand, are usually less restrictive. For example, Southwest does not charge a change fee, nor do you have to call to cancel your originally scheduled flight when using a nonrefundable ticket. Note that the rules may be different when booking online at independent travel agent sites and for international tickets. As always, be sure to check before you pay!

Other Ways Airlines Deal with Last-Minute Seat Availability

Airlines face a dilemma that is quite unique—huge fixed costs and miniscule variable costs. This means that the expenses incurred in flying an aircraft from one city to another remain relatively constant, regardless of whether the flight leaves the gate with 20 percent occupancy or has a traveler in every seat. While the additional (variable) cost to accommodate one extra traveler is perhaps a $3 meal and maybe a small amount of added fuel, airlines dare not sell seats at low prices at the last minute through conventional channels, otherwise they will lose the revenue of the business travelers needing to travel at short notice who are willing to pay a premium price if they have to.

Airlines may offload discounted seats at the last minute through consolidators, but tickets purchased through these intermediaries may be associated with significant restrictions. Increasingly, airlines are offloading last-minute fares by way of the Internet, which we will discuss in detail later in the book.

Plan, Plan, Plan

Travel suppliers, such as airlines, hotels, and car rental agencies, have structured pricing systems that penalize last-minute travelers. This typically targets business people, many who tend to be less price sensitive because they work for a large company that can afford to pay an inflated fare. But the small business person, whose pockets aren't as deep, can also get caught in a situation where he faces higher fares for last-minute ticketing, and absorbing those costs can be painful.

With just a little bit of planning, you can save big, as airlines offer price incentives to book in advance. One good example of taking advantage of the airlines' restrictions is to include a Saturday night stay in your itinerary, which almost always brings down a fare. Another is to book at least 7 to 14 days ahead—in fact, the farther out from the departure date you can book, the better. For example, 21-day advance purchases may offer better prices than 7- or 14-day advance prices for domestic travel. And 45- or 90-day advance purchases may be the most favorable with respect to ticket prices for travel to Europe. Certain promotions may have advance-purchase requirements detailed in the "small print." Be sure to check.

Start by finding some benchmark prices direct from the airlines, from your travel agent, or best yet, on the Internet. (Refer to Chapter 9 for details.)

Wait for the Sale

Another valuable money-saving strategy for getting great airfare values is to *wait for the sale*, just as you would when shopping at a department store.

But there is one advantage in exploiting airline sales over department store sales: Every airline seat is a commodity that rarely changes from day to day, season to season. You never pay for undesirable, out-of-date, or defective inventory! Furthermore, for domestic travel on most major U.S. airlines, frequent flyers who hold elite or premier status—having flown at least 25,000 paid miles on that airline in the previous calendar year—are eligible to upgrade, even when purchasing air tickets at a sale price. Finally, with the notable exception of Delta and Continental Airlines, earning frequent flyer miles or acquiring elite frequent flyer status is generally unaffected on major U.S. airlines by purchasing tickets on sale. A sale is usually started by one airline seeking to boost its cash flow, and its competitors match the sale price within hours. Airlines may sometimes offer added discounts to travelers who will fly at off-peak times or slow days. Taking advantage of sales ties in well to the concept of *planning*; if you know well in advance when you will travel, you can wait for the sale that will cover the time period you need to travel—typically two to six months following the start of the sale. For example, an airfare sale in early January will typically offer travel at reduced fares from late January or February through May or June.

A few important points about airfare sales:

- **Frequency.** Airfare sales for domestic flights occur with staggering frequency, and typically within eight to twelve weeks of each other. This means that the traveler who can plan at least sixty days in advance will have a high probability of being able to purchase his ticket on sale. But sometimes it's difficult to detect "real" sales from "phantom" sales. For example, the marathon three-month–long sales that Northwest Airlines has on occasion promoted are "phantom" sales, offering a measly 25 percent discount on selected routes. While this can still be a good value for summer travelers late in making their vacation plans, it doesn't compare with "real" sale prices, where you should receive a savings of at least 30 to 40 percent off the "standard" leisure/nonrefundable fare. How do you know what are the standard airfares? Simply keep track of fares for your desired destination(s) on a weekly basis for one to two months.

A phantom sale is an advertised sale where fares drop 20 to 30 percent from their standard level. You ideally want to purchase your tickets when fares have decreased at least 33 to 40 percent from their standard (or "typical") price. You can find out the standard price by periodically checking fares to your desired destination(s)—say twice each week over three to four weeks.

- **Keeping in the Know.** To find out about a sale, just open any major city or national newspaper. If there's an airfare sale at that time, you won't be able to miss the full-page advertisements placed by the airlines promoting their discounts. Internet sites for travel agencies and airlines will also include sale notices on their home pages. Better still, register for e-mail updates to receive prompt notifications of a sale. This is best accomplished by requesting e-mail frequent flyer statements rather than updates by way of regular mail.

Occasionally an airline will have a sale for a specific city pair or region, which may last for just a few days or even a few hours. These are typically not advertised in newspapers, so the only way to find such specials is by checking Internet sites such as *Bestfares.com* on a daily basis or at least twice each week. Another site is *Travelocity.com*, whose Fare Watcher enables you to be notified by e-mail when airfares for your selected city pair(s) have dropped below the threshold price you have designated. Similarly, *Orbitz.com*'s Deal Detector will watch for deals on up to three destinations you specify, at a price equal to or below your desired price.

■ **Notable Exceptions.** As with every rule, there is an exception to "waiting for the sale," and that is for travel on peak dates, such as the Wednesday before or Sunday after Thanksgiving, and the weekends before and after Christmas and the New Year. These used to correspond to the dreaded "frequent flyer blackout dates," which were eliminated by several (though not all) major airlines in 2002, although available award seats for peak dates of travel are few and far between! Sales *never* occur for these days, since every seat can be sold at a premium price. The ideal time to purchase a ticket and ensure the best price for peak dates is approximately 330 days in advance of travel, corresponding to the actual day the seats are entered into each airline's computer system. Prices then increase progressively as the date of travel gets closer, with virtually no possibility of a sale on airfares for travel dates corresponding to blackout dates some airlines (such as Southwest) still impose on free (award) seats over peak holidays.

■ **First Class.** Airfare sales may sometimes include discounted fares for first and business class, frequently offering 40 to 60 percent off standard premium prices. When booking online or by telephone, always check out the price of a premium seat.

Vary the Time or Date

Varying the time of day or the day of the week on originating or return flights can sometimes have a dramatic effect on price. Checking sensitivity of airfares to changes in time or date of travel can be done on the Internet or phone (though travel agents may be reluctant to spend considerable amounts of time searching for great airfares, thanks to the reduction or elimination of their commissions).

For example, suppose you want to travel late on a Friday afternoon. You probably will find fares to be higher than those for Friday morning, because of the high volume of business travel that necessarily occurs at the end of the work week. If you can be flexible and change travel times by just one to two hours on the outbound or return segment, you can sometimes cut the ticket price significantly!

Again, the Internet proves to be an invaluable tool in figuring out when to travel at the best fare. One of our favorite Web sites, *Orbitz.com,* allows you to select "anytime" rather than a specific departure time, then lists every possible combination of outbound and return flights with the number of stops you've requested on your airline of choice. As you click to view any airline by zero, one, or two stops, the associated airfares are displayed for each itinerary from lowest price to highest.

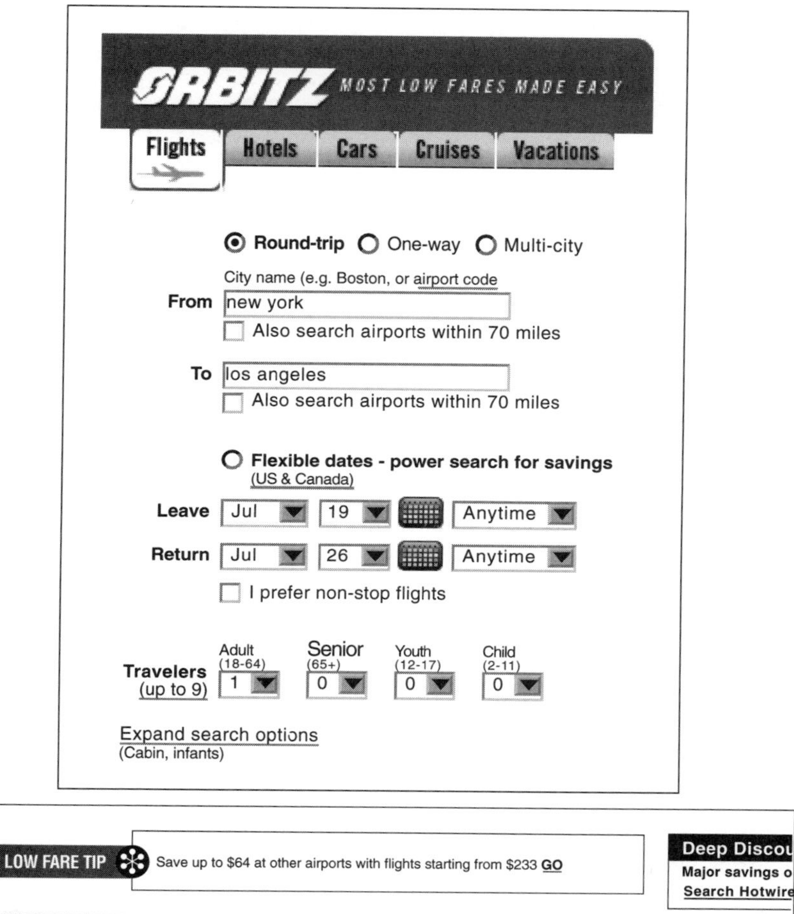

LOW FARE TIP Save up to $64 at other airports with flights starting from $233 GO

Deep Discou
Major savings o
Search Hotwire

ORBITZ MATRIX DISPLAY	Continental Airlines	US Airways	Northwest Airlines	United Airlines	America West	Delta Airlines	Spirit Airlines	American Airlines
Non-stop	$297 see below	$297		$337	$357	$357		$377
1 stop	$297	$302	$297	$317	$331	$337	$353	$377
2+ stops								

Book it **$297 per person**

Leave	**Monday, Jul 19** Depart: **9:00am** Arrive: **11:45am**	**Continental Airlines 1402** Newark, NJ (EWR) Los Angeles, CA (LAX)	Non-stop Economy I 5 Boeing 757
Return	**Monday, Jul 26** Depart: **3:40pm** Arrive: **11:55pm**	**Continental Airlines 1503** Los Angeles, CA (LAX) Newark, NJ (EWR)	Non-stop Economy I 5 Boeing 737

Book it **$297 per person**

Leave	**Monday, Jul 19** Depart: **9:00am** Arrive: **11:45am**	**Continental Airlines 1402** Newark, NJ (EWR) Los Angeles, CA (LAX)	Non-stop Economy I 5 Boeing 757
Return	**Monday, Jul 26** Depart: **9:55pm** Arrive: **6:01am** This is an overnight flight	**Continental Airlines 1803** Los Angeles, CA (LAX) Newark, NJ (EWR)	Non-stop Economy I 5 Boeing 757

Book it **$297 per person**

Leave	**Monday, Jul 19** Depart: **5:40pm** Arrive: **8:34pm**	**Continental Airlines 1502** Newark, NJ (EWR) Los Angeles, CA (LAX)	Non-stop Economy I 5 Boeing 737
Return	**Monday, Jul 26** Depart: **3:40pm**	**Continental Airlines 1503** Los Angeles, CA (LAX)	Non-stop Economy I 5

Book it **$357 per person**

Leave	**Monday, Jul 19** Depart: **6:55am** Arrive: **8:28am** **Change planes.** Time between flights: **1 hr 2min**	**Continental Airlines 1251** New York, NY (LGA) Cleveland, OH (CLE)	1 stop Economy I 1 Boeing 737
	Depart: **9:30am** Arrive: **11:18am**	**Continental Airlines 735** Cleveland, OH (CLE) Los Angeles, CA (LAX)	Economy I 4 Boeing 737 total duration
Return	**Thursday, Jul 22** Depart: **10:20am** Arrive: **5:44pm** **Change planes.** Time between flights: **1 hr 11min**	**Continental Airlines 66** Los Angeles, CA (LAX) Cleveland, OH (CLE)	1 stop Economy I 4 Boeing 757
	Depart: **6:55pm** Arrive: **8:31pm**	**Continental Airlines 1050** Cleveland, OH (CLE) New York, NY (LGA)	Economy I 1 Boeing 737 total duration

Similarly, selecting nonpeak days for travel can save a pile of money. The best and worst days to travel vary by destination, as follows:

Within the U.S.	BEST: Sa/Su (morning)/T/W WORST: F (especially late afternoon) and Su (afternoon)
Hawaii:	BEST: T/W/Th WORST: F/Sa/Su/M
Europe/Asia:	BEST: T/W/Th WORST: F/Sa/Su
Caribbean:	BEST: T/W WORST: Sa/Su/M
Mexico:	BEST: T/W WORST: F/Sa/Su

For travelers who are completely flexible with their travel dates or who want to get a benchmark price regarding the lowest possible fare to their desired destination(s), *Bestfares.com*'s Quickfare Finder may be helpful. You input your originating and destination cities, and Quickfare Finder provides you with details of the best possible fares including airfare code for each specific airline, advance-purchase requirements (such as seven or fourteen day), when the fare expires, blackout dates, as well as similar information for alternative airports.

TIP

Airfare prices on major airlines may soar for travelers wanting to stay more than thirty days. The traveler then has three options: (a) Fly with a low-cost airline since they typically do not impose maximum stay restrictions, (b) purchase a ticket from a consolidator, or (c) purchase two cheap nonrefundable tickets whose outbound and return flights fall within a thirty-day period (known as "back-to-back" ticketing, refer to details in Chapter 3). The traveler uses only the outbound segments on both tickets for a roundtrip itinerary—the first ticket to travel to his destination, the second ticket to return. The return segments on both tickets may be discarded and never used, or used for future roundtrip travel.

The Best Time to Purchase Your Ticket

There are travel experts who swear that Wednesday is the best day to purchase a ticket—especially just after midnight and the hours thereafter, when airline computers have been freshly loaded with new fares. Conversely, Friday is the worst day, since airlines test higher fares in the hope that competitors will match. If they don't, the airline rolls back the fares to their prior level.

Consider Alternative Airports

Checking prices into or out of nearby airports is another strategy that can affect ticket prices dramatically. For example, huge savings can be obtained by choosing Baltimore–Washington International (BWI) instead of Washington Dulles (IAD) or Ronald Reagan National (DCA); Newark (EWR) rather than La Guardia (LGA) or JFK; Providence (PVD) rather than Boston (BOS); Oakland instead of San Francisco (SFO); and Los Angeles International (LAX) rather than Orange County (SNA), Burbank (BUR), or Ontario (ONT). Visit the Web site *Traveltactics.com*, and click on "resources" for more information and choices. Two factors—both related to competition—influence airfares associated with any itinerary or airport, and create the possibility of lower price opportunities:

- The presence of a low-cost carrier servicing the route between the two cities. This may drive other major carriers to match the price on some seats, although often only on flights departing at similar times to those of the low-cost carrier.
- Multiple major airlines competing for passengers in certain airports. Examples include Los Angeles International, New York's JFK, and London's Heathrow.

Fly the Low-Cost Airlines

"Value" or low-cost airlines, such as Southwest, JetBlue, America West, America Trans Air (ATA), AirTran (different from ATA despite similar yet confusing names!), Frontier, and Spirit have made it possible for the traveling public to save billions of dollars. Currently, 75 percent of Americans have the option of flying on a low-cost airline, although some travelers may need to drive as much as two hours from their home to the airport or from their destination airport. Southwest has trailblazed this market niche for over two decades, with its impeccable safety record and consistently profitable operations serving to enhance the reputation of low-cost airlines. JetBlue, the best-funded airline startup ever, took the concept one step further, positioning itself as the low-cost airline with select frills, offering satellite television for every passenger and more leg room at most seats—but no meals (even on cross-country trips) or first-class cabin. Still, it's much easier to pack a gourmet lunch than a multichannel TV set!

Low-cost airlines are now recognized as the single biggest threat to the survival of the "big boys." Recognizing this, most major airlines have at some point in time set up value subsidiaries—including Continental Airlines with its short-lived "Continental Lite," United Shuttle on the West Coast, and US Air MetroJet on the East Coast. But none was able to replicate the operational prowess of Southwest, and each one was disbanded. Nevertheless, several major airlines are vowing to try setting up low-cost subsidiaries all over again, with Delta's Song and United's Ted the first of several attempts by major airlines to address the growth of low-cost airlines!

A list of low-cost airlines serving the United States and Canada is provided in Appendix C, and a list of low-cost airlines serving Europe is provided in Appendix D.

Why Low-Cost Airlines Can Charge Lower Fares Than Major Airlines

The average amount of revenue major and low-cost airlines earn per mile transporting passengers is quite similar, typically being slightly higher for major airlines that also include first-class cabins. However, the biggest advantage low-cost airlines have over major airlines is significantly lower labor costs. Additional cost-saving benefits for low-cost airlines include factors such as purchasing new fuel-efficient aircraft, never providing meals, and using secondary airports which have cheaper landing fees and which are often less congested, thereby significantly decreasing operating expenses.

After the September 11 tragedies, which coincided with a slumping economy, business travelers were forced to scale back on high-priced fares, and major airlines came under relentless attack from low-cost airlines, resulting in the bankruptcies of US Airways and United Airlines in 2002, followed by Hawaiian Airlines in 2003. American Airlines came within hours of declaring bankruptcy in 2003. There is widespread agreement that the major airlines will have to restructure their entire business model if they are to survive the onslaught they face from low-cost airlines such as Southwest, JetBlue, and Frontier.

Disadvantages Associated with Low-Cost Airlines

There are some drawbacks to flying low-cost airlines. If any of the following are important to you, you might want to steer clear of the low-cost carriers:

- Some do not have preassigned seating. This has been Southwest Airlines' most significant weakness.
- In many instances, they fly into minor airports that can require significant travel time from central locations, for example, Jet Blue (Long Beach rather than Los Angeles) and Southwest (Baltimore rather than Washington, D.C.; Providence or Manchester rather than Boston; Oakland rather than San Francisco). Several European carriers fly out of Stansted or Luton rather than Gatwick or Heathrow in London.

- Meal service is the exception (peanuts and pretzels are typically as good as it gets!), even when flying five or more hours cross-country.
- Some do not have frequent flyer programs, or the limited network of cities served reduces award redemption opportunities. (Hey—Southwest and JetBlue do not fly anywhere outside the U.S. mainland, so not even Hawaii is an option!)
- Few fly long distances—from one major airport to another—without at least one stop, although Southwest, JetBlue, and America West do have nonstops on a few of their cross-country routes.
- Southwest passengers who have purchased cheaper nonrefundable tickets must pay extra to go standby.
- Most do not have large fleets or extensive maintenance crews at all airports served, which can be a setback when an aircraft experiences a maintenance problem. Since tickets on low-cost airlines have limited transferability to other airlines, you may want to be cautious and plan for possible delays or cancellations by building in at least a two- to four-hour buffer between your scheduled arrival and a subsequent appointment.
- If your flight on a low-cost airline is canceled, you will almost always have to wait for another flight on the same airline or get a refund—but then you're left trying to find a last-minute purchase on another carrier, which could be expensive. Conversely, major airlines do have agreements with competitor airlines, meaning that a major airline can validate your ticket to an alternative carrier in the event of cancellation. Major carriers may pay for a hotel room if the cancellation strands you overnight, whereas most low-cost airlines will not. Finally, if delay or cancellation of your low-cost airline flight results in a missed connection with another airline (such as when connecting to a cross-Atlantic flight), the responsible airline will owe you nothing. However, a missed connection when transferring flights within the same major airline will get you rescheduled to the next available flight at no extra charge.
- In Europe, low-cost airlines charge significant amounts for excess baggage. For example, Ryanair levies $6 per kilo for anything over 33 pounds. This restriction could mean that U.S. travelers, who are accustomed to a two-suitcase allowance, could incur a hefty baggage charge!
- With the exception of Southwest and JetBlue, low-cost airlines have been known to operate with precarious financial support. Names that disappeared around the turn of the century include ValueJet,

Sun, Pro-Air, Kiwi, Tower, Vanguard, National, People Express, and Eastwind Airlines. Make sure you pay only with a credit card for travel within sixty days or less, so that you can dispute the transaction with your credit card company if the airline should suspend or discontinue service.

If a low-cost airline should disrupt service shortly before you travel, the cost of purchasing a last-minute fare on another airline may be prohibitive. Occasionally, a price break is given by another carrier to those who are victims of unusual circumstances, or there may be a law requiring other carriers who service the same route to pick up the slack, usually with some administrative fee tacked on. But don't count on much sympathy from the major airlines!

Given the disadvantages described above, don't blindly accept that a low-cost airline offers you the overall best deal. Before you go the value route, first compare prices and perks with your favorite large carrier(s). Where the prices are equivalent to the value carriers, we recommend you choose to fly on major airlines, such as United, American, Delta, Northwest, Continental, Midwest Express, or Alaska Airlines. The exceptions would be Southwest and JetBlue, which have managed to consistently combine excellent fares and on-time performance with financial stability.

Seek Out Free or Discounted Companion Tickets

Some of the best deals on the airlines can be had simply by traveling with a family member, friend, or work colleague. Many airlines offer programs that give the second passenger either a free or discounted ticket when travel is confined to the forty-eight contiguous states or Canada. In most cases, companion certificates can be used where the primary passenger travels at any available published airfare, even if the ticket was purchased on a sale.

TIP

***Ebay.com* is a rich source of discount coupons for all kinds of travel. However, be careful about purchasing frequent flyer miles, such as Rapid Rewards vouchers from Southwest. Since buying, selling, or purchasing frequent flyer miles is prohibited by airline rules, you are assuming a risk if you violate these heavily publicized rules.**

These certificates are relatively easy to obtain for the shrewd traveler who keeps an eye out for the best deals. For example, for just $76, travelers can purchase the Continental Executive Pack, which provides a $99 companion certificate for use within the continental United States, Alaska, and Canada, plus a variety of additional hotel and car rental discount certificates and 5,000 bonus miles. The Prestige Pack, priced at $120, provides similar benefits and 7,500 bonus miles. (Call One Pass Service Desk at 713-952-1630 to order.) The companion certificate from the Executive Pack may be used in conjunction with the lowest published airfare—even if purchased on sale—and does require a Saturday night stayover in the destination city.

Another source of discounted companion tickets is the Citibank AAdvantage MasterCard program, which has frequently offered a free companion ticket on American Airlines to travelers who apply and are approved for the credit card. United Airlines' Bank One Visa card occasionally makes similar offers. To be targeted for such specials, one should simply be a member of the airline's frequent flyer program.

In many instances, a free or discounted companion ticket may require a weekend stayover or have other restrictions, such as blackout dates. Check the fine print carefully. Furthermore, fare restrictions imposed on the use of a "free companion" certificate may occasionally mean that purchasing two regular discount tickets is the cheaper option—be sure to compare.

Certain credit cards, such as the Delta Platinum from American Express or Alaska Airlines Platinum Visa card from Bank of America, offer the cardholder a free or discounted companion ticket once each year—typically mailed when the annual renewal fee is received. The British Airways Visa card has offered a free companion ticket with one paid first- or business-class ticket. Finally, the free or discounted companion ticket must almost always be purchased at the same time as the primary passenger's ticket. Since it takes 2 to 4 weeks to receive the Executive Pack or 6 to 8 weeks to get a certificate associated with a credit card application or renewal, make sure you take the necessary actions at least 1 to 2 months before you will need to have your certificate in hand.

Other Important Types of Discount Certificates, Coupons, and Vouchers

The airlines have caught on to the coupon craze and now mail out a vast array of discount coupons and information about specials to members of airline frequent flyer programs. Since membership in these programs is free, frequent travelers have no excuse not to join the top ten airline programs. A list of phone numbers for reservations, frequent flyer/frequent-stay programs, and Web sites is included as Appendix A.

However, there are two outstanding coupon opportunities available to savvy travelers that should be noted here:

The Airline Bump

By far the best coupon you can use for travel comes from getting bumped! Passengers who voluntarily give up their reserved seats on an oversold flight receive compensation for taking a later flight, typically $200 to $400 toward future flights per passenger. (We once received $750 for each member of our family. Refer to the story that opens Chapter 9). Increasingly, airlines offer an outright free domestic roundtrip. The vouchers for discounted or free travel must usually be used within one year from the date of issue—but you can try to get an extension by writing a letter to customer service, explaining why you need to delay use of the opportunity. Use of the voucher may not be permitted during certain blackout dates—be sure you know what you are getting.

Passengers who give up their seats typically fly on the next available flight, but make sure you ask for the next flight that is most convenient for you. You might even be upgraded on the next flight; if the airline agent doesn't offer it, just ask. If an overnight stay is required till the next available flight, the cost of a hotel room may not be covered, but anything is negotiable! Also ask for a meal voucher, a calling card to phone relatives, and a pass to use the airline's lounge if you are not already a member.

Getting bumped has become a popular pastime for savvy travelers, so competition can sometimes be a bit stiff. The only way to ensure first priority for getting bumped if your scheduled flight is oversold is to arrive at the airport early and request that your name be added to the "volunteer list," either when you check in baggage or arrive at the gate. If volunteers are needed, you will be called by name before a general announcement seeking volunteers is made.

TIP

Check out *Bumptracker.com*, where travelers report their bump experiences on different airlines.

Finally, if you are bumped from the outbound (rather than return) portion of your trip, make sure that the return portion of your ticket is unchanged by having an airline staff person actually go in and check your computer record. There are occasions where the return portion will be deleted from an airline computer if you do not fly the outbound segment as originally ticketed, because the system sees you as a "no-show" with respect to the entire reservation.

The *Entertainment Directory*

U.S. mainland editions of the *Entertainment Directory* include a variety of discounts—usually good for 5 to 15 percent off the lowest price from a major carrier (or two) that differs from year to year; American, Continental, Northwest, and United Airlines have successively been offering discount opportunities most recently. In some instances, however, competing airlines will accept these coupons since they do not want to lose your business. Call (800) 445-4137 or go online to *Entertainment.com* to order an *Entertainment Directory*, available for most major North American cities and regions. Multiple charities sell the *Entertainment Directory* each year. A directory typically costs from $29 to $49, depending on the city edition you request. Directories for next year will be available after Labor Day of this year, and discount opportunities are usually valid through the end of November of the following year.

Create a Triangle

For the business or leisure traveler who wants to visit two cities in one itinerary, the triangle trip offers a great opportunity for saving time and money. Including *two* destination cities within a trip on a major airline usually adds just $70 to $150 to the typical nonrefundable, roundtrip, one-destination ticket—provided you stay in one of those two cities over a Saturday night.

The favorable pricing for triangle trips does not typically apply to *three* destination cities within a single itinerary, regardless of advance purchase with a Saturday night stayover or flying on one airline. In such instances, each flight segment will typically price out as a one-way, with a $1,000 to $2,500 total airfare being a distinct possibility, depending largely on the distances to be flown.

Keep in mind, when you book a triangle fare, the cost of the ticket will be based on the more expensive destination. If you want to travel New York–Boston–Seattle, for example, the ticket cost will be based on a New York–Seattle roundtrip, plus a few extra dollars to Boston—NOT the cost of New York–Boston, with faraway Seattle thrown in for just a few bucks.

Here's how it works. Say that you want to travel from Seattle to Philadelphia via Houston. Your base fare for an advance-purchase Seattle–Philadelphia roundtrip ticket might be around $450, with an add-on fare for including a stopover in Houston to the itinerary possibly bumping it up to around $580, provided there is a Saturday night stayover in one of your destination cities and travel remains exclusively with one airline. (In some instances, a partner or affiliated airline may be allowed. Refer to Chapter 12.) This strategy saves you both time and money, as you don't have to pay two full fares and you combine two trips into one.

When booking a triangle trip to two cities, you may actually have two itinerary choices: one going clockwise, the other counterclockwise, so to speak. If the timing of your itinerary is flexible, be sure to check out pricing for arriving in city A followed by city B, as well as city B followed by city A. One may be significantly better priced or more convenient for your needs.

Keep in mind that prices may vary from airline to airline. If you can't find a favorable pricing for a triangle on one carrier, try some others until you find the price and itinerary that works for you.

Try an "Open Jaw"

Although its name may not be very appealing, the open jaw ticket offers the traveler a great opportunity to design a creative itinerary.

"Open jaw" simply means that a traveler flies into one city (from city A to B), but returns from another (from city C back to A)—presumably covering the distance between the two cities by land or sea.

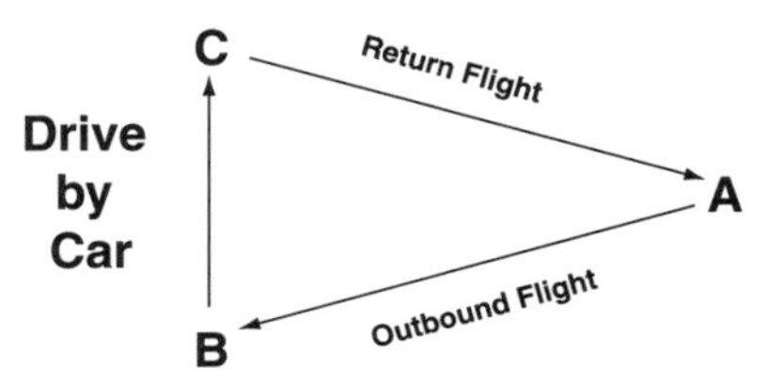

For example, consider the New York couple traveling to Los Angeles for their niece's wedding. After the nuptials, they plan to rent a car and drive up the scenic California coast, spend a couple of days in San Francisco, then return home. Their ticket from New York to Los Angeles, with a return from San Francisco to New York, will indicate "ground transportation" or "customer arrangement" from Los Angeles to San Francisco.

There is typically no price premium for open jaw ticketing, provided the closer destination city is at least 50 percent of the distance to the farther destination. For example, a traveler from New York may fly into Los Angeles (approximately 2,500 miles) and return from Denver (approximately 1,650 miles) at a low advance-purchase price since Denver is at least 50 percent of the distance from New York to Los Angeles. But the same New York traveler could not fly to Los Angeles (2,500 miles) and return from Chicago (850 miles) at a low advance-purchase price since Chicago is not at least 50 percent of the distance between New York and Los Angeles.

The Reverse Open Jaw

The open jaw doesn't always have to be in the middle of an itinerary; it can be between the originating and final destination cities. In this variation, the traveler flies from city A to city B, and returns from city B to city C after a Saturday night stayover. The benefits and rules are just the same as for the classic open jaw described in the previous paragraphs.

Let's take the example of a traveler who flies from New York to Los Angeles, then returns from Los Angeles to Boston—without paying a price premium. This works well for the business traveler who lives in New York City who has appointments in both Los Angeles and Boston. After visiting his client in Boston, he can simply return home by train. This traveler may alternatively choose to book a triangle rather than open jaw ticket, as that would allow him to fly back from Boston to New York for just a few extra dollars. (Refer to the section above for more details regarding triangle trips.)

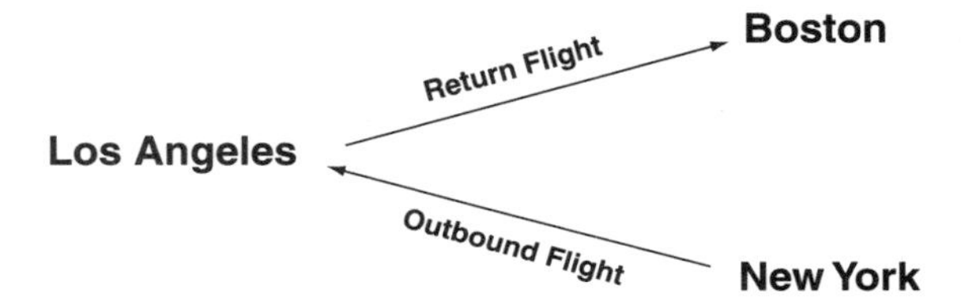

Should You Go Standby with or Without a Ticket or Confirm a Change to Nonrefundable Tickets?

"Going standby" is the aptly named practice of waiting at the airport gate to see if a flight has an extra seat you can occupy. Sounds simple, doesn't it? Well, think again.

There are a few things you need to know before you try this little maneuver—the most important being that you could end up paying much more than you anticipated. These are not seats being sold at fire sale prices. Anyone showing up at the airport at the last minute without a prepaid ticket, hoping to get a standby seat at a discounted fare, is in for a rude awakening! Unless you are a senior traveler—meaning age sixty-two or older—and you have a specific set of coupons, which select airlines may sell to mature travelers from time to time, purchasing a ticket on a standby basis is a surefire method for getting gouged. None of the U.S. carriers—not even those considered to be low-cost airlines—has discounted standby fares.

Complicating matters are the set of rules governing nonrefundable fares with respect to standby status. Not only are they complex (especially for the outbound portion of a ticket), their interpretation by airline staff can be erratic, contradictory, and sometimes just plain wrong! While there are certain times traveling standby is a good deal for the traveler who already has a 7-, 14-, or 21-day advance-purchase, nonrefundable airfare, you want to make sure you don't get stuck paying more than you want to.

The rules for major airlines are as follows:

■ **Changes to the Outbound Portion of a Nonrefundable Ticket.** Most major carriers—with the possible exception of Delta and international carriers—do not charge any penalty to passengers going standby *on the same date*—be sure to check. (An attempt by major airlines to charge $100 for standby on the same day in 2002 was quickly withdrawn due to competitive pressures.) The safest way to play it is to seek standby status only for a flight departing the same day but *earlier* than your scheduled flight. Trying to go standby *after* your scheduled time—even on the same date—is risky unless you have checked that at least one later flight has a reasonable number of open seats. If flights are full through the rest of the day, you may not get on as a standby at all. Instead, it's possible you will have to pay full coach fare to obtain higher priority waitlist status—to the tune of several hundred to over a thousand dollars! Or, if you can't get on a flight at all, you could be forced to leave the following day, incurring at the very least a $100 change fee, but possibly a much higher fare.

Southwest does not have the same policy for standby that other carriers do. To travel on a nonrefundable fare, the passenger has to fly on the exact flight that was booked. Any last-minute change or standby travel automatically requires payment of the difference between the discount and full fares, usually several hundred dollars.

■ **Making a Confirmed Change on the Outbound Flight.** If you wish to make a *confirmed* change for your outbound flight, you must do so within the rules of the ticket. For example, a 14-day advance purchase ticket will require outbound travel to occur no sooner than 14 days after the change is made. But beware of increases in the amount you must pay. First there is the inevitable change fee—usually $100 (or higher if international). Next, if the 14-day advance-purchase fare in the discount category you purchased has increased since you purchased the original reservation, you must pay the additional amount of the fare. (Conversely, if the airfare has decreased, you will receive a refund or travel voucher for the difference good for one year.) But what if a change is made to a 14-day advance purchase ticket more than 7 days but less than 14 days prior to the outbound flight? Then you are required to pay the difference between the 7- and 14-day advance-purchase ticket price, a certain increase. However, if there is no 7-day

Airline policy regarding standby is inconsistent for international flights, regardless of whether you are flying on a paid (revenue) fare or an award (free ticket). Our advice—don't try it—or at least check with the airline ahead of time.

advance-purchase fare in this instance, you may have to pay full coach price for the entire ticket.

Finally, if you anticipate the possibility of needing to make a change to the outbound flight of an itinerary reasonably close to your scheduled date of departure, you should consider either:

- Purchasing two or more nonrefundable tickets, each having the outbound on one of the possible days you will want to fly. For example, if you are uncertain whether you will start your trip on the 14th or 15th of May (and will not know till days or hours before departing), purchase two advance-purchase nonrefundable tickets, having a departure date on each of the two dates. The downside of this strategy is that according to the major airlines' new rule for nonrefundable tickets, the ticket that is not used must be changed to a new itinerary prior to the time of scheduled departure. The alternative strategy is . . .
- Obtaining an award ticket using your frequent flyer miles.

With respect to the latter option, major airlines and Southwest allow passengers with award tickets to go standby for any flight, outbound or return; and changes for the same or different dates do not incur a charge fee as long as the originating and destination cities do not change. This flexibility may change soon, as airlines look at every option to increase revenue.

Changes to the Return Portion of a Nonrefundable Ticket. I had a $400 roundtrip from Los Angeles to Cabo San Lucas in Mexico on Alaska Airlines over a long weekend in February. Just eight days prior to the trip, I needed to change my itinerary to confirm a return flight five hours earlier than ticketed. I called Alaska Airlines and happily paid a $100 change fee plus an additional $47 since the flight was almost full and the only fare code available was slightly more expensive than what I had originally purchased.

TIP

You can usually change the return portion of a nonrefundable ticket even after completing your outbound flight. Some airlines may require that you call to make the change prior to your scheduled time of return.

Bottom line—there is much less risk in modifying the return date of a nonrefundable ticket for a couple of reasons. You can get a *confirmed* new time on the same or a different date with no advance notice for a change fee that is usually $100 (or higher if international), provided seats are available for your particular fare class and category. If seats are only available in a higher fare category (as described in our example above), you will also need to pay the difference between your originally ticketed and new fare categories. And you may still go standby for any available seat just prior to departure on the same date for no charge, or on a different date for a $100 change fee—which can be your game plan if your request for a confirmed change of return date can't be granted because seats are not available for your particular fare class and category.

Timing Is Everything When Paying for Your Ticket

As shown in the chapter opening story, making a reservation on a major U.S. airline and locking in the quoted price are two very different things.

When making travel reservations for nonrefundable tickets, you are typically given twenty-four hours—and usually till midnight the following night—to pay for your reservation on a major carrier. However, many travelers are unaware that the *reservation* is guaranteed till the following day, not the fare, which is usually guaranteed only till midnight the *same* day your reservation is made. If the price in the computer increases overnight before you pay for your ticket, you are stuck with the higher price.

Sometimes—and only if you ask—the reservations agent can tell you when the favorable quoted price will expire. But even if you are told a price is unlikely to lapse by the next day, and then the price goes up, you have no recourse, as the agent has no power to guarantee the fare. Conversely, if the price decreases overnight before you have paid for the ticket, you may not always be informed of the change in your favor, so be sure to ask. When it comes to purchasing tickets on low-cost airlines, fares can change in a matter of minutes. Low-cost airlines rigorously control the number of cheapest seats available for each flight. Once sold out, only higher fares are made available.

The best policy is, if you find an excellent fare (whether with an agent, the airlines, or on the Internet), make your reservation and pay for your ticket before midnight the same day. If you are seeking a ticket on a low-cost airline and identify a great fare, purchase your ticket immediately by paying with a credit or charge card.

Air Passes

Air passes are discount vouchers that can be purchased in conjunction with a roundtrip ticket to a city abroad, enabling foreign visitors to travel to one or more additional cities (usually in coach class) at a savings of 25 to 75 percent. The air pass may either allow unlimited travel to a certain set of cities within a specified time period, or a certain number of prepaid vouchers will be issued, such as a book of four or eight, each of which is used to fly one segment (takeoff and landing). Some air passes are available year round, while others may only be offered on a seasonal basis or as part of a special promotion. While targeted at leisure travelers, there is no reason why business travelers cannot utilize the benefits of air passes.

Air passes almost always must be purchased before you leave the United States. Once you reach your destination, it is too late!

In certain instances, your choice of airline from North America may be determined by whether the airline offers an air pass option once you reach your destination—be sure to research or ask about this option when you start the planning process if traveling beyond your initial destination is a possibility. In many instances, an air pass cannot be purchased if your ticket from the United States was purchased from a consolidator or if you are using frequent flyer miles. A comprehensive list of international air passes for all major regions of the world is available at *Bestfares.com*—type "Air Pass" into story search.

Buyer Beware—Hidden Airfare Charges

One day I received a postcard in the mail from British Airways announcing: "Airfares to London starting at just $109!" Although intrigued, I thought it sounded too good to be true, and found confirmation of my suspicions in the fine print. True, $109 was the sale fare—the *one-way* fare, provided you fly on a roundtrip ticket. This type of come-on is a common practice among airlines when promoting a certain destination, one that we find misleading, as it's not possible to actually buy the advertised $109 one-way ticket! Further complications came from the fact that the price was valid for departures from New York only. As I read on, I also learned that "fares do not include government fees and taxes of approximately $93 plus a $2.50 September 11 Security fee." So what seemed at first glance like a cheap fare to London was in reality well over $300—with taxes and surcharges almost one third of the entire ticket price.

Ouch.

Hidden fees may now make up 10 to 50 percent of the total fare, depending on the price of the ticket and the number of flight segments, and include any or all of the following:

- U.S. taxes at 7.5 percent, which easily adds $20 to a ticket priced around $300 (nothing new there—but a real cost, nonetheless).
- Local taxes—typically $5 to $10.
- Flight segment taxes which go to the Aviation Trust Fund, supposedly to maintain the airline infrastructure—$3 per segment (applies only to flights within the United States).
- Facility charges, which airports may choose to impose to improve infrastructure—as high as $4.50 per segment, up to $18.

- Security fee of $2.50 per flight segment to pay for screening costs associated with post 9/11 vigilance—up to $10 per ticket.
- Fuel surcharges—which are charged at the discretion of the airline—typically $10 to $20 each way.
- For those traveling abroad, a variety of fees and taxes can easily add $40 to $100 to the ticket price—including international departure and arrival taxes, an INS user fee, customs user fee, agricultural inspections fee, as well as taxes imposed by foreign governments (such as airport security charges, terminal use charges, and noise fees).

When booking at certain Web sites, you may be surprised when the total to be charged to your credit card is considerably higher than the ticket price you were quoted. What has happened is that the site was simply promoting the "base airfare" and neglecting to include the myriad additional fees that were not disclosed till you were ready to pay.

- Expect to pay $20 to $25 if you want a paper ticket rather than an electronic ticket that simply outlines your itinerary with a confirmation number. Unless you are traveling on a complex itinerary with several airlines abroad, we do not see any benefit to requesting a paper ticket.

Dealing with Delays

Delays are a fact of life with air travel, although they are less common post 9/11, following which airlines reduced capacity. But it's how we react to the inevitable that determines how quickly we will make it where we need to be—and how well we keep our sanity.

■ **Rule 240.** This refers to an old airline rule that governed what airlines had to do in case of flight delays or cancellations. The contract governing your relationship with the airline now states exactly what the airline must offer you if it cannot get you to your destination within two hours of the scheduled time—if necessary, placing you on a competing carrier at no cost to you (even if the alternative airline only has an upgraded seat available). Rule 240 applies only to travel in the United States, and only if the delay or cancellation is caused by factors within the airline's control, such as misconnections or cancellations due to mechanical problems. It does not cover weather delays, acts of terrorism, or labor problems (an

The application of Rule 240 is slightly different for each airline. Check out *Mytravelrights .com*.

important exclusion, which may leave you powerless in the case of a strike).

If your flight is delayed or canceled, do not rush to the customer service desk to wait in line with every other angry passenger. Rather, call the airline or your travel agent and ask about alternative flights—both on the same *and* other carriers. If the delay qualifies under Rule 240, tell the airline on which you are scheduled to fly that "I'd like you to please 240 me." Depending on the length of the delay (if you are not in your hometown and the delay is expected to exceed four hours between 10 PM and 6 AM), you may also be eligible for hotel accommodations, a phone card, and meal vouchers. Finally, if the options presented to you are unacceptable, the airline is bound to refund the full price of your ticket, even if you purchased a nonrefundable fare.

■ **Preventing Delays.** The best chance of NOT being delayed is by taking the first flight of the day, since aircraft frequently are parked at the gate overnight; the converse holds true as well—the last flight has the best chance of being delayed. Many Web travel reservations sites will indicate a proposed flight's on-time history (defined as arrival at the gate less than 15 minutes after the scheduled time in the airline's computer system), or it can be obtained from the Aviation Consumer Protection site at *Acap1971.org*. The same information can be requested when you are calling an airline or your travel agent to make a reservation. Assume that an on-time arrival record under 70 percent is a warning sign that the flight under consideration is best avoided if a punctual arrival is important to you. By the way—for safety reasons, delays caused by mechanical dysfunction are exempt from being tracked as part of a flight's on-time record. However, no one monitors documentation of delays for safety maintenance reasons to see if they are, in fact, true.

TIP

When calling an airline on your departure day to learn about the status of your forthcoming flight before you leave for the airport, communicate your flight number and ask the agent to check the computer for the FLIFO (internal flight information)—specifically, the aircraft number assigned to your flight. Then ask him exactly where the aircraft with that number is now, so you can assess the likelihood of it arriving in time for your departure.

If your flight is going to arrive at its destination late and you will miss a connection and need to stay overnight, ask a flight attendant for the toll-free code number that enables direct contact with the airline's reservation system using the in-seat air phone.

Another way to minimize delays is to avoid routing through hubs where weather could be a problem, such as Chicago or Minneapolis during winter (when snow can be unpredictable) or Houston and Dallas during the summer months (when afternoon storms can wreak havoc with landings and takeoffs). Finally, before you arrive at the airport, research a "plan B" and be knowledgeable about alternative routings—"just in case."

Baggage Considerations

In an ideal world, no airline passengers would check any baggage. Business travelers already try their best not to do so. As savvy travelers, our two major concerns are:

1. Having to wait for baggage to come off the aircraft, or—worse than that—
2. Waiting for baggage that does not come off the same aircraft!

U.S. travelers are now familiar with rules allowing just two items to accompany them onto the aircraft—typically one case with clothing and the other a briefcase (including laptop). The new federally managed security personnel are vigilant about stopping passengers who try to bring three items through the initial security check, regardless of their dimensions.

If you check into the gate area less than 20 minutes prior to departure time for domestic flights (and 30 to 40 minutes for international flights), airline rules permit allocation of your seat to another passenger (be sure to ask, since each airline's rules differ). If you miss your flight, the airline may try to confirm you on another flight, but it is not obligated to do so. Most airlines state their obligation is either to refund the cost of your ticket minus a cancellation fee, or give you a voucher for use toward a future flight in the case of a nonrefundable ticket, minus a change fee.

■ **Baggage Limits.** When flying within—or to/from the United States—travelers have historically been able to check two bags, each weighing up to seventy pounds, with dimensions not to exceed 120 x 106 inches. And while airlines may historically have permitted checking in a third case or turned a blind eye toward the excess weight of checked bags, that is no longer true: Expect to pay significant charges if your baggage does not meet the specific stipulations for the airline on which you will be traveling, for example, $25 for any bag exceeding 50 pounds and $50 if greater than 70 pounds on most major airlines, as well as at least $80 for each bag above the two allowed for travel within or to/from the United States.

When your travel does not involve a segment to or from the United States, the maximum allowable weight per passenger is typically about forty-four pounds in coach class and sixty-six pounds when traveling in premium class (check exact requirements with your airline). And airlines are generally vigilant about enforcing these limits.

■ **Delayed or Lost Baggage.** In the circumstance where your bag does not make it onto the same flight as you, the airline is obligated to deliver it to you. If you need to purchase items—such as those needed for a meeting—while waiting for your bag, be sure to keep receipts. However, reimbursement will depend on the airline's goodwill rather than a legal mandate.

■ **Claims for Lost Baggage.** The ceiling for monetary liability on a bag checked within or to/from the United States is $2,500—but you have to prove the value of the loss by producing receipts. Furthermore, items such as jewelry and electronics are universally excluded, and each airline will have a list of what they will not cover detailed in their "fine print." Bottom line—don't hold out hope that you will recover very much in the case of loss.

For travel not involving a U.S. segment, airline liability is considerably less, limited to $20 per kilogram (or just under $10 per pound). This means that to file a claim, you need to know the weight of your bags at check-in and must produce receipts to verify losses. Once again—expect to recover very little in the way of monetary reimbursement if your baggage is lost.

TIP

The shrewd traveler carries key items with him onto the aircraft in a hand-carried bag rather than checking in important items with baggage, including valuables, medications, and change of clothing (for a meeting or social occasion).

■ **Minimizing Baggage Inconvenience and Preventing Loss by Airlines.** Do not purchase expensive bags—such as those from Louis Vuitton—that cry out to be targets for thieves! Rather, buy a sturdy bag that will stand the test of time and tie a bright ribbon round the handle to make your bag stand out from look-alikes circling on a baggage carousel. Finally, have an address label that matches where you are going to be (such as the hotel at your destination plus a cell phone number). And if you must have an address back home on your baggage address label, select your office address to avoid alerting thieves exactly which residential address is "ripe for the picking" because its resident is out of town!

TIP

When booking your ticket, minimize the risk of problems by:

- **Making as few stops as possible. Besides wasting considerable time, each stop enhances the probability of delays and baggage getting lost.**
- **Avoiding stops in cities that could face weather-related backups, such as Chicago or Minneapolis during winter months (snow); or Dallas and Houston during summer months (thunderstorms).**

■ **Sending Baggage Ahead of You.** Some travelers have taken to mailing their baggage a few days head of their arrival, using services, such as FedEx (*Fedex.com*/800-GO-FEDEX), Luggage express (*usxplug gageexpress.com*/866-744-7224), SkyCap International (*skycapinterna tional.com*/877-775-9227); (*skycapinternational.com* uses FedEx), Sports Express (*Sportsexpress.com*/800-357-4174), or Virtual Bellhop (*Virtualbell hop.com*/877-BELLHOP), that will pick up and drop off baggage almost anywhere. It's a great service, but if you use it, expect to pay at least $150 for an average-size case.

Round-the-World Tickets

Round-the-world tickets (RTW) may be the best bargain out there, especially when traveling first or business class. An RTW in premium class may be cheaper than a U.S.–Australia premium-class ticket—and you get to see a whole lot more. You can either purchase RTW tickets from consolidators that specialize in assembling what can be complex itineraries (refer to chapters on the Internet and consolidators for more details) or from the major airline alliances, including One World (*Oneworld.com*, click on "Global Products"), Star Alliance (*Staralliance.com*, click on "Air Passes"), and Singapore/Virgin/Air New Zealand (call 800-742-3333).

In Summary

- Planning as far in advance as possible is the cornerstone of getting great airfares.
- While 7-, 14-, and 21-day advance-purchase nonrefundable tickets are usually much cheaper than last-minute purchases, acquiring your ticket when airlines are having a sale will save you even more.
- When considering an advance-purchase nonrefundable ticket, you must understand the cancellation/change rules, preferably prior to purchase. If you decide not to use your ticket on a major airline, most require that you call to cancel prior to the ticketed departure date (be sure to check with the airline). In addition, you must pay a $100 change fee and reschedule a new trip within one year of the ticket issue date (or with some airlines, within one year of the originally scheduled departure date).
- Checking alternative cities (for both departure and destination airports) and modifying your flight times or dates wherever possible will often give you even more options for low fares.
- If traveling with a companion within the mainland United States, finding a free or discounted companion certificate for the second passenger can save a significant amount of money. There are occasionally discounted companion offers for international travel, which usually apply to first or business class.

- The best discount coupon is obtained by getting bumped from an oversold flight, for which you are typically compensated $200 to $400 (and sometimes more) per passenger or with a free ticket for domestic travel. Travel using vouchers obtained when you are bumped must usually occur within one year of the date your voucher was issued.
- The *Entertainment Directory* usually includes 5 to 15 percent discounts on one airline (the participating airline varies from year to year).
- Using low-cost airlines such as Southwest, JetBlue, and America West may also save significant amounts of money, although major airlines will frequently match the low-cost airlines' prices on flights departing at similar times. There are advantages and disadvantages associated with flying on major carriers or low-cost airlines—it is important that you understand the distinctions between them.
- The cost of doing a triangle trip (two destination cities) or an open jaw itinerary (fly to city A, return from city B) is usually not much more than the cost of a nonrefundable advance-purchase ticket to the more expensive city alone.
- The rules for going standby when using a discounted nonrefundable ticket are complex, especially when you want to change your date of travel for the outbound leg. However, going standby for the return portion is much simpler, typically incurring no fee at the airport on the day of travel or a $100 change fee (higher if international) to confirm the change ahead of time—be sure to clarify the rules (which can be quite confusing) with the ticketed airline. A notable exception is Southwest Airlines, which prohibits standby status with any discounted fare. Standby rules may vary, so be sure to check with the airline.
- Air passes allow you to travel beyond your destination abroad at a significant savings, usually on the same carrier you used from the United States. The pass almost always must be purchased before you leave the United States.
- If you find a great airfare on a major airline, pay for it prior to midnight of the same day. Even if the reservation is guaranteed to be held for twenty-four hours, you will pay the higher price if the ticket price increases overnight. For low-cost airlines, fares can increase within a matter of minutes once the cheapest seats on a specific flight are taken. So pay immediately if you identify a bargain.

- Rule 240 applies to delays or cancellations within the airline's control (*excluding* weather and labor-related delays) that keep the passenger from reaching his or her destination within two hours of the scheduled arrival time. It is only relevant to U.S. flights, and the airline is obligated to provide alternative flights, even if it means using another carrier. Minimize the chances of delays by avoiding stopovers wherever possible, especially in cities known to experience inclement weather when you will be flying.
- Given all the restrictions on baggage you can take on or check in, as well as risks of baggage being delayed or lost, travel light! The rules for checked baggage within or to/from the United States (two cases up to fifty pounds) differ markedly when traveling outside the United States (forty-four pounds in coach or sixty-six pounds in premium class), and airlines are rigorous about enforcing restrictions, meaning that overweight charges can be exorbitant. Airlines have very little liability if they lose your case—and you need to produce receipts to verify losses. Use of companies that will pick up your baggage prior to departure and deliver it on the other end is growing in popularity—but the cost is steep.
- Round-the-world (RTW) tickets provide outstanding value, especially when traveling in first or business class. Ticketing is complex and best done by specialist agents or consolidators. Various airline alliances will also price out fares for RTW tickets.

CHAPTER THREE

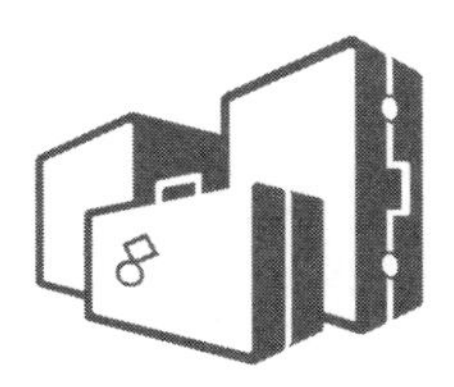

More Airfare Savings with Advance Notice

How to Save Big Without a Saturday Night Stay

During one of my business trips to the East Coast, I found I would be attending a midweek meeting in Washington, D.C., so my wife and I planned to rendezvous there. In making her flight reservation—over a month in advance of the date—we were quoted a fare of $2,200 by both United and American Airlines for a nonstop flight from Los Angeles, simply because she had no Saturday night stay in D.C. Unless I could find a more reasonably priced airfare, I planned to use frequent flyer miles—which, as always, I prefer to save for global leisure travel in first or business class or for last-minute trips that would otherwise be expensive . . .

Off I went to my favorite online travel site, *Orbitz.com*, where I found a Northwest flight with one stop each way, roundtrip Los Angeles–Washington, D.C., for under $500.

While finding a good fare is a challenge when your travel plans don't include a weekend stay, there are a number of strategies that increase your chances. This chapter focuses on travelers who have the benefit of at least seven- or fourteen-day advance notice.

Once Again—Plan!

As ever, planning is important if you want to find a great fare when you can book in advance but don't have the benefit of a Saturday night stay. As soon as you know your dates, start that search. The more time you have to plot your strategy, the better and more plentiful your options will be. You may try to locate a special fare to your destination by searching a few key Internet sites (see next section) or, if you have at least eight to ten weeks advance notice and will be using the back-to-back strategy (also discussed in this chapter), you may decide to wait for a sale. And should you decide to use frequent flyer miles, booking as far ahead as possible may improve your odds of redeeming them for the flights you want.

Remember, the more flexible you can be in your travel plans, the more likely you are to get a good fare. If you are making a reservation by telephone, ask the agent to try alternative routes as well as different departure times. For example, if you want to fly from San Francisco to Boston on United, you can request not only nonstops, but routings with a stopover in Los Angeles, Denver, Chicago, or Washington, D.C. And, if you can travel any time of day, you will have more flights to choose from and therefore more opportunities to find the cheapest fare.

Search the Internet

The Internet enables travelers to access information that was previously the exclusive domain of travel agents. To get a benchmark price for future comparison, start your Internet search at the airline-owned Web site *Orbitz.com*. Then check out fares at Internet travel agency sites, such as *Expedia.com*, *Travelocity.com*, *Overstock.com*, and *Cheaptickets.com*. Check out *Hotwire.com* to see what the airlines consider their "distressed inventory" fare (refer to Chapter 9 for more details).

Bestfares.com (click on "News Desk" from their home page) posts a variety of time-sensitive "you snooze, you lose" specials (along with the rules of the fare) that come onto the market each day, especially fare sales targeting a few specific city pairs that will almost never be advertised in the newspapers. A small percentage of these short-lived specials do not require a Saturday night stay in the destination, but inevitably do require purchasing at least seven to fourteen days in advance. Purchase of these specials may be possible from travel agents or airlines direct, but are sometimes available only to subscribers of *Bestfares.com* magazine through the publisher's affiliated consolidator travel agency. The annual subscription fee is $59, and can be requested online.

Book a Back-to-Back Ticket

Back-to-back ticketing is one of the cleverest and most powerful strategies you can use to realize big savings on air travel when you can book seven or fourteen days before your departure date, but have no Saturday night stay at your destination. Although it might seem tricky, it's really quite simple and ingenious. Here's how it works:

Instead of buying one expensive roundtrip ticket, the traveler books two cheaper, advance-purchase, nonrefundable, roundtrip tickets.

Ticket #1 has two flight segments: the outbound from home city A to the destination city B on the desired departure date, and the return from the destination city B back to home city A for some *future* date. There must be at least one Saturday night between the outbound and return flights.

Ticket #2 also has two flight segments: the outbound from destination city B to home city A on the traveler's desired return date, the return from home city A back to destination city B at some future date. Again, at least one Saturday night must occur between the outbound and return portions. The traveler uses the outbound portion of each ticket: from city A to city B on the desired departure date, and from city B to city A on the desired return date. Because the originating flights for ticket #1 and ticket #2 are used for the intended trip, no Saturday night stay is required.

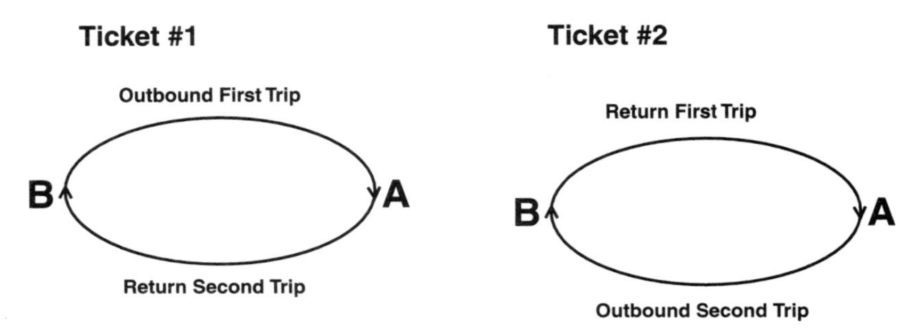

For example, let's assume that a New York business traveler needs to be in Los Angeles for two days, but does not want to stay over a Saturday night. Her preferred travel dates are departing on Tuesday, October 8, from New York to Los Angeles and returning two days later on Thursday, October 10.

Using the back-to-back strategy, she will book Ticket #1 from New York to Los Angeles on Tuesday, October 8, with return travel from Los Angeles at some future date, with at least one Saturday night between the outbound and return dates. For our purposes, let's have her return portion be ticketed for Thursday, November 7 (which could make it the return flight for a potential second trip). Ticket #2 begins with an outbound segment *starting* from Los Angeles back to New York on Thursday, October 10, with the return segment from New York back to Los Angeles at some future date, including at least one Saturday night between the outbound and return portions. Let's make that date Tuesday, November 5, which could make it the *originating* flight for a potential second trip.

From a price standpoint, a New York–Los Angeles nonstop roundtrip on a major airline with no Saturday stay can easily run $2,000 or more on a major airline, even with advance purchase. By purchasing two advance-purchase roundtrip tickets at an average price of $400 each, or $800 total, the traveler saves $1,200—and potentially receives two trips instead of one!

Now that you've mastered the basic concept of the back-to-back ticketing strategy, you're ready to move on to the finer points.

How to Use the Remaining Segment of Each Ticket

Many travelers who use the back-to-back strategy simply discard the return portions of each roundtrip ticket, content to save hundreds of dollars on the fare they originally set out to achieve. However, those discarded tickets represent a fare that can be worth $2,000 or more, which is now essentially free! In other words, to book that second trip with no Saturday stay would again cost up to $2,000, so the traveler who uses all four sectors realizes a total savings of $3,200 ($1,200 from the first trip PLUS $2,000 from the second trip).

Of course, if you use this strategy, you will most likely want to book the second trip for several weeks or months in the future, and your plans may change. Should this be the case, make sure you know the rules of the ticket and what additional charges you may incur with a change. Some examples:

1. With major airlines, there may be maximum-stay time constraints associated with the purchase of a nonrefundable advance-purchase ticket, meaning that:

(a) Trying upfront to book a ticket that has a return portion later than thirty days after the outbound may be very expensive, or

(b) The traveler may need to pay a significant amount of extra money if the original tickets permitted a maximum stay of only thirty days and a change in the ticket puts the return date beyond this time frame.

If you purchase a ticket with a return portion that exceeds thirty days from the outbound flight—or make a change to your ticket that pushes the return date beyond that thirty-day window—and the net airfare increases dramatically, it may be more cost-effective to simply discard the return portion(s).

2. Confirmed changes can be made to each ticket at any time (even after you have flown the originating portions of each ticket) as long as those changes are allowed within the rules of the ticket.

3. Major airlines will typically charge a $75 to $100 change fee for each ticket—$150 to $200 for both.

Other Important Factors to Consider When Booking

Once you have decided to book two roundtrip tickets for your back-to-back ticket, go back and review some of the key sections discussed for advance-purchase tickets, which apply to any advance-purchase nonrefundable tickets. In particular, check out other important strategies outlined in Chapter 2, including "Wait for the Sale," "Vary the Time or Date," "Consider Alternative Airports," "Other Important Types of Discount Certificates, Coupons, and Vouchers," and "Should You Go Standby with or Without a Ticket or Confirm a Change to Nonrefundable Tickets?"

Heed This Important Caveat!

The low-cost carrier Southwest Airlines, however, does not prohibit the use of back-to-back ticketing. Since back-to-back ticketing offers passengers the opportunity to save so much money on air travel, the major airlines have universally declared its implementation to be a violation of their rules. If an airline discovers back-to-back ticketing, it may try to reclaim the difference between the fare paid and the fare that *should have been paid* from the traveler, although it's more likely they would go after the travel agent who booked the tickets (if an agent was involved). The only surefire way to prevent detection is to purchase the roundtrip tickets on two different nonaligned airlines. For example, if you booked your original outbound flight on Continental (ticket #1), your original return flight might be on American (ticket #2). When using the second ticket, the carriers would reverse: outbound on American, return on Continental. There is no risk using two different airlines.

Take a Friend and Save Even More

You don't have to go to Vegas to "double down," as they say. Do it with back-to-back ticketing, compounded with companion fares.

Let's say two business colleagues will be traveling together (or perhaps your spouse wants to come along for the ride). Each traveler could buy one of the roundtrip advance-purchase tickets and use a free or discounted companion certificate for the accompanying traveler. (Refer to Chapter 2 for details.). Using the example above with Continental and American Airlines, Traveler A could purchase a roundtrip ticket on Continental and cash in a companion certificate from Continental's Executive Pack for his business colleague to use; conversely, Traveler B could purchase the second roundtrip ticket on American and use a companion certificate earned by being approved for an AAdvantage MasterCard or renewing his Delta American Express Platinum card to return the favor to his traveling associate.

When You Need to Return to the Same City Again and Again

Let's assume you are an entrepreneur in New York, and your business partner lives in Los Angeles. You need to visit him once every four weeks, and you don't want to stay over a weekend. So every fourth Tuesday you fly New York to Los Angeles, and return the next day Los Angeles back to New York. Although back-to-backs will save you tens of thousands of dollars every year, there is an even simpler solution. . . .

To prime the pump, your first flight must be a one-way ticket from New York to Los Angeles. Of course, you could buy an expensive one-way ticket, but as a veteran road warrior, you purchase a cheap nonrefundable fare and dispose of the return portion. From then on all you need to do is to buy a simple, advance-purchase roundtrip ticket from Los Angeles to New York, with the return portion four weeks later back to Los Angeles. Since there will be not just one but four Saturday nights between your outbound and return flights, you may take advantage of cheap, nonrefundable tickets. All you're doing is changing your frame of reference—your tickets suggest your departure point is Los Angeles, rather than New York. And since you're not going against airline rules—as a back-to-back does—you can safely keep using the same airline.

Because you know when you need to travel, all your tickets can be purchased at least fourteen days in advance. And you can always make last-minute changes to each ticket's return portion for a cost of $75 to $100 as late as you want—which is really the date you start your return trip from New York back to Los Angeles.

How You Can Back-to-Back from City-to-City—The Open Jaw Back-to-Back!

"Simple" back-to-back tickets that offer two trips to the same city are great for consultants who must meet with a client or work on a project in the same destination city over an extended period. The problem is, many business travelers don't need to return to the same city, so they end up tossing the return portion of each of their two roundtrip tickets. What a waste!

Ah, but for those business travelers who need to visit City A one month, then City B the next month, there *is* another strategy that may work—although I'll admit it sounds a bit like an advertisement for a contortionist. It's called the "open jaw back-to-back." The one limitation to consider regarding which cities will work for an open jaw is the requirement that the closer destination city to origination be at least 50 percent of the distance to the further destination city. Still, it's worth considering, as the significant price advantages are similar to those for "simple" open jaw tickets.

For example, let's again assume that you live in New York and have at least fourteen days advance notice to book a flight to Los Angeles in October. You also need to fly to Denver in November. Reservations could be made as follows:

Open Jaw Ticket #1 has New York City to Los Angeles on Tuesday, October 8, as the outbound portion, with a return from Denver back to New York on Thursday, November 7.

Open Jaw Ticket #2 starts with an outbound segment from Los Angeles back to New York on Thursday, October 10, with the return segment being the *originating* flight of the second trip from New York to Denver on Tuesday, November 5. Should the dates of the November trip to

Denver move, the airlines will charge $75 to $100 to change the return portion of each ticket—a minuscule sum when compared with the extraordinary savings. Don't forget that the reverse itinerary would work just as well if you needed to visit Denver for the first trip and Los Angeles for the second.

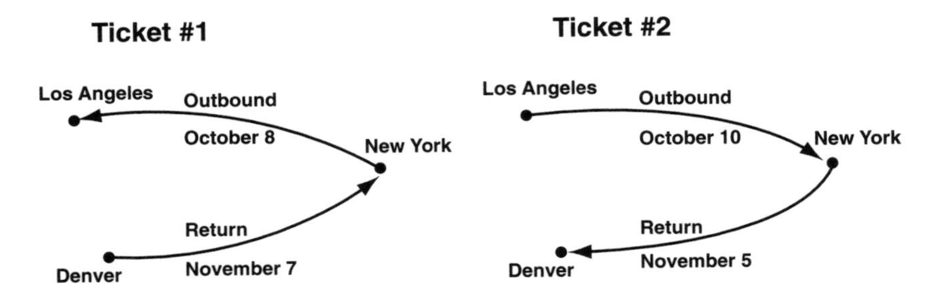

Low-Cost Airlines

As we've discussed in other chapters, low-cost airlines can typically save you a significant amount of money for simple *unrestricted* roundtrip tickets that do not include a Saturday night stay in the destination. Details regarding low-cost airlines can be found in Chapter 2.

For those travelers who want to exploit the favorable pricing of low-cost airlines and prefer to travel on major carriers—but would like to avoid higher fares—the best opportunities can be found by:

1. Checking the routes served by low-cost airlines and following up to see whether major airlines are matching the price. For example, since America West services Los Angeles and San Francisco nonstop to New York and San Francisco, travelers wanting cross-country on these routes may find that major airlines will match America West's much lower prices into those nearby cities—even without requiring a weekend stayover.
2. Finding a promotional fare from a travel agent or online; chances increase when travelers are prepared to make at least one stop. (Check out *Orbitz.com*.)
3. Using back-to-back strategies. (See above.)
4. Purchasing from a consolidator—but this arrangement may sometimes exclude eligibility for earning frequent flyer miles. (Refer to next section for details.)

Seek Out Consolidators

Purchasing a ticket from a consolidator, such as *Cheapickets.com*, *Over stock.com*, or *Flights.com*, will frequently save the traveler significant amounts of money on either the advance-purchase or last-minute ticket that doesn't include a Saturday night stayover. This is especially true for international trips, where the majority of consolidators focus their efforts.

A detailed description of consolidators is included in Chapter 7.

Take a Triangle Trip—The Minivacation That Saves You Money

For travelers reluctant to spend the weekend in their primary destination, but who are open to spending the prior or following weekend in a different city, a triangle trip may be just the ticket.

Here's how it works. Say a New York traveler needs to conduct business in Los Angeles on a Thursday or Friday, but doesn't want to spend the weekend there. She could fly to almost any other American city (San Francisco, Seattle, Chicago, Boston, even Honolulu, and so on) following completion of business in Los Angeles, spend a Saturday night, and benefit from a cheaper airfare than she would pay if she spent Saturday night at home. A New York–Los Angeles nonstop ticket with no Saturday stay could easily run $2,000; whereas a fourteen-day advance-purchase triangle ticket that also includes a weekend in San Francisco, Seattle, Chicago, or Boston could, in most instances, be purchased for under $600. It's not difficult to decide which to choose if you want to save money (and have a great weekend in a city of your choosing).

For more details on triangle trips, refer to Chapter 2.

The Magic of the Split Ticket

Travelers unable to find a reasonably priced advance-purchase, roundtrip airfare with no Saturday night requirement, or who do not want to engage in a back-to-back strategy, should check out a split ticket strategy.

As the name implies, the "split ticket" divides one longer itinerary into two shorter ones. For example, any traveler wanting to fly coast to coast should see whether purchasing two separate tickets through Las Vegas (such as a roundtrip New York–Las Vegas, and a separate roundtrip Las Vegas–Los Angeles ticket) will save money.

Las Vegas is possibly the best city for finding cheap airfares for two reasons:

1. Gamblers want to spend their money on slot machines and poker tables—not airfares. If the airfare is too high, most gamblers will simply stay home and wait till the weekend.
2. Two of the nation's low-cost airlines—Southwest and America West—use Las Vegas as a hub city and offer excellent prices with or without advance purchase. Frequently, major carriers will match the prices of their low-fare brethren in competitive markets, which may be preferable for those trying to rack up frequent flyer miles.

For tickets to Europe, the Middle East, Africa, and Asia, London may be a perfect intermediate city since economy-class prices are very competitive both into and out of the city. However, business- or first-class tickets into and out of London frequently exceed the prices for premium seats to or from major cities on the European continent. For more details regarding "split ticketing" strategies, refer to Chapter 4.

Use Your Frequent Flyer Miles

Using frequent flyer miles from an airline that does not require a Saturday night stay when redeeming a saver award is perhaps the simplest and quickest way to save when you don't want to spend the weekend in the destination city. This won't work on Continental and its partner Northwest, however, as they do require a weekend stayover in your destination when you cash in a 25,000-mile saver award. All airlines will waive capacity controls on redemption of awards when passengers are willing to use double miles. A better alternative to spending double miles may be to use a premium award for business or first class on that same flight, which frequently costs less than the double miles required for a coach-class saver award. For details regarding use of frequent flyer miles, refer to Chapter 11.

> **TIP**
>
> **As a general rule of thumb, American Airlines miles are the easiest to use, followed by United. Frequent flyer miles from Continental are the most difficult to use.**

Good Prices Come to Those Who Wait

Airfare sales provide discounts mainly for advance-purchase, nonrefundable coach tickets that require a Saturday night stay in the destination. It is unusual for regular airfare sales to include "no Saturday night stay" fares, which typically require the purchase of expensive, fully refundable tickets. Exceptions to this rule may occur during the slower summer months, when demand for business travel slows down.

Furthermore, as discussed in the Internet overview in this chapter, airlines occasionally offer sales on a few specific city pairs that will almost never be advertised in the newspapers. A small percentage of these time-sensitive airfare specials do not require a Saturday night stayover in the destination, but inevitably require at least a seven- or fourteen-day advance purchase. Checking *Bestfares.com* weekly—or better yet, daily when you have a specific need—is by far the most effective method for identifying such specials because of their "now you see it, now you don't" nature. Furthermore, there is a reasonable probability that a special discounted fare for a desired city pair will be available at least once over a two- to three-month period, especially if the originating and destination cities have major airports.

Visit the Web Sites of "Last Resort"

When all else fails, and you're getting close to your departure date, visit the Internet sites *Hotwire.com* and *Priceline.com*, where you might be able to find significant savings. But any reduced airfare you might get comes with an element of risk, as you won't know the airline, flight times, or stopovers until you have paid for a nonrefundable fare with your credit card. *Hotwire.com* does tell you the price in advance, then gives you one hour to accept the offer with a credit card. At *Priceline.com*, if your bid is accepted, your credit card is automatically charged for the nonrefundable fare. Refer to Chapter 9 for more details.

As a basic strategy, try *Hotline.com* first. If you still feel tempted to go to *Priceline.com*, bid significantly below (that is, at least 30 percent less) the price you were offered by *Hot wire.com*. Refer to Chapter 9 for more details.

TIP

If your Priceline bid for an airfare is refused, the rule is that you cannot rebid for airfare within seven days unless you change travel dates, add airports, connections, or off-peak hours, or agree to fly on non-jet aircraft. Just increasing your offer price does not work. After seven days, you can rebid on the exact same itinerary and particulars.

In Summary

- Planning is important for the traveler who has seven or fourteen days before a desired travel date, but does not want to stay over a Saturday night in his destination.
- An excellent starting point for obtaining benchmark prices and seeking out specials is *Orbitz.com*. *Hotwire.com*, which is jointly owned by the major U.S. airlines as a channel to distribute distressed inventory, is also useful for getting a benchmark "lowest fare," since it will provide you with a price the airlines consider to be "low" (without specifying airline, flight times, or stops) *before* you need to purchase with a credit card.
- If you have at least seven to fourteen days before your departure date and cannot find an excellent fare or want a nonstop that is priced too high, consider the back-to-back strategy. Buy two nonrefundable advance-purchase tickets, each with a return portion that includes a Saturday night stay. Use the outbound flight on the first ticket for your flight from your home city to your destination; then use the outbound portion on the second ticket for your return flight from your destination back home. If the return portion is more than thirty days away from the outbound segment, causing the ticket price to become excessive, simply purchase tickets with return portions on dates less than thirty days following your departure, and

discard the return portions. Since major airlines claim that this strategy is against their rules, be sure to purchase each ticket from a separate carrier. Southwest Airlines does not prohibit use of back-to-back ticketing.

- Waiting for a sale does not typically reduce the price of tickets that have no weekend stayover—but it's worth a try! However, purchasing both tickets for a back-to-back strategy on sale will enhance the already significant savings.
- The serious, creative traveler may also want to try a split ticket strategy, purchasing two tickets through an intermediate hub city such as Las Vegas, if flying cross-country in the United States, or through London for travel from the United States to Continental Europe, the Middle East, Africa, and Asia.
- The traveler who does not wish to stay over a weekend in his primary destination city can use a triangle strategy to spend the weekend in a second destination city, which may bring significant savings.
- Check the prices of low-cost airlines such as Southwest, America West, JetBlue, Frontier, Spirit, ATA, or AirTran, which will often beat major airlines on nonstop or one-stop routes.
- Consolidators such as *Cheaptickets.com*, *Overstock.com*, and *Flights.com* may be an excellent alternative for tickets without a weekend stayover.
- Using frequent flyer miles is an excellent way to save if the price of a regular revenue ticket is too high. Some airlines—most notably Continental and Northwest—require premium (double mile) awards if the traveler is not going to stay over a Saturday night. All major airlines waive capacity controls if the traveler uses double miles, meaning, if there is just one available seat, it's yours! Business- or first-class awards may be a better value than premium awards since they usually require fewer or the same number of miles (40,000 to 50,000 miles for domestic business- or first-class ticket versus 50,000 for a premium coach-class award).
- Internet sites of last resort are *Hotwire.com*, where you must accept the price offered with a credit card within one hour, and *Priceline.com*—you name your price and, if accepted, your credit card is charged for the nonrefundable and nonchargeable fare. If you try "bidding" at *Priceline.com*, start at 30 percent below the price you were offered by *Hotwire.com*. For both Web sites, the airline, time, and stopovers are revealed only *after* you pay for your nonrefundable and nonchangeable ticket with your credit or charge card.

CHAPTER FOUR

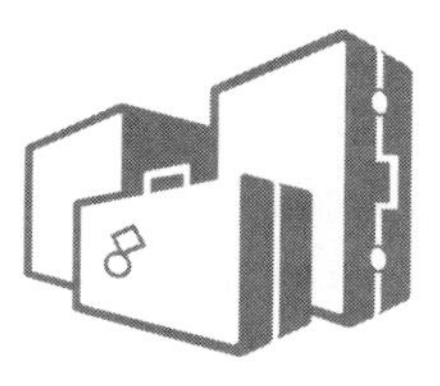

"Last-Minute Airfare Savings" Doesn't Have to Be an Oxymoron

When opportunity knocks, as it did on my door one day, you don't want to have to pay through the nose to use it.

I faced that dilemma one sunny afternoon, when a phone call brought me some good news. My contact told me that her department's senior management liked what they saw in my proposal letter and had invited me to make a presentation in Chicago. Could I be there in three days, ready to go?

"No problem!" came my confident reply, while my mind performed mental gymnastics. Although I had no doubts about the quality of my presentation, since I already had prepared well for it, I knew flying at the last minute from Los Angeles to Chicago without paying an exorbitant fare—possibly up to $2,000—would be the real challenge.

Then I remembered I had a certificate for a free roundtrip flight on Southwest Airlines stashed away in my air coupons pendaflex folder. Ten minutes later I had squared away my one-stop *free* reservation into Chicago's Midway airport.

For those of you more familiar with Chicago's O'Hare airport, which almost all major airlines use, Midway has become the preferred airport for the low-cost airlines and is situated much closer to downtown Chicago.

Of course, booking ahead of time is still the preferred way to go, as I learned when I managed a group of employees who traveled three times or so each month. Even though they knew when they would travel at least five weeks in advance, they invariably waited to make their reservation just one or two days prior to their departure. Offering small monetary incentives to encourage a change in their habits—from booking at the last minute to making advance purchases—positively impacted my division's overall travel costs. Of course, there will always be those occasions where the ever-ready businessman will need to make a last-minute trip to pitch a customer, fix a burning problem, or simply nurture an important relationship.

For the purposes of this book, we have defined the last-minute traveler as someone who needs to fly without advance notice of at least seven to fourteen days—regardless of whether or not the itinerary includes a Saturday night stay. This presents the greatest challenge in obtaining exceptional airfare value, but there are proven strategies to achieve significant travel savings.

Why Going Standby Without a Ticket Is a Bad Idea!

Let's first put to rest the one strategy you must *not* try. Major airlines recognize that it is relatively price-insensitive business travelers who most commonly need to travel at the last minute, and they will typically gouge these customers from whom they make a significant percentage of their profits. This is especially true in markets without competition from low-cost airlines. So, unless you are a senior traveler who can use coupons specifically geared to those over sixty-five years old—fares that are promoted by select airlines on an occasional basis—the idea of going to the airport to purchase a discounted standby ticket at the last minute is a myth!

Conversely, going standby when using a frequent flyer award ticket may be an excellent idea for the last-minute traveler—refer to a later section of this chapter for more details. Finally, going standby using the return portion(s) of an advance-purchase, nonrefundable ticket at a cost of the $100 fee imposed by a major airline may be worthwhile if permissible (including the return portion of back-to-back tickets), but on-the-spot changes to the originating or first portion of your revenue ticket on a major airline will *not* be permitted without reissuing an entirely new ticket—which will almost certainly be at full fare. Refer to Chapter 2 for details about the rules of going standby with an existing ticket and Chapter 3 for details regarding back-to-back ticketing.

Use the Internet for Benchmarking Prices and Seeking Out Specials

In Chapter 9, "Navigating the Internet," we shall discuss use of Internet travel reservation sites to obtain benchmark prices for your desired itinerary. *Hotwire.com* is an excellent place to start, since it offers a bargain quote you must accept within one hour that is among the lowest any major airline will offer. Next, check out the three major online retail travel agencies—*Orbitz.com*, *Expedia.com*, and *Travelocity.com*. Finally, if you can identify one airline as having a good fare, go directly to its Web site to check whether an additional online booking discount or frequent flyer mile bonus is being offered. Consolidators such as *Cheaptickets.com* and *Overstock.com* may offer lower last-minute airfares (refer to more details in the subsequent section about consolidators in this chapter).

With the exception of established Weekend Internet Faresavers described in Chapter 9, it is rare to find a special on a major airline that offers a last-minute flight at a bargain price. Weekend Internet Faresavers may work for you if the city you need to visit is offered that weekend and assuming your domestic business can be scheduled on the following Saturday, Sunday, Monday, or Tuesday. Most major U.S. carriers have weekly specials that permit outbound travel on the Saturday following posting of the fares each Tuesday or Wednesday, with a mandated return the following Monday or Tuesday. For international flights, information about each major airline's weekend specials are usually posted on a Monday for departure two weekends—or eleven days—later. The fares for these weekend faresaver specials are about the same as or slightly higher than advance-purchase, nonrefundable fares bought on sale. The major drawback is that just a few routes are offered each week, with no reliable way of predicting which routes will be selected. Refer to Chapter 9 for details about how to receive information about Weekend Internet Faresavers. Finally, the savvy road warrior will check out the following Web sites that specialize in last-minute travel: *Lastminutetravel.com* and *Site59.com*.

Varying Time or Day of Departure (or Return)

Changing the time of day or day of week of your originating or return flights can sometimes dramatically affect price. While on the Internet or when calling an airline or travel agent, assess price sensitivity by varying departures by different times of the day or different days of the week.

Varying City of Origin (or Destination)

The road warrior purchasing a last-minute ticket may find significant savings in flying out of or into alternative airports, such as Baltimore–Washington International (BWI) instead of Washington Dulles (IAD) or Ronald Reagan National (DCA); Newark (EWR) rather than La Guardia (LGA) or JFK; Providence (PVD) rather than Boston (BOS); Oakland (OAK) instead of San Francisco (SFO); and Los Angeles International (LAX) rather than Orange County (SNA), Burbank (BUR), or Ontario (ONT). It's worth your while to check various originating and destination airports that can serve your travel needs. The Web site *Traveltactics.com* provides a resource section that includes a list of alternative cities for major airports in the United States.

Packages

Booking an air/hotel or air/car rental package can often help out the last-minute business traveler. Airlines and travel agencies with a significant presence on the Internet are increasingly offering midweek packages that can save the business traveler hundreds of dollars.

You may be able to find a package that has:

1. Minimum advance-purchase requirements—as little as three days—which means the savings in airfare alone could be considerable
2. No weekend-stay requirement, although a minimum stay may be stipulated, typically two to four days
3. A rental car included at little or no additional cost
4. Airline upgrades for a reasonable add-on fee; make sure to ask about this if it is important to you

Consolidators

Consolidators—who are sometimes referred to as wholesalers or bucket shops—negotiate lower fares with an airline for resale to retail travel agents, to the public directly, or to both. (Refer to Chapter 7 for details.) Typically, a consolidator negotiates a fixed price (one that can vary seasonally) for each route the airline serves, and marks up the price a small amount. Discounts of 15 to 20 percent and even as high as 50 percent off the best available coach (and occasionally business- or first-class) fares are not uncommon when purchasing tickets from a consolidator—especially for last-minute airfares.

While consolidators can offer great airfares, they do carry some risk. Travelers should always pay with a credit card to protect themselves; be aware that they may not receive frequent flyer miles; and understand that tickets are generally nonrefundable and nonchangeable. Savvy travelers will check that the consolidator is affiliated with IATAN (International Airline Travel Agent's Network) or ARC (Airline Reporting Corporation), and will research whether complaints have been lodged against the consolidator with the Better Business Bureau.

Consolidators most commonly specialize in distributing international tickets, but the few consolidators that deal with domestic tickets (such as *Cheaptickets.com* and *Overstock .com*) can save last-minute road warriors significant amounts of money. Domestic tickets purchased from consolidators will almost always be on major carriers, and will usually require one stop since major airlines are reluctant to distribute tickets for nonstop flights through wholesale channels.

Your travel agent may have established relationships with consolidators. If your travel agent is willing to seek out a discounted ticket, he will charge a service fee if successful, and you may save a significant amount of dollars.

Refer to Chapter 7 for more details about airfare consolidations.

Using Low-Cost Airlines

For those road warriors who cannot plan and purchase tickets at least seven days in advance, low-cost airlines can help save some big bucks. Since low-cost airlines' "walk up" fares—airline-speak for last-minute fares—are typically 50 to 70 percent cheaper than those of major airlines (even for nonstop flights), checking out low-cost airlines' Web offerings is worthwhile. Even if a low-fare carrier doesn't travel to your desired city, check it out for nearby alternative cities. Lists of the low-cost airlines serving North America as well as Europe are provided in Appendices C and D, respectively.

Major airlines frequently match the prices of a competing low-cost carrier on identical routes, though sometimes only around the specific departure times of the competing low-cost carrier. The most efficient way to find such fares on major airlines is by surfing the Internet, including visiting the sites for low-cost airlines that service your nearby airport(s).

Finally, *Bestfares.com* posts information about specials for major and low-cost airlines in its "News Section" each day, and the site is a major proponent of Southwest Airlines. Unfortunately, the probability of you finding a special for the specific route you need as a last-minute reservation just when you need it is small—but worth a try!

Split Tickets

Split ticketing is a process whereby the traveler purchases two roundtrip tickets—one from his originating or home city into an intermediate city, and the second roundtrip from the intermediate city to the ultimate destination city. For example, if you want to travel from city A to city B, you would buy one roundtrip ticket from city A to intermediate city C, with the second ticket from city C to city B. Refer to Chapter 3 for more details.

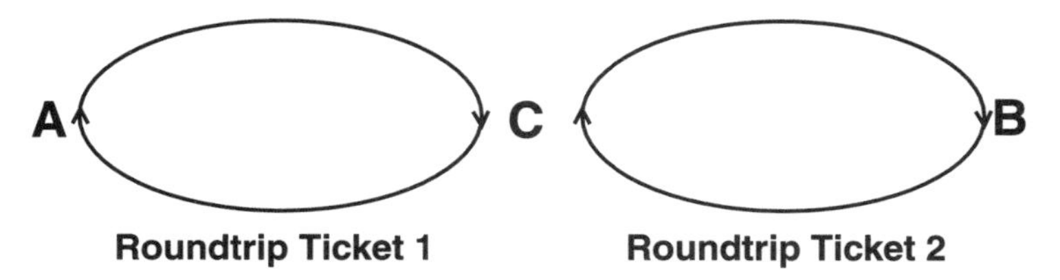

Consider the following aspects of split ticketing before you try it.

Domestic Split Ticketing

This strategy makes sense where flights into and out of the intermediate city are typically cheap. As an example, for those flying from or to the western United States, Las Vegas is a perfect intermediate city because of its inexpensive fares designed to attract gamblers who may travel at the last minute. In addition, two low-cost airlines—Southwest and America West—use Las Vegas as a hub, which means major airlines usually match prices to be competitive. Flying the major airlines through Las Vegas using two separate roundtrip tickets can result in spectacular savings.

For example, a last-minute road warrior flying roundtrip from New York to Los Angeles may purchase two roundtrip tickets: ticket #1 is a roundtrip New York–Las Vegas, and ticket #2 is a roundtrip Las Vegas–Los Angeles, ensuring at least one hour connecting time between flights in Las Vegas. While savings using split tickets vary depending on the cities involved, in the New York–Los Angeles example above, a last-minute roundtrip ticket on a major airline could be $1,500 or higher. If a last-minute New York–Las Vegas roundtrip is $550, and Las Vegas–Los Angeles is $120, the total savings could be as much as $830 ($1,500 minus $550 + $120)—or more.

> **TIP**
>
> **When you use split ticketing on two unaffiliated airlines, allocate at least *two* hours connecting time. You may need the extra time if the initial flight is delayed or if you have to retrieve your baggage and transfer it between two unaffiliated airlines, which can be based in different terminals (and, in some cases with international tickets, even different airports).**

But this strategy isn't always a money saver. A traveler from Los Angeles to Phoenix may save little, if anything, by purchasing two tickets through Las Vegas for a number of reasons:

1. Phoenix is a hub for the low-cost airlines Southwest and America West, and major airlines will frequently match the value prices.
2. Fares will often be relatively low for short-distance flights such as Los Angles–Phoenix.
3. The one-hour layover in Las Vegas will more than double the flight time, virtually obliterating any savings for the road warrior whose time has significant value.

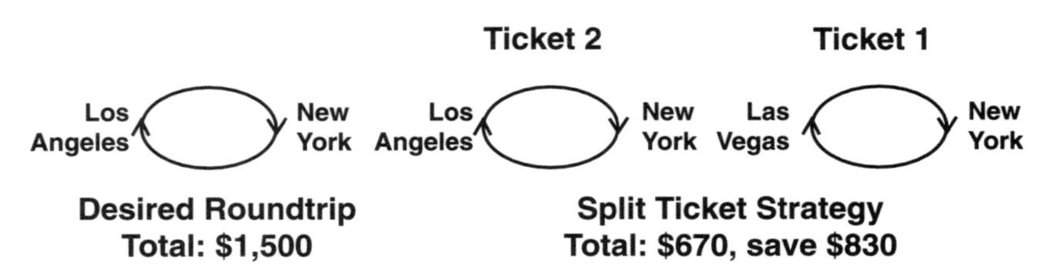

The International Split Ticket

Because of intense competition (especially for coach-class tickets), London may be an excellent intermediate or split city option when flying from the

United States to cities in continental Europe, the Middle East, or Africa—or even for flights within continental Europe. This is especially true for coach-class tickets. For example, rather than purchasing a Chicago–Athens ticket, the traveler may get better value by purchasing separate Chicago–London and London–Athens roundtrips. Similarly, flying from Venice to Stockholm may be cheaper with two tickets, having London as the intermediate city.

Once in London, the road warrior has several options for onward travel to Europe as well as the Middle East, Asia, or Africa:

1. Book your onward flight on the same or a different major airline. This option offers the greatest convenience since major airlines typically serve the major airports, and your baggage can be transferred seamlessly if you continue on the same airline or another affiliated major airline. Major European airlines have significantly dropped their fares for flights within Europe to compete with European low-cost airlines. For example, if you are flying British Airways from the United States into London and need to fly to Madrid, you can purchase your onward journey on British Airways or Iberia (affiliated), as well as on British Midland or Air France (unaffiliated). Just remember, you yourself may need to claim and then recheck your baggage if the two airlines do not have an affiliation.

ALERT

Check to be sure that you are arriving into and departing from the same London airport. The commute between two London airports can easily add two to three hours to your layover.

2. Purchase the ticket for your onward flight on a European low-cost airline. While European low-cost airlines are growing rapidly and serving virtually all major cities, they frequently use lesser-known airports that are further away from major cities and will require a significant commute if you arrive and depart from different London airports. For example, major airlines use Heathrow or Gatwick while low-cost airlines may use Stansted or Luton airports. Be sure to check those airports in which you will be originating and terminating if you select a low-cost airline.

3. If you're traveling to Paris or Brussels, consider using Eurostar, the high-speed Chunnel train that travels beneath the English Channel. But last-minute Chunnel roundtrip fares can exceed $200 ($100 for advance purchase). And you still have to spend the time and money commuting from Heathrow or Gatwick airport and making a change to Waterloo Station in central London since there is no direct connection. An alternative is to fly into London and spend some time there before continuing on the Eurostar.

4. Find a bucket shop or consolidator, which are abundant in London, but do not typically have easy Internet access for contact from countries outside Great Britain. Many of these agencies can be found around Earls Court Road and are easily identified in daily London newspapers. While the fares they offer for flights anywhere from London can be excellent—including those purchased at the last minute—the uncertainty and time expenditure lead us to suggest that only the adventurous traveler with no time constraints should even consider this option.

Split Ticket Strategy Caveats

We cannot stress this enough: When applying the split ticket strategy to either domestic or international travel, each of the two roundtrips may be purchased on the same airlines, on aligned partners, or on nonaligned airlines—-but make sure you know which is which. When you connect through the intermediate city to another flight within the same airline, or to an aligned carrier, you enjoy the magic of automatic baggage transfer. Conversely, if each ticket is on two nonaligned airlines, you may be required to pick up your baggage yourself and transport it for check-in on the connecting flight.

Be especially careful about switching to nonaligned airlines for international routes, where the change may require that you transfer to a different terminal—in addition to picking up and rechecking your baggage. For example, at London's Heathrow Airport, distances between terminals can sometimes be a mile or more, a long way to tote your luggage, recheck it, and make it to your flight on time! Furthermore, several European low-cost airlines fly out of regional London airports, such as Stansted or Luton, so the traveler may need to take ground transportation for the fifty to one hundred miles from Heathrow or Gatwick, where the majority of transatlantic flights terminate. Finally, if your inbound flight is delayed and you miss your ongoing flight on the second unaffiliated airline, the latter carrier has no obligation to accommodate you with any special treatment to expedite you on another flight to your final destination promptly.

The One-Way Split Ticket Strategy

A variant on the roundtrip split ticket is a one-way (rather than a roundtrip) split ticket. For example, instead of purchasing a New York–Los Angeles one-way ticket only, the traveler purchases two one-way tickets, the first from New York to Las Vegas, the second from Las Vegas to Los Angeles. This strategy may be especially helpful to the last-minute traveler who has seven days advance notice for the return flight, in which case he purchases a 7-, 14-, or 21-day advance ticket starting with the return portion of his trip, or to the traveler who implements a hidden city strategy to complete the roundtrip. We'll explain both of these options in more detail in the next section.

The Hidden City Strategy

The hidden city strategy may benefit the last-minute traveler who lives in or will be flying to a hub city for a particular airline. This strategy is worthwhile applying one-way from city A to city B where:

1. The intended destination (city B) is a hub city.
2. The price of a one-way ticket to another destination (city C) beyond your desired destination (with a required stop in your desired destination, with or without a change of planes) is cheaper than simply purchasing a ticket into your destination city. You get off at the hub city B, without connecting to your reserved flight destined for the ticketed destination city C.

Take as an example Detroit, the hub for Northwest Airlines. Northwest owns approximately 80 percent of the gates at Detroit International Airport, driving up airfares for travelers flying into and out of Detroit because of little competition. Let's say:

1. A traveler flying from Los Angeles to Detroit is quoted a one-way last-minute fare of $645.
2. This same traveler is quoted $222 for a Los Angeles–Birmingham, Alabama, flight, with a stop in Detroit.

The traveler simply needs to book and pay for the Los Angeles–Birmingham flights, but get off in Detroit to save $423 ($645 minus $222).

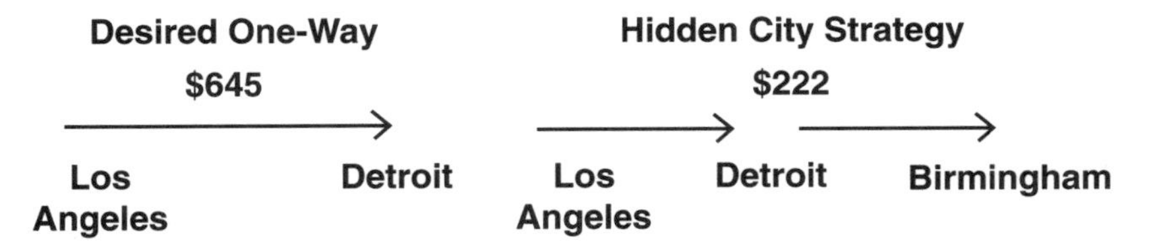

■ **Locating the Hidden City.** Finding a hidden city may require trial and error on the Internet. Try various itineraries from the originating city to other cities that involve a connection through the desired destination city, which must be a hub for an airline for the strategy to work. The most logical itineraries to search are those routes where a low-cost airline competes. For example, the traveler needing to fly from Los Angeles to

Chicago (a hub for United and American) may try Los Angeles to Kansas City via Chicago, since the low-cost airline Southwest flies nonstop from Los Angeles to Kansas City.

Use the hidden city strategy only on a one-way ticket or on the outbound portion of a roundtrip ticket on which you do not plan to use the return portion. There is a good possibility the airline computer system will automatically cancel any subsequent segments of a ticket if a passenger's absence on any segment is detected.

■ **The Hidden City Strategy Can Be Risky.** Since all checked baggage is going to the ticketed destination city, you must remember one important thing: *Do not check baggage.* And for those occasions where an aircraft's baggage racks are full, be careful about any baggage being checked to the city *beyond* your destination at the gate before you board! In addition, hidden city tickets should not be booked through a travel agent because airlines consider this money-saving practice to be a violation of their rules. Since they have been known to impose monetary penalties on travel agents implementing this creative ticketing strategy, your agent will approach you to pay the difference. A better idea is to purchase hidden city tickets from the airline direct or from a travel Web site. Finally, with increased concerns regarding airline security, your absence from the connecting flight may be detected and considered a cause for concern. Given so many risks associated with this practice, we do not suggest it as a preferred strategy.

■ **How to Reappear After Traveling to the Hidden City.** As discussed in the prior section, a hidden city ticket should be used only on the first segment of a one-way ticket or a roundtrip ticket on which you do not intend to use the return, because the return portion will likely be canceled automatically once you do not check in for the second segment of your outbound journey. For the other (outbound or return) flight where you do not have the benefit of seven days' advance notice, your options are to:

If you use the hidden city strategy, you *do not* want be asked to check your bags at the gate. Travel light and board as soon as possible to ensure that you find room in the luggage bins for your carry-on items.

1. Purchase a regular one-way ticket, either from a low-cost airline or consolidator.
2. Apply a one-way split ticket strategy, possibly through Las Vegas if travel involves a city in the West (refer to prior section on split city ticketing).

3. Use a hidden city strategy again with a separate ticket for the second "hidden city" ticket—preferably booked on another airline to reduce the risk of being detected.

If you do have at least seven to fourteen days' advance notice for the return component of your trip, review the next section.

Purchasing an Advance-Purchase Ticket for the Return Only

If you have 7 days' notice or more on the return portion (but not the outbound), purchase a much cheaper nonrefundable 7-, 14-, or 21-day advance ticket with a Saturday night stay for the return portion of your trip.

The originating flight of the advance-purchase ticket travels from your destination to originating city; the return portion back to your destination city is scheduled at least one weekend following the originating segment and can be either discarded or kept for possible future use.

Some markets may not offer 7-day advance-purchase tickets; 14- or 21-day advance fares are more common.

Check Out Whether Your Desired Flight Is a Codeshare

The prices charged by different partners on a codeshare flight may be different, for both domestic and international travel. Each airline selling seats on the flight draws from distinct inventory and is free to charge whatever it wishes. For example, if you want to fly to South Africa, you may purchase from South African Airways (SAA), which actually operates the flight, or from Delta, which as a codeshare partner purchases a set number of seats for any given flight from SAA. However, less well-known SAA often charges lower fares than Delta.

Keep Frequent Flyer Miles Ready

I once needed an "on-the-spot" ticket to Toronto and was amazed when Continental offered me a 25,000-mile saver award without charge (other than a $29 tax and security fee) when I called the airline's One Pass frequent flyer desk from my cell phone at the airport baggage check-in desk.

Want to ensure that you get exceptional value even when flying without advance notice? Keep sufficient frequent flyer miles at the ready. On most major airlines, an award ticket can be requested within two hours of a flight, either without charge or for a nominal expediting fee (typically $50 to $100). Rules for requesting award tickets within twenty-one days of departure may vary significantly from airline to airline, so check with the frequent flyer desk as soon as you know about a possible need (or better yet, an anticipated need).

With few exceptions (such as Northwest and Continental Airlines saver awards), frequent flyer programs for the major U.S. carriers do not require a Saturday night stay in the destination. Since the traveler may be using frequent flyer miles for what would otherwise be a very expensive ticket, the value of the miles used for a last-minute roundtrip can be much higher than the value for flying coach class with advance notice.

The Two Tiers for Frequent Flyer Redemption—Standard and Premium

Most of the major airlines' frequent flyer programs have two tiers of awards: saver awards, which require fewer miles, but for which fewer seats are allocated; and premium awards, which require up to double the number of miles, but usually have capacity restrictions waived (meaning if there is just one available seat, it's yours!).

TIP

Although Southwest Airlines does not allow passengers in possession of nonrefundable tickets to go on standby for any other flights without paying the difference for an unrestricted ticket, it has an explicit policy that any passenger in possession of a Southwest award ticket may go standby for any flight on any day—if there is a seat available, it's yours!

On Southwest Airlines, there is only one kind of award—the saver, for which all capacity controls are waived. However, unlike many major airlines, Southwest does have a few blackout dates around major holidays prohibiting use of award tickets.

Because saver awards are capacity controlled, you may sometimes find that you cannot use saver or lower-mileage awards for the flights you want. However, if the higher mileage (premium) award is available, it may still be an infinitely better value than paying an outrageous amount for a ticket. An alternative strategy in such instances, albeit with some risk that the flight you desire will be completely full, is to select a slightly different (preferably later) flight where the saver award is available, and then go standby for the earlier flight. On major carriers, passengers using an award or free ticket can usually stand by for any flight on the same or on a different day for the outbound or return segments, without any charge, although some airlines have attempted to introduce change fees for award tickets—for example, American Airlines introducing a $100 change fee for changing the date or time of travel with an award ticket. This strategy is considerably less risky when you ask about the current status on your preferred flight. If it's already fairly full—or worse, oversold—your chances of being successful on standby are greatly reduced. Conversely, the probability of success as a standby passenger on your preferred flight are very good if the reservations agent tells you that the flight is not especially full.

Another angle to requesting a premium award is to check the availability of a saver award in business or first class, which often costs the same or less in frequent flyer miles than a premium award ticket!

Caveats Before You Go Standby

Before you go off to the airport to stand by for a flight, give careful consideration to these four points:

1. **Rules of Your Ticket.** East airline has specific standby rules for the different types of revenue and award tickets. Be sure to check.
2. **Frequency of Flights.** Using the standby technique works best in those airports where your preferred airline has departures to your destination at least every three to six hours. If flights are infrequent, failure to hop on your desired flight could mean long delays.
3. **Holiday Travel.** Since flights are often oversold around the holiday season, going standby can be difficult, if not impossible.
4. **International Travel.** Certain airlines may not permit standby status with international flights—be sure to check ahead of time if you intend to try this strategy.

The Opportunity Cost of Frequent Flyer Miles

Some small business travelers who pay for their travel out of pocket fail to recognize the opportunity cost concept, resolutely holding their frequent flyer miles for inexpensive vacation tickets while overlooking their use for more expensive business travel. Even if business travel costs are tax-deductible, travelers will typically keep more of their money by using frequent flyer miles for those costly business trips—where the luxury of a cheaper fare isn't an option—than for their vacation tickets, which can often be found at bargain rates.

Taking Advantage of Foreign Currency Differentials

The last-minute international traveler purchasing an international ticket to Europe or Asia should check out flights originating from Toronto or Vancouver if the price in Canadian dollars is similar to the price in U.S. dollars. For example, a ticket price of CN$1,000 would be much less in actual cost than one sold for U.S.$1,000, as long as the U.S. dollar is considerably stronger than the Canadian dollar. However, the additional cost of a roundtrip ticket from the actual departure city in the United States must be factored in, which, of course, will be priced in U.S. dollars.

This strategy can be especially beneficial for business- or first-class tickets that retail for several thousands of dollars. Check prices out of Canada for all classes of service at *Expedia.ca* and *Travelocity.ca*.

Similarly, flying from Mexico City to Europe or Asia may save a significant amount, especially if you can obtain a cheap ticket to pick up your flight in Mexico. Call a travel agent or airline to check out prices from Mexico. This strategy may also benefit those seeking premium-class tickets on world-class carriers at a significant discount.

For those traveling without advance notice to a country whose currency is much weaker than the U.S. dollar, you may try booking a one-way to your destination country and have a travel agent price the return for you in the foreign currency (variant of the split ticket—in this instance splitting one roundtrip ticket into two one-way tickets). For example, if you're flying last-minute coach from San Francisco to Malaysia, the SFO–Kuala Lumpur segment may cost $1,700, with a one-way return segment purchased in Malaysia only $1,200—a $500 savings. This strategy can benefit the last-minute road warrior as well as any savvy traveler purchasing tickets in business or first class. The business traveler who returns to the same destination abroad frequently should consider purchasing an initial one-way ticket to his destination, and thereafter purchasing roundtrips that originate from the foreign destination for future trips if the savings are worthwhile.

When All Else Fails . . . Visit the Auctions Sites

Using *Hotwire.com* or *Priceline.com* is the strategy of last resort. With *Hotwire.com*, you are offered the lowest-priced published airfares for your dates, and you must purchase the ticket within one hour of receiving the quote. However, with *Priceline.com*, you have no knowledge of the lowest available fare stored in the company's database, so we suggest bidding 30 percent lower than the price you were offered by *Hotwire.com*. Tickets purchased from both sites are nonrefundable and nonchangeable. Refer to Chapter 9 for more details about these sites.

In Summary

- When you must travel without the benefit of at least seven days' advance purchase, start with the Internet. Visit *Hotwire.com* to find the lowest fare an airline will accept, keeping in mind that you will not know which airline, routing, or times you will fly before you have paid for a nonrefundable and nonchangeable ticket. Then compare the price with retail sites, such as *Orbitz.com*, *Expedia.com*, and *Travelocity.com*, airline sites, and consolidator sites, such as *Cheaptickets.com* and *Overstock.com*, as well as *Flights.com* for international tickets. Vary the times and days of travel as well as your cities of departure and destination.

- Check out prices from low-cost airlines that serve your city from major or secondary airports. Then look at the fares of the major airlines serving the same routes, as they may match the prices of low-cost airlines.
- Road warriors—especially those booking at the last minute—may find a package that beats high airfares as long as they book three days in advance. Hotels and car rentals may be included. Some packages enable the passenger to upgrade to business or first class for a reasonable add-on fee.
- Consolidators are wholesalers who sell either direct to travel agents or the public, and which may offer fares that benefit international travelers with fewer than twenty-one days before their date of departure or whose length of stay in their destination will be less than the minimum required for a discount ticket (usually at least five days).
- A split ticket strategy—purchasing two or more one-way or round-trip tickets through an intermediate city—can be especially helpful for travelers looking for inexpensive, last-minute fares. In the United States, Las Vegas is a popular intermediate city for those traveling to or from the West (for example, New York to Los Angeles is ticketed as New York–Las Vegas and Las Vegas–Los Angeles). For international travel, London can be an excellent split ticket intermediate city for those traveling from the United States to continental Europe (for example, Philadelphia to Milan is ticketed as Philadelphia–London and London–Milan) or within continental Europe itself (for example, Athens to Stockholm is ticketed as Athens–London and London–Stockholm). The major drawbacks to a split ticket strategy are:

  1. You may have to transfer your own baggage, sometimes between terminals or even airports, when traveling on nonaffiliated airlines.
  2. The second airline, if not aligned with the first, has no obligation to expedite you on a later flight if your inbound trip is delayed and you miss your connecting flight. Allow at least two to three hours between flights when using a split ticket on two nonaffiliated airlines. To check affiliations, call the airlines' frequent flyer desk.

- The hidden city strategy may benefit the traveler wishing to fly on a major airline into a hub city where the one-way price is very expensive. For example, the road warrior flying from Seattle to Chicago may find an excellent fare on United or American by purchasing a ticket from Seattle to Baltimore via Chicago. He simply disembarks in Chicago—having made sure not to check any baggage, which would be sent to Baltimore!

- Ultimately, using frequent flyer miles rather than purchasing an expensive ticket may be the superior strategy. This is especially true if the road warrior can use a saver award for the least amount of miles. If the saver award is not available, a premium award (using double frequent flyer miles)—or a business- or first-class award ticket for double the miles of a saver award (or less)—can still be a cost-effective option.
- As long as the U.S. dollar is considerably stronger than its Canadian counterpart, purchasing tickets to Europe or Asia from Toronto or Vancouver can help the last-minute international traveler save significant amounts of money, especially for those seeking business or first-class tickets. Remember to factor in the additional roundtrip ticket from your home city to Toronto or Vancouver when calculating your savings! Check out fares originating from Canada at *Expedia.ca* and *Travelocity.ca.* Flying from Mexico City to Europe or Asia may provide similar benefits, especially for travelers seeking a business- or first-class ticket.
- For last-minute travelers to countries whose currency is considerably weaker than the U.S. dollar, having a travel agent purchase a one-way ticket for the return portion denominated in the weak foreign currency can result in huge savings—including for business and first class (the outbound portion originating from the United States must be purchased in U.S. dollars). For the traveler visiting the same destination abroad regularly, purchasing roundtrip tickets denominated in foreign currency that originate from the foreign destination city may be a cost-effective option if that country's currency is weak relative to the U.S. dollar.
- As a last resort, the cost-conscious road warrior could go to *Hotwire.com* or *Priceline.com*—but he will only know his airline and times of travel once he has purchased a nonrefundable and nonchangeable ticket! This is rarely a good option for the time-sensitive road warrior—notwithstanding that frequent flyer miles will not be earned on such flights—and all fares are ineligible for upgrades.

CHAPTER FIVE

First Class for a Fraction of the Cost

Tax day—15 April, 2002—the day I had to ante up approximately $20,000 in federal and state taxes. Ouch! Even though I didn't relish handing over my hard-earned money, I had found a way to ease the sting a bit, thanks to one of my affinity credit cards.

American Express saw a way to capitalize on tax day by offering holders of its Delta credit card the opportunity to receive *double* frequent flyer miles if they used it to pay their income taxes. The ceiling for payment of taxes was $10,000, which would earn a maximum of 20,000 miles—while incurring a 2.5 percent "courtesy" fee. (I love how they use those euphemisms!)

I already possessed an American Express Delta card, so I opened a new and separate account for my business. Between the two accounts, I was able to overcome the $10,000 maximum payment and earn the full 40,000 miles for the $20,000 tax bill.

A roundtrip cross-country first-class ticket within the United States on Delta retails for about $4,000, but can be obtained for 40,000 miles. Our transaction fee for earning 40,000 miles was 2.5 percent (applied to the $20,000 only—remember, the promotion was for double miles) or $500. When I redeemed the 40,000 miles for first-class cross-country tickets from Los Angeles to Boston, the effective cost for the ticket was $500—or 12.5% of the retail price!

Granted my tax bill was pretty high, one that most people probably won't have to pay, so racking up a lot of miles this way may not be possible for everyone. An alternative strategy would have been to purchase the frequent flyer miles from American Express Membership Miles program, through which regular cardholders may purchase up to 500,000 miles per year at a cost of $25 per 1,000 (no tax is charged on miles purchased through American Express). Purchasing 40,000 miles from American Express would cost $1,000 or 25 percent of retail price—still an outstanding deal.

A further option would have been to purchase the miles direct from Delta over two years, which permits annual purchases of 20,000 miles for each individual account. However, purchasing direct from an airline is usually about $30 per 1,000 miles and incurs a 7.5 percent tax charge as well as a transaction fee. (Refer to the section "Purchase Those Extra Miles" in this chapter for additional details.)

Using Your Frequent Flyer Miles

Savvy travelers for whom luxury travel is very important recognize that by far the greatest value they can reap from their hard-earned frequent flyer miles is for premium (business- or first-class) travel—especially for international travel, where flight times typically exceed eight hours and frequently include overnight travel. There are two ways that frequent flyer miles can be used for domestic or international upgrades:

TIP

Round-the-world first-class award trips may go for up to 400,000 miles on Star Alliance, which includes United Airlines, Air Canada, and their worldwide partners.

1. For an outright business- or first-class award ticket, which may cost anywhere between 40,000 miles (domestic, with capacity controls that limit available seats and blackout dates on some airlines) and 240,000 miles (international, with no capacity controls or blackout dates).

2. By purchasing a coach-class ticket and using a smaller amount of frequent flyer miles to upgrade. For example, a United saver award in business class from the United States to Australia may be 90,000 miles—or can be obtained with 50,000 miles in conjunction with an advance-purchase, nonrefundable, roundtrip ticket priced around $1,600. The benefit of the latter is that the traveler will earn miles because he is flying with a paid (or revenue) ticket.

Continental, Northwest, and Delta's international routes have only one level of premium class, which combines business and first class. American has similar configurations on some of its international flights. This strategy significantly limits inventory for potential upgrades. Other major airlines, such as United and British Airways, may feature both first- and business-class offerings, which results in significantly larger upgrade seat inventory.

In some cases, frequent flyer miles cannot be used for an upgrade in conjunction with the cheapest nonrefundable airfares, but that doesn't mean you need to purchase a full coach fare to benefit from the miles-for-upgrade option. For example, when I had to fly from Los Angeles to Vienna, the cheapest coach fare was $1,110. The lowest upgradeable fare was just $90 higher, at $1,200, while the full coach fare was almost $2,000.

It is extremely important to recognize that upgrade policies and upgrade seat availability differ vastly from airline to airline, and change from time to time. Go online or call an airline's frequent flyer desk to request the most up-to-date mileage requirements for the award you have in mind.

One more point: If you can't redeem your frequent flyer miles for the seat you want on your primary carrier, consider its partner airlines, especially for international flights. Check with your preferred airline's Web site (click on "partners") or frequent flyer desk to find out which alliances are in place that may offer alternatives; or look at any airline's in-flight magazine, which always lists partner airlines and can be ordered—usually without charge—by contacting the customer service desk.

TIP

Saver awards are capacity controlled, meaning just a few seats are allocated for these awards on each flight. In contrast, awards requiring double use of miles are not subject to capacity control of award seat availability.

The Co-Pay Solution

American Airlines offers an option that enables travelers to co-pay on their awards for certain routes. For example, if you only have 30,000 miles available to you and the first-class domestic award seat you want is 40,000 miles, American will allow you to use your 30,000 miles and pay $275 in lieu of the additional 10,000 miles needed. Furthermore, if you do not have any American Airlines miles in your frequent flyer account, the airline has staged promotions whereby you can obtain up to 30,000 miles in the form of 15,000 personal miles purchased by you for immediate deposit into your account, with the other 15,000 miles purchased as a gift to you—by your spouse, child, parent, or friend. Given that buying 30,000 miles at $25 per 1,000 miles will cost you approximately $832.50 ($750 plus 7.5 percent tax plus $1/1,000 miles transaction fee), your total first-class roundtrip fare—including the $275 co-pay—will be $1,107.50 instead of the retail cost exceeding $3,000, which represents a 63 percent discount.

If the aircraft you select has three classes of service—coach, business, and first—you will be upgraded to American's business class by following the strategies outlined above. But American Airlines will also allow you to purchase your way into first class by paying the difference between what the first-class and business-class fares are.

For example, let's assume you are traveling on a flight that has three classes of service; the retail cost of a first-class ticket is $4,200, and business class is $3,600. If your co-pay and mileage purchase has cost you the $1,107.50 we figured above and you have upgraded into business class, you will be able to upgrade again by paying an additional $600—the difference between the first-class and business-class fares. In this scenario, your first-class roundtrip ticket will cost $1,707.50 ($1,107.50 plus $600) instead of a retail price of $4,200—a savings of 60 percent!

Sound complicated? It's really not, just a formula anyone can follow. Let's go through the steps:

Step 1: Purchase 30,000 miles (15,000 purchased for yourself and the other 15,000 purchased as a gift for you) at $25 per 1,000 miles for a total of $832.50 ($750 plus 7.5 percent tax plus a transaction fee of $1 per 1,000 miles).

Step 2: Add the $275 co-pay with the cost of purchasing 30,000 miles (described in Step 1) to get to a total of $1,107.50 for business-class roundtrip versus the retail cost of $3,600, which represents a 70 percent discount.

Step 3: Pay an additional $600 to upgrade from business to first class for a final total cost of $1,707.50 for first-class roundtrip versus retail cost of $4,200, a 60 percent discount.

Purchase Those Extra Miles

World travelers and road warriors who anticipate the need to make last-minute business travel arrangements will make a point of purchasing on a regular basis—meaning every year—the maximum number of miles from as many airlines as possible. They look on this as an investment or a long-term plan to build up their "savings." An even smarter traveler will not limit purchases to his own account, but will buy miles for his spouse, parents, and children—for their use or his own. (An award ticket requested from frequent flyer miles may be gifted to anyone you please). Since frequent flyer miles no longer expire, visionary travelers will eventually have a stockpile of miles for as many leisure and business trips flown in coach, business, or first class as they may desire.

TIP

Another source for purchasing is American Express Membership Rewards, where you can buy 500,000 miles per year.

For the last-minute business traveler, a 25,000-mile domestic coach-class award using purchased miles obtained at $25 for 1,000 miles will cost $695.30 ($625 + 7.5 percent tax + a transaction fee of $1 per 1000 miles) versus a retail cost of $1,000 to $2,400 on a major airline. (Keep in mind that frequent flyer miles purchased through American Express do not incur tax or transaction costs.) Even using a double miles "anytime" award priced at $1,397.76 ($698.88 x 2) may offer a significant savings if the regular fare exceeds $2,000. The benefits of purchasing frequent flyer miles for business and first class are discussed in the previous section "Using Your Frequent Flyer Miles."

The shrewd traveler also watches out for special promotions that enable him to purchase frequent flyer miles at a discount (and perhaps enable him to exceed the standard annual purchase limits imposed by an airline). For example, the author once purchased 180,000 Qantas miles by taking out thirty magazine subscriptions at $60 per subscription (pity the poor mailman!). The effective cost was $10 per 1,000 miles—a bargain!

Capitalize on Your Elite Status

When it comes to easy and inexpensive upgrades, elite frequent flyer status is "where the action is" for frequent business travelers who fly at least 25,000 miles on the same carrier within a calendar year. Different airlines have slightly different qualification requirements and upgrade rules, but elite flyers are always assured of separate check-in lines (usually with business- or first-class travelers), bonus frequent flyer miles when flying on their primary—as opposed to partner—airline (typically 25 to 100 percent), and unprecedented upgrade opportunities which will allow free domestic upgrades, provided space is available, even when flying on cheap tickets.

ALERT

Delta and Continental have pioneered a policy whereby only 50 percent of miles flown on discounted tickets contribute toward elite status the following year.

Elite frequent flyers have two unique opportunities for upgrading without using frequent flyer miles, especially when flying within North America—even when flying on most nonrefundable advance-purchase tickets:

- **Free.** Airlines such as Continental and Northwest allow their elite frequent flyers to upgrade without extra charge on domestic routes and occasionally outside the United States, such as Canada. Those elite flyers who have the highest status based on the prior year's flight activity naturally have the highest priority.
- **Using Inexpensive Certificates.** For example, American and United Airlines will award certificates that are:
  1. Offered free in limited amounts depending on flight activity (the more miles you fly, the more certificates you receive).
  2. Purchasable for a reasonable amount that will permit a cross-country one-way upgrade for around $250, even if the passenger purchased a cheap ticket.

American and United also reward their highest level elite members who traveled in excess of 100,000 miles in the prior year with six or eight free upgrades for international flights, which are confirmable when making the reservation and can be used with some advance-purchase nonrefundable discount fares. In addition, United regularly offers its elite 100,000 mile flyers free confirmed upgrade certificates for domestic travel, which enable travelers to confirm their upgrade when making the reservation—no matter how far in advance the ticket is purchased.

While upgrade certificates cannot officially be used to upgrade with domestic award tickets (that is, frequent flyer) on domestic or international flights, passengers enjoying the highest level elite status or the million-miler status have been upgraded just for the asking! This is more likely to occur if the flight is oversold in coach class, and the airline has to upgrade a few coach passengers—known as an "operational upgrade" in the industry.

Upgrade from Full-Coach Fare

Some airlines will allow coach-class passengers paying a fully refundable economy-class fare—which is usually the most expensive, between $1,000 and $2,000 for a roundtrip cross-country nonstop flight—to upgrade without charge or use of certificate or frequent flyer miles on a space-available basis, even if the passenger does not hold elite frequent flyer status with that airline. However, airline rules for upgrading with full-coach fares are quite variable and change frequently. For example, Northwest has put on promotions that allowed "free" upgrades to full-fare passengers who connect through one of their hubs and change planes. US Airways may permit an upgrade to the passenger paying full-coach fare even if no connection is made. United Airlines allows full-fare passengers to upgrade by purchasing the same inexpensive upgrade certificates its elite frequent flyers use (refer to prior section) without any connecting flight requirement. In fact, on United, nonelite flyers paying full-coach fare have higher priority status for upgrading than all elite flyers except for United's highest level 1K elites—those passengers who flew at least 100,000 miles in the prior year.

Paying in Increments to Upgrade

Some of the smaller U.S. airlines have unique and individual upgrade policies distinct from the major carriers, regardless of whether the traveler enjoys elite status with the airline. Expect to see many variations as airlines experiment with policies to gain loyalty and maximize revenue. Here are a few examples:

- Hawaiian Airlines offers a $250 one-way upgrade on a standby basis at the gate up to four hours ahead of departure time for most fare categories.

- Low-cost carrier America West enables upgrades at a cost based on distance flown, not to exceed $150 on a cross-country flight.
- American Trans Air (ATA)—which is based out of Atlanta and has become a serious competitor for Delta—is unique among the value carriers in having a business-class cabin on all its aircraft. Full-fare passengers may upgrade at any time in advance for $25 one way.

The Exception to the Rule—Midwest Airlines

Perhaps the best kept secret among domestic travelers seeking first-class comfort at coach price is the "not-so-little airline that could"—Midwest Airlines. Midwest Airlines operates as a scheduled carrier to all major U.S. cities from its hub in Milwaukee. Every seat is leather and as wide as other airlines' first-class seats, all offered at coach prices. Unfortunately, Midwest Airlines does not fly outside the U.S., although miles accrued in its frequent flyer program can be redeemed for tickets on American (which has an extensive network throughout Europe and Asia). Another disadvantage is its limited schedule, making it an impractical choice for time-sensitive travelers who live outside Milwaukee.

Take Advantage of Small Business Program Awards

Check with your favorite airline as to whether it has a small business award program (such as Continental's Reward One and American's Business ExtrAA). Each airline's program for small business includes awards that can be used for upgrades and free tickets. The individual flyer may find it a challenge to accrue sufficient points for upgrades or free tickets from participating in small business reward programs, but a company with several travelers may have sufficient volume to meet the required earning threshold.

Get a Free Companion Ticket from Prestige Charge Cards or Credit Cards

American Express Platinum (annual fee $395) offers members the benefit of obtaining a free companion first- or business-class ticket on twenty different airlines that change from time to time, usually including Virgin, Air France, Alitalia, Lufthansa, Cathay Pacific, Aer Lingus, Air New Zealand, Delta, and Continental Airlines, with one paid premium-class ticket. Both passengers must fly together on all flights booked using this promotion. Although American Express supposedly "invites" its members to be Platinum cardholders, anyone with a good credit record and annual income exceeding $100,000 per year will have a reasonable chance of being approved. Proof, such as tax returns verifying claimed income, may be required.

Purchasing two separate premium-class tickets when the airline has a special promotion may be cheaper than using the American Express Platinum card companion ticket offer. Be sure to check!

The Diners Carte Royale card (annual fee $300) offers a free British Airways companion certificate on British Airways usable for any class of service.

Finally, Bank One offers a British Airways Visa credit card that earns miles in British Airways' Executive Club frequent flyer program. Using the card to purchase a business- or first-class ticket entitles the traveler to take a companion in the same class of service.

For more details, refer to Chapter 18.

Bump Yourself Up

Chapter 2 describes the process for assuring you will be first in line for the opportunity to be bumped if a flight is oversold, as well as what you can reasonably ask for in terms of compensation. One important compensatory benefit to request if you voluntarily offer your seat for an oversold flight is first class on the next available flight. I obtained this perk for my entire family when we gave up our seats on a Los Angeles–Honolulu flight over the Easter weekend (and walked away with whopping $750 vouchers toward future Northwest flights for each of us to boot!).

Travel Agents Specializing in Discounted Premium Class

Several travel agencies specialize in selling discounted premium tickets direct to the public, either through negotiated contracts or creative routing. While we cannot testify to the quality of service or financial stability of either company, we can bring two examples to your attention:

1. *1stair.net* (or call 888-467-3040)
2. *Flyfirstclass.com* (or call 800-883-5937)

Originate from Mexico or Canada

When flying abroad to another continent, it is easy to obtain a cheap ticket from most U.S. cities to Mexico City, Toronto, or Vancouver. Then purchase your first- or business-class ticket from one of those cities to Europe or Asia. For example, if a Los Angeles–Frankfurt business- or first-class ticket can be purchased for $8,000 and $12,000 respectively, you may find a ticket from Mexico City to Frankfurt for less than $3,000 in business class, and double that in first class.

Check our *Travelocity.ca* or *Expedia.ca* to review first- or business-class fares originating from Canada. Contact a travel agent or major airlines by telephone to get premium-class fare quotes originating from Mexico.

Go RTW (Round-the-World)

Round-the-world (RTW) tickets really become bargains when we consider premium class, and typically allow use of several carriers within a global alliance (such as Star Alliance, One World, and so on). For example, a San Francisco–London business fare may approach $10,000, while a first-class ticket costs almost $15,000. But RTW tickets in business class may be purchased for $5,000 to $7,000, with first class approximately $7,000 to $10,000.

Most RTW fares require continuous travel in one direction (east/west), but do allow several stops. Contact a travel agent or any major airline for more details on RTW tickets. And shop around. Refer to Chapter 2 for more details.

The Right Gate at the Right Time—Just Ask for It!

Sometimes, if you're at the right gate at the right time, just asking for an upgrade may reap rewards. My standard question is: What will it take to get an upgrade today? Your chances for success will be greatly enhanced if you are well-dressed, attentive, and exhibit a genuine friendly attitude. Chatting with the gate agent, bringing him a gourmet cookie from one of the vendors, just showing any kindness and empathy can only help your cause.

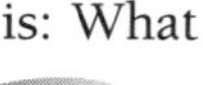

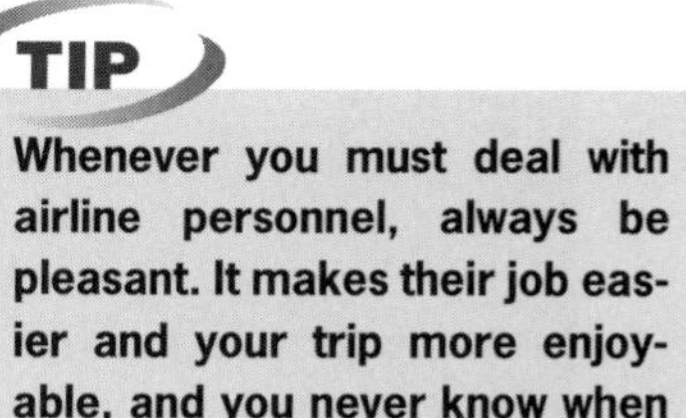

Whenever you must deal with airline personnel, always be pleasant. It makes their job easier and your trip more enjoyable, and you never know when your cheerful disposition will win you special consideration.

If you are turned down, simply ask what is the lowest amount you would need to pay for an upgrade. You may be pleasantly surprised by how little extra is asked for the privilege!

In Summary

- The most powerful strategies for upgrading at a fraction of the retail price are using frequent flyer miles and attaining elite frequent flyer status.
- If your frequent flyer miles account is deficient, you can purchase additional miles either from the airlines or American Express Membership Miles.
- The savvy world traveler or road warrior wanting to travel in premium class or at the "last minute"—especially those with limited flight or credit card mileage-earning opportunities—will buy frequent flyer miles on a regular basis, taking advantage of several airlines' maximum purchase allowed during each calendar year to ultimately accumulate a significant number of frequent flyer miles

over several years, or will purchase frequent flyer miles through his American Express card. Watch out for special promotions that offer a significant amount of frequent flyer miles at a reasonable price.

- When seeking upgraded travel options for using frequent flyer miles, always consider partner airlines if award seats are not available from your primary airline, especially for international flights. Two ways to upgrade using frequent flyer miles are to purchase a relatively inexpensive ticket and use miles to upgrade, or to use more miles for an outright premium-class ticket.
- Elite frequent flyers have the opportunity to upgrade free or to use inexpensive certificates with several major carriers, even when they have purchased a cheap nonrefundable airfare.
- Full-fare coach passengers have excellent opportunities for upgrading with most major U.S. carriers when traveling within the domestic United States, but some carriers require that the passenger make a connection and change planes to be eligible.
- Other diverse options for "upgrading" when traveling domestically include flying Midwest Airlines through its hub in Milwaukee (all coach seats are equivalent to other airlines' first-class cabin), or American Trans Air (ATA) through Atlanta (upgrades are surprisingly inexpensive but only distributed on a space-available basis, which means they are not guaranteed). America West enables upgrades for a nominal amount, typically $50 to $150.
- American Express Platinum cardholders may obtain a free companion ticket when purchasing a first- or business-class international ticket on a variety of major U.S. and international carriers, with a similar privilege afforded to Diners Club Carte Royale cardholders on British Airways that enables a companion to fly free with a paid ticket in any class of service. However, these prestige cards incur annual fees of $395 and $300, respectively. The British Airways Visa card from Bank One offers a free companion ticket with purchase of a business- or first-class ticket.
- If you are bumped from an oversold flight by voluntarily offering your seat in exchange for compensation, make sure to ask for a first-class seat on the next flight.
- Contact travel agents that specialize in discounted premium-class tickets. Two examples are *1stair.net* and *Flyfirstclass.com*.
- Check out premium-class ticket prices originating from cities, such as Vancouver or Toronto in Canada at *Expedia.ca* and *Travelocity.ca*,

which may be much cheaper than originating from the United States. Similarly, contact major airlines or a travel agent to check premium fares out of Mexico City.

- Round-the-world (RTW) tickets can save huge amounts on premium-class tickets. With the emergence of global airline partnerships, you can use several carriers and make multiple stops as you circle the globe in comfort at prices much lower than you would pay for a simple premium-class roundtrip.
- Just ask. If you are empathetic and well-dressed, who knows which gate agent may be willing to accommodate your polite request? If you are turned down, you can still inquire, "What would it cost to upgrade?" You may be surprised at how inexpensively that premium-class seat can be taken by you!

CHAPTER SIX

Comfort in Coach Class

It Could Happen to You!

"Great news!" the perky airline staffer told me as I checked in to get my boarding pass. "Your upgrade has come through. You'll be flying first class."

She gave me a benevolent smile, confident that she had used her powers for good and succeeded in making another passenger happy. But before she could hand me the golden pass, I stopped her with a question.

"Tell me," I asked, "is there an aisle seat available in coach, one that has a guaranteed open middle seat next to it? Or better yet, do you have a row of three empty seats?"

She gave me a confused look, then quickly clicked the keys on her computer.

"Yes, I have that too, but perhaps you didn't understand that you have a *confirmed* seat in *first class . . .*"

Now it was my turn to smile at her. "I know, thank you," I replied graciously, "but would you cancel that upgrade, please, and put me in the aisle seat on that empty row in coach?"

As she processed this unusual request, I could practically hear what was going through her mind: *What's with this guy, choosing coach over first class?*

You, too, might be wondering what kind of person would trade elegant first class for common coach. It's true, most passengers covet the more spacious seats in first class that recline to a greater degree and sometimes include a footrest. The food is generally superior as well, especially when flying abroad—although the service frequently falls short of excellent, especially when flying on U.S.-owned airlines. Business class is almost always crowded, and open seats in premium classes are rare, especially when flying in the United States where many passengers are competing for upgrades by virtue of their elite frequent flyer status.

But as a savvy world traveler, I will often choose coach over first class, and I'll tell you why.

Unless I am flying overnight and need a business-class seat that reclines so I can get some sleep, I will always choose a seat next to one or two vacant seats in coach over an upgrade. I find the space and relative privacy those adjacent unoccupied seats give me are much more desirable than sitting next to another passenger in comfy-but-close first class. Since most airlines charge at least a nominal amount for an upgrade, it doesn't make sense to pay for a standard of service that frequently falls short of my ideal. And the perks in first class—the marginally better food, free drinks, slightly larger seats, and opportunity to scrutinize the other passengers as they crowd their way down the aisle—are certainly not worth the added expense.

Having elite status on an airline helps snare adjacent open middle seats on most airlines—but there are several important steps the average traveler can take to ensure maximum comfort in coach class, whether an elite flyer with the airline or not.

Requesting Desirable Coach Seats in Advance: Ask and You Shall Receive

Just as it is true in life, if you want something in the world of travel, you must ask for it. Nowhere is following this rule more important than in getting a good seat assignment. Try these strategies next time you book a flight, whether requesting advance seating assignments for regular revenue tickets or award tickets:

Book as Early as Possible

Most airlines offer at least 60 percent of seats on a flight for assignment prior to the day of travel, no matter how far in advance a flight is booked. The earlier you book, the more seats you'll have to choose from.

Request Your Seat at the Time of Booking

Make asking for your seat assignment part of your reservation routine. If you wait until later, or forget altogether, you dramatically diminish your chances of being assigned a good seat. Should you arrive at the airport without an assigned seat and your flight is fairly full, you face the possibility of being wedged into an uncomfortable middle seat and waging a silent war with your seatmates for those coveted armrests.

Certain tickets—such as those purchased through a consolidator—may not be eligible for advance seat allocation. Rather, seat selection must be made when checking in.

Which is the best kind of seat to request? Most aircraft have a 3-3, 2-3-2, or 3-4-3 configuration. If two passengers are traveling together, select two spots together in a two-seat configuration. In a three-seat configuration, request aisle plus window or aisle plus aisle, asking for seats where the middle seat is currently open, preferably as far back as possible, because those middle seats go last! If the middle seat is assigned when you board, you will not have difficulty exchanging the middle seat for an aisle. For one person traveling alone, do not select the aisle in a two-seat configuration, since the window is likely to be allocated if the flight starts filling up. Rather, request the aisle in a three-seat configuration, where the adjacent aisle seat is already assigned but the middle seat is open—again, as far back as you can get.

Nowadays, you can book your flight and seat assignment in a variety of ways. In instances where an online seat selection capability is not available or if you do not select a seat, the computer system will automatically assign you a seat. When registering at online Web sites, you may be able to prespecify a seat preference such as aisle or window as well as a special meal preference, which will then become your default assignment.

- **By Telephone.** If you book by telephone directly with the airline or through a travel agent, ask for a seat assignment (and any other considerations, such as a special meal) when making your reservation.

Certain travel agents may have software to either allocate a seat as soon as one becomes available (if none was released to you when you booked) or to improve a seat assignment if you're unhappy with what you first received. Be sure to ask about this service if you book through an agency.

- **Online.** When you book online at an airline or travel agent site, you will find that many Internet sites allow you to select your seat before you pay for your ticket. Where this capability is available, you will often be able to see a configuration of available seats from which you can make your desired choice (this is especially true when booking at branded airline sites such as *Americanairlines.com*, *United.com*, *Delta.com*, and so on).

If there is no online mechanism to select your seat, call the airline or online agent contact phone number immediately after you have purchased your ticket to request an advance seat assignment.

You may want to visit *Seatguru.com* before you book, as it enables you to view seating configurations for all major U.S. airlines (refer to the later section "The Best Seat in the House").

Be Prepared to Jump a Hurdle or Two

One obstacle to seat selection you may encounter when you book your ticket far in advance occurs with codeshare flights (refer to Chapter 12 for details)—that is, where the airline from which you purchase your ticket is selling seats on its partner's aircraft. In such instances, you may also need to call the partner airline to request advance seating. Naturally, it is worth the effort to ensure you do not get stuck in an undesirable seat allocated at the airport.

Sometimes you may get a representative on the phone who is not especially helpful with your request for seating preferences. When this happens to me, I usually just call back and talk to someone else. You can also ask to speak to a supervisor, especially if you are an elite frequent flyer on the codeshare airline or are paying a full-coach fare.

Don't Forget Those Frequent Flyer Numbers

Make sure your frequent flyer number is inserted into the reservation when you call or book online—especially if you enjoy elite status—since that may open up superior seating options and automatically block the adjacent middle seat.

Take Advantage of Your Elite Status or Full-Coach Fare

Some airlines will block middle seats for their elite frequent flyers or those travelers (we can't imagine who they are or what they are thinking!) paying full-coach fares. Here are examples of what different airlines will or will not do for you:

- United designates the first few rows of coach on all its aircraft (including international) as its Premier or "Economy Plus" seat section for its elite frequent flyers and full-fare passengers, which offers extra legroom and "blocked" middle seats that remain open unless the flight is full.
- Continental, on the other hand, is the absolute worst for frequent business flyers relegated to coach—cramped legroom throughout, irrespective of elite frequent flyer status.

By the way, anyone paying full-coach fare should have a relatively easy time getting an upgrade. Most airlines give full-fare passengers almost the same upgrade priority as their "super elite" highest level flyers who travel at least 100,000 miles in a year.

Travel with a Friend

If you're traveling with someone else on an aircraft with three-seat configuration, book the aisle and window seats and hope that the middle remains empty. If someone does get plugged in there, you can bet she will be happy to switch for the aisle or window. Better yet, reserve two aisles, one behind the other, to double the possibility of an open middle seat. The chances of the middle seat remaining open are higher as you get further back since most passengers resist being seated in the rear of the aircraft!

Conversely, if traveling alone and only middle seats are available, ask for one between two passengers having the same last name. The couple obviously knows the strategy discussed above—and will be happy to give you an aisle so they can sit next to each other.

Airport Tactics

What if you arrive at the airport and you still have a less-than-desirable seat assignment or no seat at all? Don't give up yet. You still have a chance to do better, since you will probably have several opportunities to enhance your seat.

- **Check-In.** If you have baggage that has not been checked with a curbside skycap, you will need to check in using an electronic kiosk or with an airline staff person at the airline counter in the terminal. This is another chance to request a better seat selection. Electronic check-in software frequently enables the user to check for alternative seats and switch if available. Because of immigration clearance issues, however, electronic check-in can only be used for travel within the United States. If you are being checked in by an actual person, see whether you can get an upgrade simply by asking or using an upgrade certificate (refer to the previous chapter for details) or request an open seat adjacent to your assigned one in coach.

- **Plan B—At the Gate.** Don't despair if you are unsuccessful at the check-in counter. Most of the final seating arrangements for any flight are made at the gate, starting about thirty minutes prior to departure on the assumption that all passengers with advance reservations have checked in. Since up to 30 percent of passengers who have confirmed tickets and reserved seats do not show up, seats originally allocated to those no-shows will be reassigned at the gate as the attending staff finalize seating arrangements.

Once you're face-to-face with the gate agent, here is the golden commandment you must never forget . . .

Treat the Gate Agent as the Most Important Person in the World

At a seminar I presented in Toronto, a lady sitting in the front row who had not said anything throughout the whole session put up her hand. When I called on her, she said, "I'm a gate agent for Air Canada. May I tell everyone the real scoop?"

"Please do!" I replied.

"For anyone who is nice to me, I do my best to provide them with a great seat. But, for those who are nasty to me, I return the favor."

She went on to tell a story about one particularly obnoxious traveler who harassed her, impressing on her what an important person he was and threatening that if he did not get upgraded, he would never fly Air Canada again. The gate agent assigned him to a middle seat, next to a mom traveling with a baby!

When asking for special consideration, from a gate agent or anyone in the travel industry, your pleasant appearance and cheerful demeanor will go far in helping you get what you want.

I heard another story about a gate agent that is certainly humorous, though I cannot tell you whether it is truth or fiction. A businesswoman standing in line to see the gate agent witnessed the man ahead of her being very nasty. When her turn to talk to the gate agent came up, she empathized, promising to be kinder than the previous guy. The gate agent responded, "No worries. That passenger is on your flight to Seattle. But I've routed his baggage to Hong Kong!" Do gate agents even have that kind of power? I don't know. But it's a good story with a great lesson.

Being nice to gate agents can pay back in spades, not least since these overworked staff people are far more used to being abused by irate passengers not getting what they want. If the agent says that he cannot improve your seat, ask if it may be worthwhile waiting until twenty minutes before departure for the possibility of a better seat opening up. In some cases, the agent will tell you to return to the desk within a certain time frame; or better still, will offer to hold your boarding pass to see whether something better may open up. As a last resort, ask to speak to a "special services" manager or supervisor.

I have been upgraded without using certificates or miles just by schmoozing the gate agent and simply asking, "What will it take to be upgraded today?" Bring some cookies—or buy some at an airport newsagent or nearby coffee shop. It takes so little to add a bright spot to someone's day, and your courtesy may very well be rewarded. Treat overworked airline employees with kind thoughtfulness. Your tasteful gift will be remembered.

Airline Lounges

The staff who work in airline lounges have access to computers capable of finding seats for their members. However, I have only occasionally found that lounge staff can improve my seat assignment when I really needed some help. Again, it is the gate agents who are often the final word. Furthermore, airline lounge staff are often overworked and primarily dedicated to checking in the members who arrive at their lounge—they may simply not have the time to search for optimal seating for one individual.

Still, it's worth a try. Since you've perhaps forked over a hefty annual membership fee, you might as well try to get your money's worth and check out what the lounge staff can do to help you.

One Final Strategy—On Board

Once you have boarded, be hyperalert and look around for a better seat. As soon as the chief flight attendant announces that the door has closed, *immediately* move to the better seat before you are preempted by some other alert passenger. Since empty seats are much more likely to be at the back of the plane, keep an eye toward the rear. The only exception on many airlines is the very last row of seats, which may be reserved for the flight attendants during their rest periods—and understandably they can become annoyed with anyone who commandeers "their space." Feel free to ask flight attendants about moving to any seemingly vacant seat—they can help you if you have the right attitude.

A variation on this strategy is to make sure you are the absolute last passenger to board if your flight does not look full (that is, if the gate area looks relatively empty) or by asking the gate agent how full the flight is. Once the final boarding call is made, just walk to the best open seat and claim it. The only problem may be a lack of storage space if you wait to be last, but that should not be a problem if the flight is less than two-thirds full.

Finally, if the plane is full and you don't like your seat, you can try trading with other passengers. For example, a novice flyer may be happy to take your window seat in exchange for an aisle. A couple who is seated separately may trade one of their window or aisle seats for your middle seat. Once again, ask the flight attendant or head purser, who is the most senior attendant, to help you.

Extra Pillows and Blankets

If you want extra blankets or pillows for the flight, ask as soon as you board. During the boarding process or soon after takeoff, these coveted items are quickly snapped up by other passengers, especially on overnight flights. Extras are frequently stored in a few designated overhead bins which you may see open as you board. If you can, grab one for yourself then; otherwise, ask the flight attendants before the aircraft pushes back from the gate.

What do the savviest travelers who want the most comfortable blankets or pillows do? They bring their own! You can purchase a small pillow, which may be inflatable, from a travel store. An additional cushion for extra lumbar support might be a good idea as well.

Finally, if you will be flying overnight, invest in a pair of ear plugs—rarely offered in even the premium classes—as well as an eye mask, which usually is offered in international business or first class. An excellent online source for travel comfort items is *Magellans.com*.

The One Airline That Won't

If you're flying on Southwest, forget about trying to get advance seating. In fact, forget about trying to get an optimal seat at any time ahead of boarding. Southwest does not offer assigned seating to any of its passengers—ever! Theirs is a true "first come, first served" system. The earlier you check in, the lower the boarding number you will be allocated. When boarding begins, those with numbers 1 through 30 or 40 are allowed on first and get to choose whatever seat they want, followed by the second group of 30, and so on. Passengers who arrive last have a good chance of having only middle seats to choose from, especially if the flight is relatively full.

Frequent flyer? So what. Paid full coach fare? Big deal. Bringing up these points will get you nowhere with the Southwest Airlines gate agent. All that matters is what time you checked in, so the earlier the better. There is one way to get first group seating priority on Southwest Airlines without arriving at the airport early: Print your boarding pass at home by visiting *Southwest.com* any time after midnight on your scheduled day of travel.

I know what you're thinking—if that's their attitude, you'll just request an upgrade. Sorry, but you can abandon that tactic, too, as Southwest has no first-class section! Everybody gets narrow leather seats, with just enough legroom for the average adult to avoid "tasting his knees"!

However, you can still enjoy a great meal on your Southwest flight, even though drinks and peanuts are as much as will ever be served by the flight crew. Every flight, without fail. Just bring your own!

The Guaranteed Open Seat—On Any Airline

There is one strategy that will guarantee you an open adjacent seat: Buy it. If the price you are paying is so low, as may be the case when flying on a fourteen-day advance-purchase nonrefundable or sale fare, just buy an additional seat, especially if you will be flying over peak periods such as a Friday afternoon or around major holidays. Paying for the extra seat may still be much cheaper than purchasing a business- or first-class seat!

Requesting Advance Seating (and Special Meals) When Booking Online

If you book online—especially at an airline's proprietary Web site rather than a travel agent site—you will be able to preselect your seat (and special meal) before you pay for your ticket with your credit card. If you were not offered this option, simply call the airline direct to request an advance seating assignment and special meal, if preferred.

The exact same principles for requesting advance seating assignments (and special meal requests) apply when booking award tickets as when obtaining revenue tickets, regardless of whether you book by phone or online. Most airlines now offer the capability to book free—that is, award—seats online using your frequent flyer miles. Make sure you request seating in advance.

The Best Seat in the House

Where's the best place to sit on the airplane? Well, that's a matter of personal choice. Here are some choices to consider.

- Many people like to sit as close to the front as possible. We're not sure why; could it possibly be because they believe they will arrive sooner?! They do disembark first, but the difference in time is minimal and probably won't help if you need to pick up checked baggage.
- Our preference is just the opposite. Because most flyers seem to prefer to sit toward the front, the odds of being seated next to an open middle seat get better further back in the plane. That's where you will almost always find us—unless we are seated in business or first class.
- Often people don't want to sit by the bathroom, but we've never found it a problem, as lines are rarely long and the ventilation systems are usually very good. Sitting by the galley, however, can sometimes be noisy.
- Some passengers always try to snag the bulkhead seats at the front of a cabin because there is extra legroom and no one in front of them. However, there is no forward under-the-seat storage area, either, which can be inconvenient. And the middle seat will almost always be taken.
- Unless it's a short flight, be cautious about accepting the very last row. Those seats sometimes don't recline, and sitting in the same position for hours on end can be uncomfortable.
- Emergency row seats also may not recline, but they generally have much more legroom. These are often assigned at the airport to ensure that the passengers are able and fit to assist in the event of an emergency, and sometimes doled out preferentially to elite passengers. Still, it never hurts to ask.

If you'd like to know what your options are before you request a seat, visit *Seatguru.com*, which has smart graphics explaining seating charts and information that is frequently updated based on passenger feedback.

Tired of Regular Plane Food?

You may want to request a special meal when booking on a major airline for a flight that will have meal service (low-cost airlines do not serve meals), which can usually be done up till twenty-four hours ahead of the departure time. Airlines spend more money per special meal versus regular meals, and special meals are often served before the regular meals (which can be especially beneficial if you are seated toward the back). Each airline offers several special meal options, ranging from vegetarian to kosher, low-fat to seafood. Any phone reservations agent will be able to list the possibilities and insert your request.

One final thought about guaranteeing a meal perfectly suited to your needs. Bring your own—whether from home, your favorite deli or restaurant, or one of the many food outlets available in airports! We note with interest the founding of Skymeals in Santa Monica, California, which delivers meals to travelers. Check out *Skymeals.com* or call 866-SKY-MEAL.

Sound Reduction Strategies

You may also bring your own headphones rather than using the cheap ones provided by the airline, although some airlines may charge you for the movie when you use your own pair. Road warriors and world travelers may prefer to invest in a pair of noise-reduction headphones that plug into an accompanying unit comprising a microphone and digital processor to analyze noise and issue an opposite sound wave. Here are a few products that might suit your needs—we recommend the first three offerings:

- QuietComfort 2 headset from Bose Corporation is the top-of-the-line product by which all others are measured. "Over-the-ear" rather than "on-the-ear" design makes the headset very comfortable to wear and improves noise reduction. All electronics are built into the earcups, so no external box is needed. One AAA battery built into the right earcup is needed to operate—including while plugged in to the aircraft entertainment system. Storage is in a compact hard-sided and reasonably sized carry case. ($300 from *Bose.com* or call 800-WWW-BOSE/800-901-0199 to order—a thirty-day "no questions asked" money-back guarantee is standard)
- Plane Quiet Noise-Reducing headset looks very similar to the Quiet Comfort 2, and also includes "over-the-ear" rather than "on-the-ear" design. Electronics are built into a compact external box. One AA

battery built into the right earcup is needed to operate—but will transmit music from the aircraft entertainment system when the battery is dead. Storage is in a drawstring protective bag. Overall, an excellent value for the money. ($80 from *Planequiet.com* or call 800-720-5076)

- NoiseBuster Extreme offers a much cheaper alternative to the Bose QuietComfort, although it's not in the same class. Value for money is excellent, however. ($39 from *Nctgroupinc.com* or call 800-278-3526)
- Etymotic ER4 earphones comprise soft rubber ear tips that seal comfortably inside the ear canal to eliminate virtually all external background noise. ($330 from *Etymotic.com* or call 847-228-0006)
- Sennheiser Noise Reduction headphones are less expensive, but not as good at reducing cabin sound. ($150 from *Sennheiserusa.com* or call 860-434-9190)
- Sony Noise Canceling headset comprises compact earbud headphones. ($110-$150 from various vendors such as *Amazon.com*)

The above products may be available at competitive prices from "bricks and mortar" electronics stores or a variety of online sources. Search online at sites such as *Google.com*, inputting "airplane headphones" or "noise canceling headphones."

Fast Track for Checking In

As we all know, September 11 dramatically increased the length of time waiting to check in baggage. Since then, American and Northwest pioneered the ability for e-ticket holders—those with an electronic as opposed to a paper ticket—to print out a boarding card from their home or office before leaving for the airport. (If the flight isn't full, you can even change your seat.) Alternatively or in addition, using curbside baggage check-in (where skycaps can also provide you with your boarding pass) will save you significant amounts of time when you fly within the United States and should be your preferred option when traveling over peak periods. Either of these options will free you to proceed straight to the gate to discuss seating options, stopping only once to clear security.

Most airlines now enable e-ticket holders to print their boarding pass from an automated electronic machine before proceeding to the security screening location. The passenger inserts either a credit card or his frequent flyer card to activate the process. Staff members are present at these special machines to facilitate baggage check-in. Automated electronic check-in may also allow passengers to view a seating map, including which seats are and are not available, and to change a seat assignment.

To sum up, since new regulations always require that you have a boarding pass in hand before clearing security—automated check-in can be a significant timesaver!

In Summary

- Book your flight as early as possible and request your seat assignment at the same time.
- If a flight is not full, an open middle seat next to you offers excellent comfort. Your best chance of getting one will be by asking for a seat toward the back; be sure to ask for one that has an open seat next to it. If the agent is not being helpful, call back as many times as needed until you find someone who will work with you!
- Use every advantage you've got, such as frequent flyer or elite status or your full-coach-fare ticket.
- If you want to be guaranteed an open adjacent seat in coach—consider purchasing the additional seat if the price is reasonable!
- Several airlines now enable you to print your boarding pass at home by logging on to the airline's Web site. If your flight is not full, you also have the option to change seats from your computer.
- If you arrive at the airport with an undesirable seat or none at all, try improving your seat assignment at the electronic check-in kiosk, baggage check-in counter, the airline lounge, the gate, and possibly even on the plane. Ideally, request an aisle or window seat with an adjacent open middle seat. For two traveling together, ask for an aisle and window which has an open middle seat at the time you make your reservation. Naturally, the airline cannot guarantee that the middle seat will remain open.
- For travel within the United States, electronic check-in kiosks can speed the check-in process and enable you to improve your seat assignment—even if you have baggage to check in. Or leave your baggage with a skycap—it's worth the gratuity!
- Be nice to the gate agent, and he will be nice to you. Ask: "What will it take to get an upgrade today?" If unavailable, ask him to help find you an ideal seat.
- Always present a neat appearance, a genuine smile, and an appreciative attitude.

- Once on board—if you have not been able to secure an upgrade—keep an eye out for any seat that may be preferable, and move quickly when the aircraft door closes.
- Requesting a special meal can improve the quality of airline food. You will likely receive a higher-quality meal, even though airlines spend less than $5 on airline meals. Or, to guarantee great food, simply bring your own.
- Purchasing your own pillows, blankets, and noise-reduction headphones can significantly enhance your onboard experience.
- Grab some extra pillows and blankets as you board! Investing a few dollars in an eye patch and ear plugs may help you sleep in-flight.

CHAPTER SEVEN

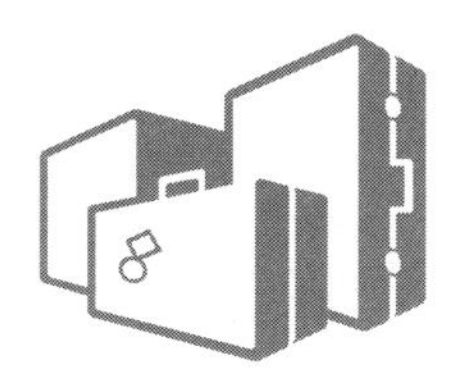

Airfare Consolidators

Hacking Through the Jungle of Savage Wholesalers

One April morning, my parents, who live in Sydney, Australia, called with some good news: My cousin was getting married in just under three weeks and they hoped I would be able to come. The question for me was not whether I would go, but how much I would have to pay. Without the benefit of a twenty-one-day advance-purchase price—and no time to wait for an airline sale—I knew I faced having to pay a premium for an international ticket. Time for guerrilla tactics.

> **TIP**
>
> **Airlines will frequently discount seats on international routes where they are not a known carrier because both originating and destination cities are outside their home country—provided the airline has obtained approval for carrying passengers from both external nations. Two examples are Singapore Airlines (arguably the world's best) from New York to Frankfurt and Air New Zealand from Los Angeles to London. Tickets may be purchased direct from the airlines or through consolidators.**

I called the airlines and found the going rate for a ticket to be $1,800—a bit steep, I thought. I then contacted several consolidators and found a nonstop Los Angeles–Sydney flight for a more reasonable price of $850—a guerrilla-sized savings of $950! Interestingly enough, the flights were on the same carrier that I contacted direct.

On another occasion, I sought tickets for my family of four from Singapore to Bali, Indonesia. The retail price per ticket offered by the two major carriers between these destinations (Singapore Airlines and Garuda Indonesia) was $450, but I found a consolidator selling Qantas seats for $250—a savings of $800 for the four of us.

What Is a Consolidator?

Consolidators are travel agents who purchase tickets direct from an airline at an agreed-upon discount price in return for promising a guaranteed volume, which they accomplish by exclusively promoting the airline and its destinations. Unlike the traditional travel agent, who earns his living from service fees charged to clients and commissions from the airlines and tour operators, the consolidator either marks up the ticket price from its "wholesale" cost or receives an inflated rebate (or refund) on the regular retail cost of the ticket. Either way, the consolidator will usually make more per ticket sold than the traditional travel agent selling published airfares.

While the majority of consolidators sell exclusively through traditional travel agents and do not work with the general public, a significant number do sell direct to the public. Some consolidators are tour companies that package the various components of travel, including airfare plus hotels and other components of an inclusive trip, for sale through travel agents or direct to the public. In many instances, tour operators are happy to sell airfare alone to clear excess inventory and move closer toward meeting the volume they've agreed to in their contract with an airline.

Consolidators—Best Friend of the Last-Minute International Traveler (and Sometimes the Advanced Planner, Too)

Any savvy world traveler purchasing an international ticket, who does not meet advance-purchase requirements (typically seven to twenty-one days advance) or who cannot stay the minimum required number of nights at his destination (frequently at least five) to qualify for an advance-purchase discounted ticket, will almost always be able to find a better airfare through a consolidator. The same may be true for travelers purchasing well in advance of their travel date, especially for travel to a country where there is less airline competition or which is served by a less well-known national carrier.

What About Consolidators for Domestic Tickets?

By far the cheapest way to travel within North America is to obtain "Visit USA" fares, but these are only sold to visitors from abroad and must be purchased outside the United States, requiring presentation of a foreign passport and an airline ticket originating outside the North America. Certain U.S. airlines selling a Visit USA ticket may require that you fly into the United States from abroad on its airline or a partner. Using a search engine online, type in "visit USA air ticket" to see which airline(s) may have special offerings for visitors from abroad. But what about those of us who live here in the good old U.S. of A?

Most airlines have shifted distribution of last-minute airfare specials to the Internet, hoping to reduce the costs incurred via "the middleman," including consolidators. Examples of this emerging practice include Internet sites that include last-minute offerings and airlines offering weekend specials (refer to Chapter 9). However, consolidators still play a role in obtaining last-minute savings on domestic tickets. The best-known consolidator that sells direct to the public is *Cheaptickets.com*, which started out as a "bricks and mortar" agency, but now offers its services almost exclusively on the Web.

The Great Consolidator Hunt

Unfortunately, there is no one, definitive list of well-established consolidators, as these companies tend to come and go or focus their sales efforts exclusively through travel agents. Still, there are a number of sources you can consult. We advise you to seek multiple channels for identifying consolidators, including:

■ The *Airline Consolidators Quick Reference Chart* ($22), which lists consolidators that sell direct to the public (as opposed to travel agents only). You can do so by visiting *Onthegopublishing.com* and clicking on "airline page."

■ The newspaper travel sections, which often appear in the Sunday edition. Since a significant number of U.S. consolidators are based in New York, the back pages of *The New York Times* Sunday travel section are filled with tiny consolidator advertisements promoting myriad world cities at seemingly ridiculous prices. Call each one that includes your destination city in its advertisement. Note that advertisements rarely mention any airlines, since the consolidator-airline contracts prohibit providing such information.

Other U.S. cities in which a significant number of consolidators may advertise in the major newspaper(s) are San Francisco (*San Francisco Chronicle* and *The Examiner*) and Los Angeles (*Los Angeles Times*) for cities within Asia, and Miami (*The Miami Herald*) for Central and South American destinations.

Some savvy travelers have been known to purchase an air and hotel package with no intention of using the hotel component, because the combined price is so low and the air component cannot be purchased alone.

■ The Internet, for consolidator sites. The best-known consolidator for domestic tickets is *Cheaptickets.com*, which only lists its special consolidator fares, so be sure to check another site such as *Orbitz.com* for standard published prices before purchasing. Our favorite consolidator for international flights is *Flights.com*, which includes the capability to book online. Many major international airlines participate, and prices for several airlines are displayed for each requested itinerary (although on occasion just a few or none may be available for the date(s) you request). *Overstock.com* (click on "travel" at the home page) is an emerging consolidator with a significant array of airlines offering last-minute bargains. Search engines, such as *Google.com*, offer another powerful strategy especially useful in locating consolidators that specialize in selling to specific ethnic communities and expatriates at excellent prices. Simply type in "consolidators" or "package tours," followed by the name of your destination country. Consolidators sell airline tickets only; tour operators may either sell tickets only or offer an air and hotel package that can save you significant amounts of money.

■ An expatriate of the country you wish to visit will know where his community purchases their air tickets. Consolidators who serve the local community wishing to visit their homeland may offer outstanding prices.

■ *Jax Fax* is a monthly magazine specifically produced for travel agents. *Jax Fax* is by far the best resource for identifying all the consolidators specializing in your selected destination, including those focusing on your city as the originating airport, if you live in a major U.S. center. For example, you may find a listing of all the consolidators selling tickets from New York to Sydney, Detroit to Tokyo, or Seattle to Budapest! Additional information includes low and high fares for the route you review with applicable dates, as well as the consolidator's phone and fax numbers and address (and sometimes their Web site and e-mail address). While none of the listed information specifies which consolidators will sell only to travel agents and not to the public, it is still worth contacting as many as possible to obtain the best possible prices. If the consolidator offering an excellent fare refuses to sell direct to you, have him contact your travel agent, who will charge you an additional transaction fee—which you should negotiate down as low as possible since you did all the legwork! The fastest way to contact several consolidators is by fax, using the following sample template:

JOHN SMITH
9108 HILLSBORO LANE
ATLANTA, GA 40034
PHONE (410) 555-5678
FAX (410) 555-1234
E-MAIL JSmith@earthlink.net

ATTN: RESERVATIONS

February 8, 2005

Dear Sir/Madam:

I am looking for a consolidator air ticket from Atlanta to Johannesburg, South Africa. My departure date is March 1, 2005, with return date March 12, 2005.

My preferred choice would be nonstop on South African Airways, but I am open to one-stop travel with a European airline, such as British Airways or Air France, if the price is excellent.

Please fax your response as soon as possible to (410) 555-1234.

With thanks,

John Smith

The response you receive from consolidators will inevitably include the price, airline, and flight numbers. Visit *Jaxfax.com* online to subscribe. The annual fee for twelve editions is $30.

■ Consolidators who sell only to travel agencies advertise exclusively in travel industry newsletters and magazines. Travel agents are increasingly willing to purchase tickets from consolidators for their customers, mainly because commissions direct from airlines for regularly published fares have either diminished or disappeared altogether. And because many travel agents can now access consolidator tickets from their regular computer systems, it's quick and easy for them to help you locate the best consolidator fare. Best of all, the agent enjoys higher margins on consolidator tickets even though you pay less—a true win-win situation. Travel agents may also have a close relationship with a select few consolidators who have a proven track record of operational and financial stability.

Dreams May Come True, but Not Without Drawbacks

Everything in life is a trade-off, and purchasing consolidator tickets is no different. While the savings can be spectacular, the smart traveler must be aware of potential disadvantages, including:

- Tickets purchased from a consolidator are almost always nonrefundable and often nonchangeable, meaning you cannot get your money back or change the date of travel—be sure to check before you pay.
- Tickets purchased from a consolidator go to the bottom of the priority list for attention or reassignment when a scheduled flight is delayed or canceled. When you fly on a consolidator ticket, you usually cannot switch to another carrier, so you may need to wait up to twenty-four hours (or more) for the next flight in the event your flight is canceled. Inexpensive, nonrefundable fares purchased direct from the airline or a regular travel agent enjoy higher priority—so the savvy traveler will prefer to purchase his ticket through retail channels during a sale period if there is sufficient lead time.

An airfare purchased from the airline direct or a retail travel agent during a sale will almost always beat the consolidator ticket price without incurring any of the disadvantages associated with a consolidator ticket.

- Because powerful reservations software is extremely expensive to develop, consolidators will rarely offer online reservations capabilities. *Cheaptickets.com* and *Overstock.com* are two exceptions, both offering Web searches for domestic and international tickets.

- Consolidators have been known to go out of business—after receiving payment but before sending out the purchased ticket. The consumer's only recourse against taking a loss in such a case is through paying with a credit card, which gives the purchaser the legal right to dispute the charge and request a refund. Even if the consolidator charges a 2 to 4 percent markup on a credit card purchase, it's worth the extra expense.

  Additional safeguards regarding the viability and integrity of the consolidator are:

  1. Checking for complaints that may have been lodged with the Better Business Bureau in the city where the consolidator is located.
  2. Ensuring that the consolidator is accredited either by IATAN (International Airline Travel Agent's Network) or, for U.S. consolidators, affiliated with ARC (Airline Reporting Corporation). Since the requirements for membership of IATAN and ARC are financial strength and experience, lack of affiliation should be an automatic disqualifier.
- Consolidator tickets may be ineligible for frequent flyer miles. As a general rule of thumb, consolidator tickets to Europe will not accrue miles, while those to Asia will. Domestic tickets purchased from a consolidator may or may not accrue frequent flyer miles. You simply need to calculate whether the savings outweigh the value of miles you may not receive. If mileage earnings are important to you, be sure to ask—and check the consolidator's affirmative response by calling the airline's frequent flyer desk with your reservation information (preferably *before* paying!).

When you receive your consolidator ticket, which will usually be a paper ticket, check that your name and flights are correct, that there is a coupon for each sector of your trip, and that each segment of your trip is designated OK in the status box.

- Consolidator tickets are usually nonrefundable, and may also be nonchangeable (meaning that you cannot change your date[s] of travel).
- Advance seating assignments may not be permitted in certain cases.

Beware Those Hidden Costs

When inquiring about the pricing of a consolidator ticket, don't forget to check into various taxes, service fees, security charges, and delivery costs that will be added on to the quoted price of your ticket. Most of these added charges also apply to the purchase of regularly published air tickets, but may be a significant add-on portion of a consolidator ticket that initially seems quite cheap!

Round-the-World Tickets and Complex International Tickets the Consolidator Way

Pricing of round-the-world (RTW) and multiple-stop international tickets can be difficult and complex, a specialized activity best left to the expertise of agents who do nothing else. For example, an expert in RTW travel will know how to build an itinerary using multiple segments and airlines, possibly obtaining certain portions from overseas consolidators that will beat the retail RTW prices offered by airline alliances such as Star Alliance and One World. The best U.S. consolidator for RTW itineraries is *Airtreks.com.*

TIP

For more information on consolidators, go to *Travel-library.com/air-travel/consolidators.html.* Written by Edward Hasbrouk, this site will provide you with every detail you should know (and then some) about purchasing tickets from consolidators. Or, you can visit *Amazon.com* to order *Air Travels Bargain Basement* by Kelly Monaghan, a book about consolidators ($10). Two guides, used mainly by travel agents, but that also include consolidators who sell direct to the public are: *Moffitt's Consolidators' Guide* ($45) at *Travelknowledge.com* (or call 800-322-3834) or *Schmidt's Index to Air Travel Consolidators* ($56) available from *2.bitstream.net/~schmidt/iatc.htm* (or call 800-241-9299).

Outside the United States, consolidators are sometimes known as "bucket shops" and are concentrated in London, Athens, Kuala Lumpur and Penang (both in Malaysia), and Bangkok (Thailand). Bucket shops frequently specialize in single-segment (one-way) international trips, sometimes purchasing segments from consolidators in other countries with whom they have an established relationship. Such possibilities can make using a bucket shop a good idea when constructing round-the-world itineraries, and U.S. consolidators may purchase multiple segments from these bucket shops abroad to incorporate into an itinerary for a U.S. client.

Bucket shops outside the United States may be identified by Web searches—again using a search engine such as *Google.com*—by inputting "bucket shop" followed by your destination countries, or by looking in the travel sections of foreign newspapers available at specialty newsstands or in major bookstores.

In Summary

- Consolidators are wholesalers who sell either direct to travel agents or the public (and sometimes to both). They offer the best advantage to international travelers who do not meet advance-purchase requirements (with seven to twenty-one days prior to their date of departure) or whose length of stay in their destination will be less than the minimum required for a discount ticket (usually at least five days).

- Domestic consolidators such as *Cheaptickets.com* and *Overstock.com* also enable Web searches for domestic tickets. Check fares against those offered by retail sites to make sure you are getting an excellent deal. Because powerful reservations software is extremely expensive to develop, consolidators will not usually offer online reservations capabilities.
- Consolidator tickets are typically nonrefundable and may be nonchangeable, and you may not earn frequent flyer miles or be able to reserve seating ahead of time. Be sure to check before you pay for your ticket!
- If a scheduled flight is delayed or canceled, travelers holding consolidator tickets receive lowest priority for reassignment to other flights, and alternative carriers will rarely honor a consolidator ticket.
- Since consolidators may be financially unstable, always purchase a consolidator ticket using a credit card to protect yourself should a problem arise. The savvy traveler will also check that the consolidator is affiliated with IATAN (International Airline Travel Agent's Network) or, for U.S. consolidators, with ARC (Airline Reporting Corporation). An additional safeguard is to check for complaints that may have been lodged with the Better Business Bureau in the consolidator's location of business.
- There is no single list that provides information about all consolidators who deal direct with the public. Still, steps you can take to identify consolidators include:
  1. **Browsing the Internet.** Go to search engines and type in "consolidator" plus your destination.
  2. **Reading the Sunday travel section of your newspaper.** Also, check the travel sections of Sunday edition newspapers in areas where consolidators are concentrated, including New York (for flights to Europe), Los Angeles and San Francisco (for Asia), and Miami (for Central and South America).
  3. **Subscribing to the magazine *Jax Fax*.**
  4. **Using a travel agency that has the capability to book consolidator tickets through its regular computer system or has close relationships with a select few consolidators.**
- Find out from expatriates which consolidators serve an ethnic community for return visits to their homeland.

CHAPTER EIGHT

Far from the Madding Crowd

Is Airline Lounge Membership Worth the Cost?

Russian caviar and French croissants, fine chocolates and imported cheese, expensive champagne and exquisite smoked salmon. These were just a few of the delicacies my wife and I savored in British Airways' posh Concorde lounge prior to boarding our flight at London Heathrow. Truly a lounge fit for royalty—were that all airline lounges came even *close* to this . . .

Alas, they do not. Not even close. And the Concorde, too, is a thing of the past!

Consider my experience in the Japanese Air Lines business-class lounge at Los Angeles airport. The elevator to the lounge on the fourth floor was out of service. When I finally reached the lounge with my wife and six-month-old infant, there was not a single seat to be had. A limited range of soft drinks were offered, and if you wanted coffee, you got it yourself from a vending machine. Snacks consisted of a few less-than-fresh-looking apples and pears and packages of cookies and peanuts. Hardly a tranquil haven for travelers paying $5,000 and up for their round-trip ticket.

Although having access to an airline lounge may sound appealing, the fantasy may be better than the reality. The wisdom of purchasing a lounge membership depends on each individual traveler's needs. Although I've considered doing so in the past, I never found the expenditure to be worthwhile for several reasons:

1. One of my most treasured activities at an airport is sitting down at a gourmet coffee bar, such as the ubiquitous Starbucks, to enjoy a chocolate brownie frappacino after clearing security. The cost of the experience is the drink alone—and even if the area is crowded

or no seats are available, I can always find a quiet corner at a nearby gate where I can relax, unwind, and await my flight in peace.

2. I find the snacks and drinks in most traditional airline lounges to be average at best, certainly not worth the cost of a membership. Almost all lounges prohibit members from bringing in outside food and drinks.

3. As a guerrilla traveler, I am not loyal to just one airline. Joining several airline clubs would be expensive and counterproductive.

4. My American Express Platinum card allows me and up to two companions to use Continental, Northwest, and Delta Airlines' lounges if I am flying any of those airlines that day, while my Diners Club charge card enables me to use at least one lounge in most international airports serving major cities worldwide, and even to bring along a companion for little or no additional cost.

The Perks of Airline Lounge Membership

Once upon a time, airline lounges were like exclusive clubs where the upper crust could gather to sip whisky *gratis* and quietly read the newspaper—all the while sheltered from the hustle and bustle of backpacking students and crying babies.

That was then—when travel was typically more of a leisure activity for the affluent. In this brave new world, travel is often an essential part of our busy professional lives, and whiling away time waiting for a flight is no longer a luxury most of us can afford.

Airlines claim that their lounges offer a "haven of tranquility," insulating members from the turmoil of activity inherent to airline terminals. For business travelers, this benefit can be significant when their flight is delayed or they have a long wait between flights and need to take care of business. Not only do airline lounges offer comfortable seating and complimentary snacks and beverages, but they also provide a pleasant and efficient place to do some work. With ports to plug in a laptop—and often meeting rooms that can be rented by the hour—lounges can function as an extension of the office. Naturally, phones can be used to hold conference calls. In many lounges catering to business- and first-class passengers found in international airports, such amenities as showers, sleeping rooms, computers, and more may await the dedicated traveler.

Lounge staff can be of service, too, as they have access to computer terminals and can (at least in theory) help with seating and upgrades.

In short, if you are a traveler who flies at least once each month on the same airline and can benefit from using work or meeting space at an airport location, membership may be a worthwhile expenditure for you.

When a Lounge Offers Less Than What's Advertised

Unfortunately, airline lounges are not always the secluded oasis of comfort and luxury their public relations department would lead you to believe. Here are a few of the reasons I've found to avoid the lounge experience:

- **Inconsistency of Product.** For example, the lounge in Atlanta may be run with relaxed Southern charm, while the staff in the same airline's Chicago lounge are harried and overworked; the meeting rooms in Phoenix may be light and spacious, while they are nonexistent in the airline's Boise lounge. This lack of a reliably acceptable standard in airport lounges around the country is hardly surprising, given that the airline industry is not typically known for dependability and excellence.
- **Too Many People.** At certain times of the day, especially around peak times for business travel, airline lounges can be crowded. On occasion, it can be an ordeal just to find an open seat—or a seat far enough from screaming toddlers!
- **Less Than Desirable Refreshments.** While tea, coffee, and soft drinks are offered without charge, alcoholic drinks are sold at typical airport bar prices (exceptions being Delta's lounges and most international first-class lounges). Packaged peanuts and cookies are frequently the "food" on offer, while bringing in one's own food or beverage is not just tacky, it's forbidden.
- **Poor Service.** Although you'll sometimes find staff people who can be extremely helpful with seating and upgrades, often they are not. For example, I have found United lounge staff to be very accommodating (which explains why United's Red Carpet Clubs have consistently been voted the best by the readers of *Business Traveler* magazine), while Continental's staff are often indifferent.
- **Inaccessibility.** Planning a meeting in the lounge can be a great idea until you find out that not all of the participants qualify for entrance.

The Bottom Line

Each major airline has its own lounge program, which costs, on average, $400 per year. Discounts of 25 to 50 percent are usually available to elite members of an airline's frequent flyer program.

Is Membership Worth the Annual Fee?

Start out by considering how many times you fly, how often you might use the lounge, and the average time you would spend in the lounge. For example, if you use the lounge twenty times in a year and pay a $400 membership fee (or frequent flyer miles valued at roughly the same amount), each visit effectively costs $20. Is that outlay commensurate with the value you will receive?

Check out that the airline you select actually has lounges in the cities you will be visiting. For example, if you fly a lot internationally, United and American have far more lounges than Delta; if you spend a lot of time in connecting airports, the airlines' biggest and best lounges are often those in their hubs. In some instances, lounge membership also opens the doors to an extensive network of partner lounges. For example, when you join United's Red Carpet Club, you also gain entry to US Airways' lounges as well as those for all foreign carriers which are part of the Star Alliance.

One last note—you want to join a club which has quality standards compatible with your needs.

One important caveat to consider before you purchase a lifetime airline lounge membership is what will happen to it should that airline cease operations or be acquired by another. For example, when American Airlines purchased TWA in 2001, lifetime TWA lounge memberships were not honored by American.

Alternative Access Strategies

Sometimes access to a lounge can be gained through means other than money. Delta rewards its Platinum Elite members (those passengers who flew at least 100,000 miles on nondiscounted tickets—or greater than 100,000 miles if discounted tickets were used—in the current or prior year) with complimentary entrance to its Crown Rooms. All major U.S. airlines offer memberships in exchange for miles—usually the higher the elite status, the fewer the miles needed.

Travelers flying on a paid or free international business- or first-class ticket are given complimentary access to airline lounges, with the same privilege offered by partner airlines. Similarly, elite members of most major U.S. airlines are eligible to use the business-class lounges of the primary airline (on which they earned elite status) as well as with partner airlines when flying on an international coach-class ticket—even if the ticket is an advance-purchase nonrefundable fare. Consolidator tickets may be eligible as well. For example, United Premier Executive and 1K frequent flyers have complimentary access to any Star Alliance partner lounge when flying on an international ticket on a partner airline—even if the passenger is traveling in coach class.

At least two charge cards offer the opportunity to use an airport lounge. American Express Platinum cardholders (refer to Chapter 18 for details) has an extensive network of U.S. lounges but just a few abroad, enabling members to use Delta, Continental, and Northwest Airlines lounges if flying on one of those airlines that day. While the card itself carries a stiff annual fee of $395, it is approximately the same price as purchasing an annual lounge membership for just one airline! And the Diners Club card enables travelers to use at least one airport lounge in airports serving most major cities abroad; in the U.S., however, access to lounges in only two airports—Miami and Newark—are offered. Also, note that the Diners Club lounge may not be in the same terminal from which you will be departing. Bottom line—the American Express Platinum card may be an excellent choice for those who travel within the United States, while Diners Club is the better alternative for those whose travel takes them abroad.

Passengers who have voluntarily offered to be bumped for monetary compensation or a free ticket should also request complimentary access to the airline's lounge as compensation for the inconvenience while waiting for their flight. Similarly, passengers whose flight is significantly delayed will, on occasion, be granted free entry if they ask—especially if they are elite frequent flyers.

Most airlines offer a one-day pass for approximately $50. Alternatively, travelers who are new to Continental's One Pass frequent flyer program (or members for less than one year) may purchase the Executive Pack ($79.95) or Prestige Pack ($119.95) from that airline's One Pass program (call 713-952-1630 to order). Besides the $99 companion certificate and 5,000 (Executive Pack) or 7,500 (Prestige Pack) bonus miles that make this package a spectacular value, two passes to any of Continental's lounges worldwide are provided.

Finally, Priority Pass (*Prioritypass.com*) is the world's largest independent airport lounge access program, providing members with access to over four hundred airport VIP lounges in seventy-five countries, regardless of their class of travel, choice of airline, or membership in an airline airport lounge program. The program has a wide array of independent lounges and, in select instances, uses the lounges of major U.S. (including Continental, Delta, Northwest, and US Airways) and Mexican airlines. The major disadvantage is that the Priority Pass lounge may be in a different terminal than the airline you will be flying. Annual membership fees are as follows:

- Standard Membership is $99 plus $24 per person for each lounge visit. A guest costs an additional $24 per visit.
- Standard Plus Membership is $249 for ten free visits and $24 per visit thereafter. A guest costs an additional $24 per visit.
- Prestige Membership is $399 for free unlimited personal visits. A guest costs an additional $24 per visit.

Bottom line—choose Standard if you anticipate six or fewer visits in a year, Standard Plus for seven to sixteen anticipated visits, and Prestige for seventeen visits or more.

Luxury Oases

There are a few top-notch lounges still available to international first-class travelers. Virgin Airlines Upper Class lounges offer massages, haircuts, and a huge buffet that will change the way you think about an airline lounge (and spoil you for any other "regular" lounge!).

In Summary

- Lounges can offer a haven away from the hullabaloo of the airport; complimentary drinks and snacks; power plugs, meeting rooms, faxes, copiers, and Internet access; at least one staff person to assist with seating and upgrades; and various other amenities.
- But they can also suffer from overcrowding, mediocre food and beverages, indifferent or overworked staff, and inconsistent products and services.
- Before paying an annual fee for a lounge, consider the frequency you will use the lounge, whether the airline you fly actually has lounges in the cities you frequent (including partner airlines whose lounges can be used), and the overall quality of the lounges.
- Lounge access can sometimes be attained through means other than paying the cost of the membership, such as trading in frequent flyer miles or using either the American Express Platinum card (better for domestic travel) or the Diners Club card (superior choice for international travel). Priority Pass provides access to over four hundred lounges in the United States and abroad, and has three levels of membership ranging from $100 to $400 per year.

CHAPTER NINE

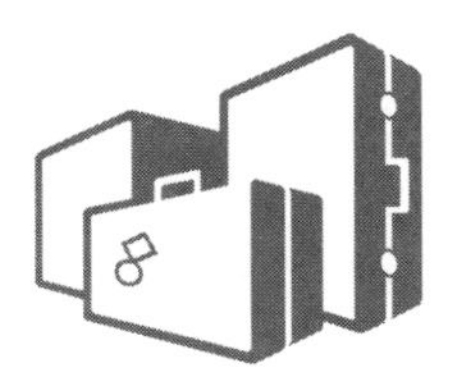

Navigating the Internet to Discover Unbelievable Airfares

While my family and I waited at the gate to board our flight to Hawaii, an announcement was made that the flight was oversold. As a collective groan rose from the other waiting passengers, we immediately made our way to the podium and offered to be bumped. For our few hours of inconvenience, we received four $750 certificates for flights wherever Northwest and KLM fly—anywhere in the world.

A few months later, we decided to redeem this unexpected windfall to book a visit to Israel, even though we knew that the airfare from Los Angeles to Tel Aviv would likely exceed the value of our award. To find the best deal, I checked a few Internet sites every few days, looking for deals on two itineraries:

1. Los Angeles–Tel Aviv, using one ticket
2. Los Angeles–Amsterdam and Amsterdam–Tel Aviv, using "split ticketing"

Why investigate the second option? I knew that if we flew on KLM, our flight would automatically make a stop in Amsterdam, KLM's hub. A "split ticket" strategy—buying two roundtrip tickets, Los Angeles–Amsterdam and Amsterdam–Tel Aviv—would be easy to do and possibly cheaper than a one-ticket strategy.

By visiting Internet sites often, I soon got an idea of the regular retail prices for the routes I wanted, and noticed that split ticketing was indeed looking like the better deal.

One morning, while cruising the Internet, I noticed the fare had dropped about $350 per ticket (using the split ticket strategy). I immediately called Northwest to make our reservations, and later that day went into a Northwest ticket office to present the certificates and purchase the tickets. The average out-of-pocket cost per ticket from Los Angeles to Israel was $267.

This story illustrates just one example of the power of the Internet to do fare searches on a frequent basis. Had I not have been using discount coupons, I could have booked online.

In general, applying a discount certificate toward your ticket purchase cannot be done when booking on the Internet. That may eliminate the possibility of using Web-only specials. If you intend to use a discount voucher, you must do so by calling the airlines direct.

The Internet—Opening a Whole New World for Travelers

Imagine calling a travel agent every morning for two months and asking him to price the same itinerary as you patiently wait for a bargain airfare to emerge. You would drive him crazy! Yet that's what you can now do on your own in a matter of minutes, thanks to the Internet.

There is no question that the Internet has revolutionized airfare searches, giving the "industry outsider" the same access to flight information, pricing, and availability that only travel agents enjoyed up until end of the twentieth century. It is essentially a huge marketplace, where you can find travel bargains, special discounts, last-minute opportunities, and easy ways to compare prices.

Online travel sites have been one of the real success stories of the Internet, thanks to rapidly improving technologies and competitive travel agent companies that relentlessly focus on creating user-friendly Web sites. Now, with a few clicks of the mouse, you can:

TIP

***Travelocity.com*'s Fare Watcher offers a feature (click on "my stuff") that lets you input a desired itinerary and threshold price you'll pay. If the price on any airline should drop below that threshold price, you receive an e-mail letting you know. *Orbitz.com*'s Flex Search enables you to find the best fare by identifying the cheapest weekend deal, search to see what you can save by departing or returning a few days earlier or later, or find the cheapest time to travel within a thirty-day period.**

- Make flight reservations.
- Select a seat (and even find out which are the "best seats in the house"!).
- Check on-time statistics for flights under consideration.
- Pay for the transaction online.
- Receive instant fare change alerts for a selected itinerary.
- Be notified of flight delay warnings.
- Book complex multiple-segment itineraries (that is, for more than simple roundtrip tickets), inclusive holiday packages, and even cruises.

The Internet also offers at least three distinct advantages over a travel agent:

1. Many sites offer Web-only fares that are not available through regular travel agents' computer systems.
2. You won't be charged more than a $10 Web service fee, whereas most travel agents charge at least $25 per ticket.
3. Online travel sites are ready to serve you twenty-four hours a day, seven days a week, holidays included!

To begin, imagine a possible vacation and visit a few Internet reservations sites to become familiar with how they work and what they offer. At minimum you can use the information you uncover for an itinerary you are considering as a benchmark for prevailing prices to help you comparison shop. And if you register at any major travel reservations Web site, purchasing online is simple and fast, especially when a site has stored all your key identifying information, such as your name, address, phone number(s), and credit card details.

While there is no one Internet site that consistently provides the lowest fare, there are a few that stand out above all the rest. They will be the focus of this chapter.

Web Searches—What to Watch For

Just like any skill, learning how to use the Internet for travel searches takes a little time. As a novice, allow yourself thirty to sixty minutes for your first few Internet searches. With experience, you'll cut your time down considerably and find yourself zipping around the Internet for travel deals like a pro. Bookmark your favorite travel Web sites for even faster action!

TIP

Any time you're gathering information, print out the itineraries and fares that could possibly meet your needs. This will save you from having to go back to sites you've already visited and help you comparison shop as you visit new sites.

As you check out various Web sites, look for the following key components, charges, and options:

- **Viable Connections.** For example, you don't want a stopover in Denver when booking a San Francisco–Honolulu roundtrip!
- **Reasonable Connect Times.** At least forty-five minutes for domestic flights and sixty minutes for international itineraries should be allowed (especially if you will be checking baggage).

- **Access to Any Flight You May Need.** This is rarely a problem with the big three—*Orbitz.com*, *Travelocity.com*, and *Expedia.com*—but less common routes may not be available from other smaller sites. We especially prefer *Orbitz.com* for the vast range of flight options each search presents.

- **Last-Minute Bookings.** Some sites cannot book flights scheduled to depart within twenty-four or forty-eight hours.

- **The Site's Ability to:**
- Check out nearby airports.
- Select whether to search by your desired schedule or best price.
- Indicate number of stops acceptable or nonstops only.
- Choose seating.
- Change a variable while booking, for example, easily modify your result by the date or time of departure/arrival or by price (you don't want to start over again to check the price if you leave on an earlier or later flight).

All of the above capabilities are almost always available on the three major retail sites and to a lesser extent by the smaller sites.

- **Service Fees.** Several sites do have nominal ticketing charges, for example, $5 with *Orbitz.com* or *Expedia.com*. From time to time, a site may impose higher service charges for a particular airline if the airline has scaled back on the terms by which it compensates the site.

- **Web-Only Fares.** Some sites offer fares that are at least as good as sale fares, but sometimes accessible even when there is no sale. *Orbitz.com* appears to have the best range of Web-only fares on a significant number of airlines, with *Expedia.com* and *Travelocity.com* having more limited offerings.

- **Change and Cancellation Policies, Procedures, and Fees.** These can differ significantly from what you would expect if purchasing online at an airline's own site. Be certain you know what you are getting into if there is a reasonable chance you will want to change or cancel!

TIP

When doing a Web search for two or more passengers, always check the price for one adult first. Then come back and redo the search for two (or however many are traveling) passengers. If the latter search is more than double the former, there was only one seat left at the lower fare, in which case you should check other Web sites that may draw their seats from a different inventory.

- **"Opaque" or "White Label Fares."** These are highly restricted, deep-discounted, nonrefundable, and nonchangeable tickets offered by some sites. Typically, the name of airline and exact flight times are divulged only after you have paid with a credit card.

Keep in mind that when booking airline tickets online, the basic principles for getting great airfares still apply: Book at least seven to twenty-one days in advance of your desired departure date, wait for an airfare sale, and check out alternative (nearby) airports for both origination and destination airports.

Can Travel Agents Beat Web Fares?

Unless you have had a close relationship with a travel agent for many years, there is a good chance that you will at least match or often beat a travel agent's search, for several reasons:

- Travel agents have little incentive to spend considerable amounts of time in search of rock-bottom fares since commissions are low or nonexistent.
- The computer systems used by agents are frequently the same as online agents and airline Web sites.
- In certain circumstances, travel agents do not have access to Web-only fares offered by the major travel reservations Web sites.
- An agent will typically charge an additional service fee—most likely at least $25.

When a New Fare Beats the Fare You've Already Paid

Let's imagine that you have paid for your air ticket, either online or by calling the airline or a travel agent, and you subsequently notice a special lower Internet fare. You must call the airline or travel agent direct to request the lower fare; if the reservations agent cannot bring it up in his general computer system as a published rather than Web-only fare, your previously purchased ticket cannot be reissued at the new lower special price.

However, if you notice a lower airfare in a newspaper advertisement as part of a sale, and those seats can be found by an airline reservations agent, the airline will reissue a ticket that was originally purchased on the Web, unless it was purchased as part of a Web-only special or "white label" fare and is designated as nonrefundable and nonchangeable.

Cruising the Internet—Where to Go and What to Do

Finding any travel site you want is really quite easy when you use a search engine, such as *Google.com* or *Yahoo.com*. Once you've accessed the search engine, you simply type in:

- The name of the company whose site you want to visit, such as Delta Airlines, plus the word "home" for that company's home page; or you can put ".com" on the end of the company's name, as in *Delta.com*, and usually reach its site.
- A phrase, such as "vacation packages Miami," and the search engine will instantaneously take you to definite or potential matches.

The following are ten key steps to follow when using the Internet to find the best bargain airfares—-ultimately you will discover which steps work best for you to speed up the process:

Step 1. Check for Any Special Discounts You Have

As a savvy traveler, you first check whether you have a discount certificate you can use, perhaps one given to you as a result of being bumped (refer to the opening story of this chapter) or as compensation for an adverse experience. Doing this *before* you go online is important for two reasons:

1. Ticketing with a discount certificate can rarely be done online, but will usually require making a reservation directly with the airline, followed by presenting the coupon at the airline's local or airport ticketing office. Sometimes a discount coupon can be mailed in. While a coupon's rules will occasionally allow a travel agent to issue the ticket, agents loathe handling such reservations because of very low airline commissions and the complexities that come with applying a coupon.

2. Knowing which airline has provided your certificate will help in your comparison shopping. For example, if you have a $200 United discount certificate and find that the best prices for different carriers are competitive, you know that using your coupon on United is your best bet. Conversely, if Southwest offers a fare that's $400 less than United's, you can take the lower fare on Southwest and save your United certificate for another trip.

If you own an *Entertainment Directory,* you may have another discount opportunity. (Refer to Chapters 2 and 14 for details and ordering information.) Each directory includes discounts of 5 to 15 percent on some airlines—most recently on United, previously on Continental and Northwest Airlines—by calling direct or (in some instances) booking online and presenting a special discount code.

ALERT

If you find an excellent fare online, but your discount certificate does not apply to Web prices (meaning it cannot be used when booking online), you must call the airline for the lowest available published non-Internet fare to which you can apply your coupon. The airline's regular published fare quoted by a phone agent will, however, typically be identical to the online fare you identified.

Step 2. Visit the Three Giant Retail Travel Sites

As you cruise various travel reservations Web sites, you'll find that most "guarantee" their prices are the lowest. Do not be deceived by such claims and continue to check all sources. And keep in mind that airfare availability and fares can and do change minute by minute, day by day. What may seem like a low fare at 3 PM may be superseded by an even better (or worse) fare at 3:05 PM! We have seen instances where a great airfare that was available one minute had vanished the next!

> **TIP**
>
> ***Tripadvisor.com* is an excellent way to quickly access all three sites. Type your desired destination into the "search" field to view articles and reviews by fellow travelers.**

By far the most established and best-known retail travel reservations sites are *Orbitz.com*, *Travelocity.com*, and *Expedia.com*. These should be the starting points for any airfare search to set the standard retail price.

Orbitz.com

Orbitz.com was founded by several major U.S. airlines to compete with private retail travel agent sites such as *Travelocity.com* and *Expedia.com*. Its key advantages include:

- An underlying technology initially developed at the Massachusetts Institute of Technology and commercialized by ITA software that searches multiple airline databases and presents each airline's lowest prices for your selected dates and time—for nonstop, one-stop, and multiple-stop flights.
- Web-only special airfares for thirty-five different airlines that are frequently unavailable elsewhere—sometimes not even at that airline's own Web site.
- Travel alerts via phone, e-mail, pager, or voice mail that advise ticket holders who bought through the Web site of delays, gate changes, and weather problems.
- Information regarding virtually any itinerary imaginable (including international destinations) while many other sites may be unable to access flights for uncommon routes.
- *Orbitz.com* allows you to automatically include into your search alternative airports (for both originating and destination cities) within 25, 50, or 100 miles.

Quite simply, *Orbitz.com* presents far more alternatives for flight inquiries than any other site, including Web-only specials for its founding airlines that competing sites have deemed anticompetitive (but still offer you great savings!). These features make it especially attractive to the traveler for whom scheduling is critical or who is not especially loyal to any one airline.

Two disadvantages to using *Orbitz.com* are it does not include offerings from low-cost airlines such as Southwest Airlines, which are available only from those airlines' own Web sites; and at the time this book went to press, it does not book flights originating outside North America.

We recommend *Orbitz.com* as the best starting point for an airfare search.

TIP

Many travel experts will only fly with an old-fashioned paper ticket that includes a separate stub for each segment of a trip, each of which is extracted at the time one checks in. However, a paper ticket is no longer necessary; in fact, airlines now charge at least $10 as a way to direct passengers towards electronic ticketing, which is less costly for the airlines. This electronic ticket is by far the most common form of airline reservation today and is nothing more than a sheet of paper with your itinerary and a confirmation number. We strongly prefer the electronic reservation since there is nothing to lose! The only exception to our recommendation in favor of electronic ticketing is for an itinerary that includes more than one airline, which introduces the possibility of an error between different reservations systems. In this case, ask for a paper ticket if it is not offered.

Expedia.com

Expedia.com offers every type of travel product imaginable, including air, hotel, car rental, cruises, and packages. Some of this site's benefits are:

- The Fare Calendar, which allows you to select a destination and receive information on available dates and rules surrounding the best available fares for that route several months into the future. The user who has no special date in mind will learn when a certain airline is offering special fares; for example, the best fare for a traveler who has selected Copenhagen may be Aer Lingus in November for $397, with a weekend stayover required.
- Time-sensitive bargain fares similar to *Hotwire.com*, where you know the price for your selected city pair, but the airline and actual flight times are revealed only after you accept the offer and your credit card has been charged for a nonrefundable, nonchangeable fare.
- The capability to check the on-time performance of suggested flights.
- The ability to make and hold a reservation for twenty-four hours, allowing you to do comparison shopping while securing a good

option. Again, while it's always a good idea to hold a flight with a good fare, prices are frequently guaranteed only until midnight that same night. So if you come across a great fare, lock it in by purchasing the ticket with your credit card before that deadline—or even better—before midnight that same day.

Note that, like *Orbitz.com*, *Expedia.com* may charge a $5 to $10 fee per ticket for routine reservations such as air tickets, hotel bookings, and car rental reservations.

Travelocity.com

This site includes offerings for approximately 700 airlines, 50,000 hotels, and 50 car rental companies worldwide. However, a simple search will usually offer just five to twenty alternatives, a fraction of the information the same request will provide at *Orbitz.com*. As a starting point, however, *Travelocity.com* will provide you with the option of setting the date and time of your desired flights—or search for the earliest and best fare available for the city pair you have specified. Additional capabilities include:

- The opportunity to use an express booking function with just three clicks if you have already registered (registering requires your name, address, and a credit card number with expiration date, all of which are stored for speedy transactions in the future).
- "Fare Watcher" (click on "my stuff" once you have registered) provides the ability to input up to five destinations and receive an alert if there is a lower fare to or from a nearby airport at a future time.
- The Dream Map (accessible by clicking on flights), through which you specify your desired type of vacation and target airfare, and *Travelocity.com* presents possible destinations from your home city.
- An online concierge service that allows you to make bookings for theater tickets, restaurants, and golf courses.
- The ability to make and hold a reservation for twenty-four hours—definitely well worth the effort—following which you can do some comparison shopping while holding the reservation. However, as suggested in Chapter 2, to make sure you get the fare quoted with your reservation, you should pay for the ticket by midnight that same night.

The principal disadvantage that comes with using *Travelocity.com* is poor customer service. We have found that letters addressed to three successive CEOs regarding unacceptable services went unanswered (perhaps they should fire the third CEO, too!). Therefore, be cautious about booking at this site, since you may be ignored if you experience a problem.

Step 3. Give the Consolidator Sites a Look

Consolidator sites may offer significant discounts, but airfares purchased at these sites usually come with numerous restrictions. For example, tickets will almost always be nonrefundable and may also be nonchangeable. And certain flights purchased from consolidators may not be eligible for frequent flyer miles. Be certain to check on applicable restrictions before you pay for your ticket.

There is no clear leader when it comes to consolidator sites. Furthermore, because of the complexity and expense of building online reservations capabilities, few consolidators have developed efficient and easy-to-navigate sites that allow users to find the best flight and price.

The best known consolidator—based on a long and profitable history as a "bricks and mortar" travel agent—is *Cheaptickets.com*, which offers domestic tickets on multiple airlines. However, *Cheaptickets.com* fares are frequently bettered by the best-known retail sites.

Cheaptickets.com offers both an express search and a "power fare search," which allows you to find the lowest fares and best travel dates for your itinerary. In addition, this site may offer the best fares to Hawaii, and is increasingly offering competitive fares abroad.

Another consolidation site worth checking is *Overstock.com*. Click on "travel" from the home page.

Other travel sites to check out in your "spare time":

- *Allcheapfares.com*
- *Travelnow.com*
- *Cheap-airfares.us*

Step 4. Compare Airfares Side by Side

"Site scrapers," such as *Farechase.com*, *Qixo.com*, and *Sidestep.com*, claim to scan vast numbers of Web travel sites to find the best airfares and hotel rates, providing a simple way to compare airfares side by side. Each site has capability to scan different sites, so none is able to access the entire universe. One benefit of accessing these sites is that their searches include fares offered by major discount airlines such as Southwest and JetBlue, which you frequently cannot obtain from *Orbitz.com*, *Expedia.com*, or *Travelocity.com*. If you see an attractive fare,

***Sidestep.com* requires that you download an application program onto your hard drive. *Farechase.com* requires registration.**

you simply click on a link that takes you directly to the reservations site offering the fare.

However, prices are not necessarily the lowest possible, and their technology still has a ways to go to be fast, user friendly, and consistently effective. But give it a try if you have some extra time!

Step 5. Don't Forget to Click on the Major Airlines' Web Sites . . .

Each major carrier and low-cost airline has its own Web site, which you can easily access through any search engine (also refer to Appendixes A–D). Three key benefits to booking on an airline Web site are:

1. Some sites offer frequent flyer miles for purchasing at their sites.
2. Airlines are typically more customer friendly when it comes to making changes if the ticket was purchased direct from them rather than a travel agent.
3. You will be able to access all flights offered by an airline to your desired destination versus just select offerings at independent travel Web sites.

If you can find a better fare at a retail site or consolidator, however, you will have to decide whether these advantages outweigh the lower price.

In general, proprietary airline sites are user friendly and provide information about specials such as:

- Discounts that may be time sensitive
- Vacation packages
- Frequent flyer promotions
- New routes

Notwithstanding, we strongly recommend that you check out prices at supplier-neutral retail travel agency sites, such as *Orbitz.com*, *Expedia.com*, or *Travelocity.com*, as they are less likely to be biased in their presentation of information.

Step 6. . . . and the Low-Cost Airline Web Sites, Too

If you are interested in the low-cost airlines which may not be available from the neutral retail travel agent Web sites, check out Internet sites for low-cost airlines, such as Southwest Airlines, JetBlue, America West, Frontier, ATA, AirTran, Spirit, and so on. (Refer to Appendix C for a listing of low-cost airlines' Web sites.)

Southwest Airlines is widely regarded as the "champion cheap airline," having been profitable every single quarter since 1972. Its operational prowess, including on-time performance and customer service, is excellent; and the proportion of tickets purchased at its Web site *Southwest.com* beats out every other major airline. The reason for this phenomenon is really quite easy to understand: Using *Southwest.com* rather than the phone to make reservations is extremely easy and fast, may offer extra frequent flyer credits, and makes understanding Southwest's clear pricing structure remarkably simple.

But be forewarned—Southwest's fares may not always be the cheapest, and there are a few disadvantages to flying Southwest, such as:

- Long lines to check in baggage (especially over peak holiday travel periods)
- No preassigned seating at the time of publication (those who arrive earliest board first, and get priority selection of seats)
- No opportunities to upgrade
- No in-flight meals

Taking these drawbacks into consideration, the savvy business traveler may want to choose a major carrier over Southwest, even if it means paying a slightly higher price.

A list of U.S. and European low-cost airlines' Internet sites and phone contact information is provided as Appendices C and D.

Step 7. Check *Bestfares.com* for the Best Bargain Info

Bestfares.com focuses on providing information about specials for specific city pairs—over one hundred each day. Sounds pretty good, doesn't it, until you find out that the majority of offerings will be irrelevant to you!

This site is simply a billboard for bargains; no reservations can be made online. Although targeted mainly at leisure travelers, *Bestfares.com* will occasionally include information about short-notice fares and fares not requiring a weekend stayover. Click on "News Desk" when accessing *Bestfares.com*'s home page to view a long list of available specials, one of which *may* be useful to you. For example, the site may notify you that a major airline has started a sale in certain markets, meaning you should check out the airline's Web site to access the special fare.

One feature that may be helpful to the leisure traveler is *Bestfare.com*'s Quickfare Finder. You input your originating and destination cities, and Quickfare Finder provides you with details of the best possible fares, including the airfare code for each specific airline, advance-purchase requirements (such as seven or fourteen days), when the fare expires, and blackout dates, as well as similar information for alternative airports and member-only prices if you book through *Bestfare.com*'s consolidator agency. But these are just benchmark prices to help guide you when you book online or call to make a reservation that unfortunately cannot be booked instantaneously.

Bestfares.com makes most of its money by selling $59-per-year subscriptions to its monthly magazine, which is essentially useless to time-constrained business travelers because its focus is on special leisure fares (many of which are dated by the time the magazine is published) and detailed tourist information about various featured destinations. Membership also grants the right to use the *Bestfares.com* discount travel consolidator agency, using phone numbers listed in the magazine. However, becoming a member to gain access to *Bestfare.com*'s consolidator fares is hardly worth the expenditure, given that phone agents are frequently poorly informed about specials, customer service and response times are widely considered unacceptable, and almost all worthwhile and timely information is free at the *Bestfares.com* Web site.

Because of the changing nature of *Bestfares.com*'s special fares, it is unlikely you will find something relevant to you unless you are prepared to return every few days for several weeks and even months to find something that is perfect for your needs. Conversely, the leisure traveler may find certain offers irresistible, and premium-class deals may be featured on occasion.

Step 8. Call a Major Airline or Travel Agent

Once you have ascertained which airlines are offering the best value online, you may want to check to see if you can get an even better price by telephone from those airlines direct, or from a travel agent with whom you have an established relationship and who will be prepared to spend time doing a search for you, even though they make almost nothing from selling airline tickets. Many articles in mainstream publications have documented how a knowledgeable travel agent may beat the best Internet fare, either because she uses a different reservations system or she has learned where to look or how to use creative ticketing strategies. For example, a veteran agent may know how to plug in alternative airports, apply a stopover, use an airline that you had not considered, or have a preferred relationship with an airline that lowers the ticket price.

If the travel agent or airline offers the same best price you were able to identify on the Internet, it is your choice whether to purchase immediately or go back to the Internet. Internet reservations at an airline site may occasionally offer bonus frequent flyer miles. Furthermore, travel agents almost always charge additional fees for issuing air tickets to compensate for vanishing commissions—usually from $35 per ticket, and sometimes higher.

For international trips—especially those without the benefit of advance-purchase discounts—an agent may provide access to a reputable consolidator the average person doesn't have (most times you will need to specifically request that the agent seek a consolidator fare), or be able to book two one-way tickets, with the return priced in another nation's currency that provides a foreign exchange advantage. Now that you know, be sure to ask if these opportunities are available.

Step 9. Go Back Online and Buy the Best Fare—Even If You Have to Register

If you decide to purchase your ticket online from an airline site or Internet travel agency Web site, you may have to register with the site, providing details of your name, address, and other miscellaneous information. Alternatively, certain sites may allow you to purchase a ticket as a guest; but given all the information you must provide (including address, phone contact information, and credit card number), you should register and have all this information stored electronically for a much faster ticket purchase next time around. Typically, your credit card number and expiration date will be requested just prior to completing your transaction, and with your permission, be kept on file to facilitate ease of completing future transactions.

Step 10. As a Last Resort . . . Make an Offer at the "Auction Sites"

Okay. So now you've tried every airline Web site we recommend and talked with a travel agent. But you still cannot find an airfare that will take you where you want to go, when you need to go, within your budget. Fortunately, there are two sites that may come to your rescue, as long as you understand the trade-offs inherent in snagging a bargain, and how to optimally use the sites to ensure you truly come away with a great deal as compensation for your flexibility.

Hotwire.com

With *Hotwire.com*, you provide your departure and destination cities and dates, the maximum number of stops you will accept, whether you only want jet travel or will fly turboprop aircraft, and whether you will accept overnight or off-peak flights. The best available price then pops up, but you are not told the airline, time of flights, or routing. You then have one hour to decide whether to go ahead. If you wish to accept the price you are being offered, you provide your credit card number with expiration date (plus additional identifying information unless you have previously registered), and only after your credit card has been charged for a ticket are you told the airline, routing, and flight times.

As with *Priceline.com* (discussed in the next section), your purchased ticket is nonrefundable and nonchangeable. *Hotwire.com*'s advantage over *Priceline.com* is that you receive a specific price quote before deciding whether to proceed, so you can be sure you have not overpaid if you have done your homework and checked other retail sites.

Since *Hotwire.com*'s fares are typically no lower—and may even be higher—than retail or consolidator air fares, especially when the airlines have sales, this site should be avoided by the time-sensitive business traveler who has at least seven to fourteen days' advance notice before his date of departure and is able stay over a weekend. (Note that advance-purchase requirements vary in different markets.) However, this site is an excellent place to start an airfare search since you are free to ascertain what the airlines consider to be their "rock bottom" inventory price without being forced to commit to a nonrefundable, nonchangeable purchase. This site also offers hotels and car rentals.

Priceline.com

Priceline.com has been described as an auction site because you bid on a flight by naming your price, indicate the number of stops you will accept and whether you will fly overnight or on a commuter aircraft, and provide your credit card. Within fifteen minutes, you receive an e-mail response, and if your bid has been accepted, your credit card has been charged for a *nonrefundable*, *nonchangeable* ticket. Only then do you find out the airline, flights, and times. Flights booked through *Priceline.com* are not eligible for frequent flyer miles or upgrades. If you don't like what you have purchased, it's too bad—your credit card has been charged and no changes or cancellations are permissible. Of note is that *Priceline.com* also represents itself as a regular Internet travel agent, requiring each visitor to first use a conventional booking engine similar to other online travel sites prior to offering the capability to "name your own price."

To label *Priceline.com* as an auction site is a misnomer, for two reasons:

1. At authentic auctions, bidders always know the characteristics of the product for which they are bidding. At *Priceline.com*, the airline and times of travel are not known until after you have been charged for a nonrefundable, nonchangeable ticket—which are critical components of the product you are purchasing.

2. You are not "bidding" against another buyer, but exclusively against an airfare stored in a database. Your bid is either accepted or rejected based on whether you have met or (more often) exceeded

a predetermined threshold amount. Your chances of success have nothing to do with some other individual who may outbid you.

Most major U.S. airlines participate by listing in *Priceline.com*'s database the lowest fare they are prepared to accept for any given routing on a specified date. However, the user has no idea what that lowest acceptable price is, which works to *Priceline.com*'s advantage. Countless articles have been written by travel writers who compared prices obtained at retail (not sale fares, but regular fares) and wholesale Web travel sites—meaning consolidators—to those from "successful bids" at *Priceline.com* and found the following facts:

1. The traveler who spends some time seeking fares will often beat the lowest successful bid from *Priceline.com*.
2. If a traveler books a fare on *Priceline.com*, the savings are insignificant and certainly not worth giving up flexibility of time or airline.
3. Independent research has shown that many customers bid too high, meaning they could have obtained a ticket at a lower amount.

Given that the purchase is irrevocable and flight times and airline are unknown, should the business user even consider using *Priceline.com*? The simple answer is no, unless the business traveler can be flexible on both outbound and return flights, and has not succeeded in obtaining a reasonably priced ticket using all the other airfare strategies outlined in this book. *Priceline* states that a future upgrade will enable selection of departure times in segments such as 6 AM–noon and noon–6 PM. This has not been implemented at the time of this writing.

> **TIP**
>
> **If you want to bid for a hotel alone at *Priceline.com*, checking out which hotels are offered with the vacation package to your desired destination will help guide you to what you may get!**

Bottom line: *Priceline.com* should only be used as a last resort for the business traveler to whom time is not critical. If you do choose to bid at *Priceline.com*, research several retail sites first for the lowest standard price, then bid at least 30 percent lower than the best fare you found (or at least 15 to 20 percent below *Hotwire.com*'s best price, as discussed below).

You might want to check out several sites that post information based on user feedback about successful bids from *Priceline.com*, including *Biddingfortravel.com*. Even though *Priceline.com* is barred from divulging any information about successful bids, it encourages use of other sites that reveal *Priceline.com* "bidding secrets," since the profitability of its business model depends purely on customers placing successful bids.

Priceline.com also offers hotels, car rentals, and vacation packages that can benefit both leisure and business travelers (especially if they're traveling at the last minute). Bidding for a hotel room at *Priceline.com* involves a similar process to airfares, whereby the potential customer does not know which hotels are available. However, bidding for an air–hotel package does reveal the hotel upfront with details before you bid with your credit card—but the airline and flight times remain transparent unless the bid is accepted.

Finally, since the airlines that participate in *Hotwire.com* and *Priceline.com* are similar, the traveler who has resolved to use an auction site should first get a price quote from *Hotwire.com*—then offer a bid at *Priceline.com* at a 30 percent discount to *Hotwire.com*'s price.

Skyauction.com

This site auctions specific airfares, hotel stays, cruises, or packages, either for a specific date or a range of possible departure dates. Auctions include coach and first-class tickets for domestic and international tickets as well as hotel rooms, all-inclusive island getaways, African safari adventures, and student travel.

Luxurylink.com

This site's database contains thousands of products of interest to the sophisticated traveler—tours, cruises, specialty travel, hotels, resorts, inns, lodges, yacht charters, villas, spas, and more (and frequently excludes airfare—you're on your own for that). Users may search by destination and product type as well as via more specialized criteria. Special rates, promotions, new cruise itineraries, special events, and scores of items of note to luxury travel buyers are available via the Luxury Link News service.

By special arrangement with the site's suppliers, a number of packages are offered for auction each week at a fraction of retail cost. There is no charge to register to bid on any of the auction properties. Click on "auctions" to view the current listing.

An Easy Way to Get Weekly Travel Updates

Register at *Traveltactics.com* to receive free weekly updates about value in upscale travel. The site also has a variety of special reports topical to major issues in travel, as well as an extensive array of carefully selected links to the best travel sites. This site can save you significant amounts of time and money. Other sites to check out for weekly travel updates include *Joesentme.com* (excellent fare for business travelers run by Joe Brancatelli), *Elliott.org* (Chris Elliott is the ombudsman for *National Geographic Travel* magazine and an advocate for travelers), *Frequentflier.com* (Tim Winship is an expert on frequent flyer miles), and *Johnnyjet.com* (Johnny DiScala is an Internet travel expert with a weekly e-zine describing his travels).

Be the First to Know About Weekend Specials

Several sites will e-mail free travel information on a weekly basis. The best site we've found offering information on weekend specials is *Smarterliving .com*.

Smarterliving.com targets the leisure traveler with its information on specials, but also offers the flexible last-minute business traveler one key feature: Those registered will be e-mailed a well-organized listing of weekend specials, specifically flights departing from all local airports the user has indicated. Such weekend specials may also be obtained by registering at the Web site of all major airlines, but e-mail notifications will typically include a majority of flights that involve city pairs irrelevant to the traveler. Weekend special fares for domestic travel are usually announced each Wednesday for a Friday or Saturday departure, returning the following Monday or Tuesday. International specials are posted on Mondays for travel seven to ten days later and returning within a few days. Fares are about the same as sale fares, and may be 65 to 80 percent off full-coach fares. Refer to Chapter 4 for more details about Weekend Internet Fares.

Other Niche Web Sites

- *Airtreks.com*—Focuses on round-the-world fares. Also try *Air brokers.com* and *Bootsnall.com/rtw*. *Thetravellerslounge.co.uk* discusses various deals and schedules associated with RTW flying.
- *Travelzoo.com*—Lists sale fares, specials, and hot deals from hundreds of sites.

Package Vacations

For the savvy leisure traveler or road warrior needing three or more days in a major city, an air and hotel package may be cheaper than purchasing each component separately—even if the hotel isn't used! This is especially true for last-minute travel, that is, booking less than seven to fourteen days prior to the departure date.

Using any search engine, type in your destination city and "package" or "tour." You can access the major airlines' vacation desks (such as American, Delta, or Continental Airlines' Vacations) from their home page by clicking on "vacations" or "packages." For other sites that may be helpful regarding last-minute bookings, refer to the next section.

Last-Minute Travel

Certain Web sites specialize in last-minute vacations, which can be a wonderful benefit for the spontaneous leisure traveler. There is, however, no reason why the savvy road warrior cannot take advantage of the offerings if they are compatible with his business needs.

1. *Site59.com.* Now part of *Travelocity.com*, this site aggregates the components composing packages, and bookings can be made online three hours to fourteen days prior to departure. Be aware, however, that certain components may be more expensive when changed or combined, such as switching to a superior hotel or adding a car to the air and hotel combination. Make sure to check the price for the components if they were to be purchased separately before you proceed to book a package on this site. If you don't like the hotel being offered, you can usually select a more upscale option at a clearly designated price. If you consider the air and hotel component to be reasonably priced but find adding a car is expensive, simply rent the car independent of the package.

2. *11thhourvacations.com.* This site offers cruise and vacation packages, as well as air- and hotel-only purchases to a wide variety of domestic and international destinations.

TIP

Before purchasing a travel package, check with airlines and hotels as to what their independent prices will be to ensure you are truly getting a great deal. And watch out for hidden charges such as taxes that can negate your savings!

3. *Concierge.com.* This is the Web site of the travel magazine *Condé Nast Traveler*. Click on "deals" for daily specials. Register to receive daily updates that include "Quick Getaways."

4. *Lastminutetravel.com.* This site is really nothing more than a middleman, listing other companies' packages offering air, hotel, and car from major cities. Links to the suppliers are provided for booking. Despite this site's name, bookings can be made months in advance.

One final note about last-minute packages: Check with your travel agent, who is typically inundated with information about such specials.

Booking Business- or First-Class Seats Online

Several airline Web sites allow frequent flyers to redeem their earned miles to book free business- or first-class tickets online. Airline Web sites and neutral travel agent reservation sites also offer online purchase of full-fare business- or first-class tickets online—but the retail prices will almost always be extremely high.

It may be worthwhile checking out business- and first-class fares from your home city as well as other nearby cities within a 1,000-mile radius. If you find a reasonable premium-class fare from a nearby city, simply purchase a cheap coach fare from your home city to meet your connection. For example, a friend living in Fort Lauderdale who needed to visit Paris found an excellent first-class fare from Boston to Paris. She then purchased a discount fare from Fort Lauderdale to Boston, and saved more than $3,000.

Finding discounted premium-class tickets online is more challenging as airlines try to eliminate the middleman and offer special pricing—occasionally for premium seating when demand is low—especially at their own Web sites. Even consolidators (refer to Chapter 7 for details) that sell airline tickets at discount prices will rarely offer business- or first-class seats at discount prices. However, it may be worthwhile checking *1stair.net* and *Flyfirstclass.com* to seek premium seats at reduced prices.

Other Sites for International and European Travel

For those traveling abroad, check out the following sites:

1. ***Flights.com*** is a consolidator that focuses mainly on international routes, although it may on occasion also have favorable prices for U.S. domestic routes. Since *Flights.com* is a consolidator, tickets may not be eligible for frequent flyer miles.
2. ***Economytravel.com*** specializes in international fares.
3. ***DestinationsEurope.com*** is an affiliate site of the car rental Web site *AutoEurope.com* that provides low airfares from the United States to Europe.
4. ***Faremax.com/Cheap-getaway.com*** offers airline tickets to Europe and other international destinations for up to a 60 percent discount. It also provides hotel and car reservations, all-inclusive packages, and cruises.
5. ***Opodo.com*** (short for "Opportunity To Do") was established by Europe's major airlines—including British Airways, Air France, Lufthansa, KLM, Alitalia, Aer Lingus, and Iberia—as an equivalent to *Orbitz.com*. Many additional European airlines have signed on as marketing partners and can be booked on this site, as can hotels and car rentals. You should definitely check out this site if you will be purchasing flights within Europe.

   Since *Opodo.com* does not include flights of European low-cost airlines such as EasyJet, RyanAir, Go, and Virgin Express, you should check those airlines' Web sites separately as well as *Aerfares.net* and *Easyvalue.com* (see below).
6. ***Lastminute.com*** is a competitor of *Opodo.com* and should be checked out before purchasing a ticket at *Opodo.com* for flights to be taken within the forthcoming three months.

7. ***Aerfares.net*** claims to search for the best airfares across all the European low-cost airlines.
8. ***Easyvalue.com*** is the partner site of European low-cost airline EasyJet and compares prices across the board on low-cost airlines from the United Kingdom by searching numerous low-cost airlines' Web sites simultaneously.
9. ***Europebyair.com*** searches over twenty airlines. The user may also purchase a flight pass for intra-European travel at $99 per flight.
10. ***Travel.guardian.co.uk*** provides a detailed overview of European low-cost airlines, including route maps for the larger ones.
11. ***Lowcostairlines.org*** links to low-cost airlines worldwide.

Online Travel Sites for Business

The big three online travel agencies (*Orbitz.com*, *Expedia.com*, and *Travelocity.com*) are now courting companies large and small, to have their business travelers book through the site rather than dealing with traditional travel agencies. Each of the three enables negotiated rates to be input into the system, and promotes unique features such as the ability to display corporate negotiated fares and rates integrated with the Web site's regular fares and rates into one combined screen display. Any of the three may also offer hotel discounts the Web site has negotiated (typically 15–20 percent off rack rates).

Service fees may be as low as $5 per transaction, and $15–20 for travelers who interact with a human. This is in contrast to $40–60 charged by traditional corporate travel agencies. However, the online sites may also charge a setup fee to load a company's negotiated rates into their system.

McDonald's selecting *Orbitz.com* as its corporate travel agent in 2003 was the first instance of a major company moving into the online travel world in a big way—expect many more to follow. One benefit of having business travelers book online is research showing lower overall fares when the traveler is presented with multiple options on a screen versus having a travel agent do the search. For companies that need a managed program with regular activity reports and the ability to keep track of travelers, the online travel agent option may be a viable option that can save significant amounts of money.

Customer Service Associated with Online Reservations

Customer service for online reservations pertains mainly to response time to e-mail inquiries as well as how change fees are handled. The big three (*Orbitz.com*, *Expedia.com*, and *Travelocity.com*) are best in this area—and they are not especially good when it comes to customer service—but as always, check change fees and cancellation rules before providing your credit card whenever you book. Typical rules for changes are the same imposed by the airline from which your ticket is issued—usually $75 to $100 to change a nonrefundable ticket—but there may also be a site-specific additional fee ranging from $5 to $10 or even as much as $50. Some tickets may be changed or canceled online, while other sites require that you call the customer service number, which is usually but not always toll-free, and hold times can be considerable.

Remember that cancellations or changes to nonrefundable tickets for flights on most major U.S. airlines must be made prior to scheduled departure time or the entire ticket becomes worthless. This rule applies irrespective of how you purchased your ticket (online or by phone).

Changing a regular airline ticket, as opposed to one bought through a consolidator—and especially when the ticket is nonrefundable—is much simpler if it was purchased from the airline direct rather than through a travel agent or an online travel site. We therefore strongly suggest that you book at the airline's own Web site or with the airline direct by phone if you believe there is a reasonable chance you may need to make a change or cancel your reservation.

Best Seat in the House

Want to know how to get a better seat? *Seatguru.com* has smart graphics explaining seating charts and is frequently updated based on passenger feedback.

Airport Information

Airwise.com provides information about sixty major airports in the United States and abroad, including transportation options and restaurants, as well as news and travel schedules. *Airwise.com* will also update you on airline industry news by e-mail each day if you register at its Web site.

Advisories for International Travel

Visit *travel.state.gov* to check out the U.S. State Department's list of travel warnings and information for all countries abroad. The British government's site *fco.gov.uk* provides more detailed and objective advice that is less politically oriented.

Credit Card Security Online

We have absolutely no concern about online credit card security, which has improved considerably over the past few years. Credit card companies never hold the consumer liable for more than $50 of fraudulent use of a credit or charge card. Identity theft rarely arises from transactions made online when purchasing from established vendors that build in multiple security safeguards.

Caveats

A final note about booking on Internet travel sites. Be mindful of the following key points:

1. When transferring from one flight to another, ensure that you have at least 45 minutes for domestic flights, and 60 to 90 minutes for international. Flying into Mexico City from New York en route to Puerto Vallarta in Mexico, I had to clear immigration in Mexico City—and missed my onward flight because 50 minutes was insufficient to make the connection. I had to sleep over at an airport hotel.

With experience, the savvy world traveler and road warrior will develop his own flow chart combining his own site preferences and preferred airlines.

2. Online sites may not be as vigilant as travel agents or airlines in notifying customers of schedule changes and delays, although some sites have developed excellent systems for informing customers of such by phone, cell phone, PDA, e-mail, and so on. Confirm your flight times a few days before you travel, especially if your reservation was made several months in advance.

In Summary

- When you have a free hour or so, sit down at your computer and, just for the fun of it, go to the Web sites described in this chapter. Then, when you're ready to plan a serious trip, you'll save time by already being familiar with several sites. With experience, you will ultimately find two or three favorite sites you can navigate quickly.
- Don't forget basic airfare principles discussed in Chapters 2, 3, and 4, including planning as far in advance as possible, so you can research a variety of options, watch for airfare sales, be flexible with your travel dates and times, and check out alternative airports.
- For travelers who just want to focus their comparison shopping on those few major retail sites offering the biggest bang for the buck, go to *Orbitz.com*, followed by *Expedia.com*, and possibly *Travelocity .com*. Also check *Hotwire.com* to find out what a bargain basement fare should be. *Tripadvisor.com* links you to all these sites as well as to articles and travel reviews about destination hotels when you

search for a destination. For more extensive links to the best travel Web sites, go to *Traveltactics.com*.

- After checking the three major retail travel agent sites *Orbitz.com*, *Expedia.com*, and *Travelocity.com*, determine which airlines offered you the best prices and schedules and visit those airlines' own proprietary branded sites. You may realize additional benefits, such as a possible 5 percent discount or bonus frequent flyer miles for booking online.
- If you are compulsive in your quest for a spectacular fare, check the two discount sites—*Cheaptickets.com* (especially for Hawaii) and *Overstock.com*.
- For last-minute travel, check out *Site59.com*, *11thhourvacations.com*, *Concierge.com*, *and Lastminutetravel.com*.
- For international itineraries—especially for last-minute travel—visit consolidators such as *Flights.com* and *Economytravel.com*.
- The three major online travel sites (*Orbitz.com, Expedia.com,* and *Travelocity.com*) now offer special online booking programs for business that provide access to the Web site's regular offerings as well as the company's negotiated fares and rates. These programs promote savings around 75 percent off the standard lost working with a regular travel agent.
- For information about weekend special fares (domestic and international), register at *Smarterliving.com* to receive weekly e-mail travel updates.
- For updates on stability and safety of countries you wish to visit abroad, visit *travel.state.gov* and *fco.gov.uk*.
- Check out *Seatguru.com* for details about best seats on major U.S. airlines' aircraft.
- *Airwise.com* provides information about sixty major airports in the United States and abroad, including transportation options and restaurants.
- Follow ten key steps when using the Internet to find bargain airfares:
    1. Review special discounts or coupons you may have that could reduce the price of a ticket. Most discount certificates cannot be used when purchasing your ticket online, but it is still worth seeking out great fares—or at least obtaining some benchmark prices—before calling to make a reservation.

2. Visit the three largest retail sites: *Orbitz.com*, *Travelocity.com*, and *Expedia.com*.
3. Check wholesale/consolidator sites: *Cheaptickets.com* and *Overstock.com* (as well as *Flights.com* if traveling abroad).
4. Compare airfares with side-by-side travel sites (also known as "site scrapers") such as *Sidestep.com*, *Qixo.com*, and *Fare chase.com*.
5. Visit the major airlines' sites.
6. Check one or more low-cost airline sites (such as Southwest, JetBlue, and Frontier).
7. Check the bargain information Web site *Bestfares.com*, in particular assessing the lowest price available for your city pair by using its QuickFare Finder.
8. Go offline and call a major airline or your travel agent.
9. Return online to purchase the best fare.
10. As a last resort, go to an "auction" site such as *Priceline.com* or *Hotwire.com*.

- The authors' Top Ten travel Web sites for purchasing a routine air ticket are:

1. ***Orbitz.com*** to review standard retail prices for all major airlines and look for Web fare specials
2. ***Hotwire.com*** to check out what the major airlines consider to be a "distressed fare" for your itinerary
3. ***Travelocity.com***
4. ***Expedia.com***
5. ***Traveltactics.com*** for its updates, extensive links, and special reports
6. ***Tripadvisor.com*** for its traveler reviews and articles, as well as links to the major online travel sites
7. ***Priceline.com*** as a last resort
8. ***Airtreks.com*** for round-the-world tickets
9. ***Flights.com***—which is a consolidator specializing in international flights
10. ***Luxurylink.com*** for the elegant vacationer seeing a top-of-the-line package!

CHAPTER TEN

Maximize Your Opportunities for Earning Frequent Flyer Miles

One day I received a flyer in the mail presenting a unique opportunity: If I were to switch my long-distance carrier to Sprint, I would earn 40,000 miles from Northwest Airlines over an eighteen-month period—receiving 10,000 miles upfront and an additional 10,000 miles every six months thereafter as long as I remained a customer with Sprint. Since 35,000 miles provides a free trip to Hawaii or the Caribbean, and 40,000 miles is half the number of miles required for a business-class ticket anywhere Northwest Airlines or its partner KLM flies, this decision was a no-brainer. My wife and I switched both of our home phones and my home office line, which netted us each 40,000 miles into our Northwest WorldPerks account. Total cost in time—about thirty minutes; total dollar cost to switch—zero. In essence, two free tickets to Hawaii just fell into our laps.

> **TIP**
>
> **An unexpected offer for discounted or free travel may come in the guise of junk mail. Take a moment to quickly scan every piece of mail you receive—just in case a great travel deal is hidden there somewhere.**

> **TIP**
>
> **Most discussions about frequent flyer miles in this and subsequent chapters apply to the major airlines. Many of the low-cost airlines do have frequent flyer programs, but earning and redemption characteristics are quite different—and are discussed in a later section of this chapter.**

Many frequent flyer aficionados do silly things to earn miles—like avoiding a much lower fare on a nonpreferred airline (especially when their company is paying), charging unnecessary purchases with their mileage-earning credit card, and perhaps even carrying a significant balance that incurs annual interest rates around 19 percent.

And then, there are the "fanatics" . . .

Do you remember the "Pudding Man"? This gutsy maverick took advantage of an

American Airlines frequent flyer promotion, which offered one hundred frequent flyer miles for each purchase of a certain brand of pudding. The "Pudding Man" bought thousands of packages of dessert from a discount grocery store at a reduced price, then donated it all to charity, which not only made his massive purchase tax-deductible, but mobilized the volunteer help he needed to cut out the bar code from each box! He accumulated 1 million miles!

Creative, yes. Practical for the everyday traveler, no. For those of us who are pressured for time in our quest for the best mileage-earning opportunities, there are simpler, effective ways to accumulate frequent flyer miles, as you will see.

When It Comes to Flying, Not All Miles Are Created Equal

In general, the amount of frequent flyer miles you earn is equal to the actual distance you fly. Just be aware that some airlines may give fewer miles when flying on discounted tickets; for example, British Airways only offers 25 percent of actual miles flown when using a nonrefundable ticket. Delta offers only 50 percent of actual miles flown on certain discount fares. But the savvy world traveler and road warrior knows that when it comes to airlines and flying, base miles are just the starting point.

We all know that miles earned apply to free trips. But miles have two other key applications:

1. Counting toward elite status that offers frequent flyers lots of benefits (refer to a subsequent section in this chapter for more information).
2. Contributing to the achievement of million-miler status on some airlines, such as United, American, and America West. Since these million-miler programs are not usually published, check with the frequent flyer desk for information.

Let's explore the different kinds of miles you can earn when flying:

1. **Flight Miles**—What you earn when flying from city A to city B. In addition, most airlines offer minimum miles for short trips—typically 500 miles, which means that if your actual flown mileage is just 385, you will still earn 500 flight mileage for your flight.
2. **Base or Qualifying Miles**—Those flight miles that count toward earning elite status the following year. With the advent of extensive airline alliances, the miles you earn on many partner airlines usually apply toward elite status the following year. Be sure to check with your preferred airline's frequent flyer desk if in doubt whether

miles earned with a partner will count toward your elite status qualification.

3. **Elite Bonus Miles**—Those extra miles you earn from flying once you have achieved elite status—typically 100 percent or double the flight miles if you are highest- or intermediate-level elite with an airline, 50 to 100 percent for intermediate level, and 25 percent if you are entry- or first-level elite. Bonus miles do not apply toward elite qualification the following year.
4. **Class-of-Service Miles**—Miles offered to travelers who actually pay full fare for a business- or first-class seat (what are they thinking?), typically earning additional bonuses of 25 and 50 percent, respectively (but the percentage may vary from airline to airline). Class-of-service bonus miles may count toward elite status the following year.
5. **Promotional or Special Route Bonus Miles**—Miles offered by airlines to a traveler flying either a new route or a route the airline is promoting heavily (frequently against an aggressive or new competitor). Earning these bonus miles often requires that you register by phone or online.
6. **Credit Card Bonus Miles**—When you pay for your airline ticket with a credit card affiliated with the same airline, the miles you earn from the transaction may be doubled. A surprising exception that does not give double frequent flyer miles is the American Airlines credit card issued by Citibank.

To demonstrate the power of these different kinds of miles, let's imagine a highest-level elite flyer traveling one way with a paid business-class seat on a new route from Boston to Ontario (near Los Angeles). His earnings for a $500 ticket could be as follows:

- Flight Miles: 2,500 (only these miles count toward elite status the following year, meaning that these are also Base or Qualifying miles)
- Class-of-Service Bonus Miles (25 percent for business class): 625
- Elite Double Miles: 2,500
- New Route Bonus Miles: 2,000
- Credit Card Miles Plus Double Bonus from Ticket Purchase: 1,000
- Total Earned for Flight: 8,625, which is more than three times the actual miles flown

Just How Valuable Are Those Miles?

The value of 1,000 miles can range from a low of $12 to a high of $100, depending upon how the miles are used. Let's look at the following two examples:

1. The most popular frequent flyer mile award is 25,000 miles for a free coach-class ticket within the United States or Canada. If you use this award to fly coast-to-coast for an itinerary that otherwise costs $300—a fare that can be obtained when purchased in advance with a Saturday stayover—then redeeming 25,000 miles saves $300. To determine the value of 1,000 miles in this instance, divide $300 by 25 and you come up with $12 per 1,000 miles (1.2 cents per mile).
2. A traveler who wants to fly first class on an international flight uses 100,000 miles for a flight that retails at $10,000. The value of his award is calculated by dividing $10,000 by 100, which equals $100 per 1,000 miles (or 10 cents per mile).

As you can see, scenario #2 gives the traveler a whopping eight times greater value than #1! Do the math—it's worth it!

Why is this math so important? For two reasons:

1. Simply because when you receive notification about a promotion that includes frequent flyer miles, you must calculate the value of those miles to judge whether you are getting a good deal—or not. For example, when a hotel offers you 1,000 bonus miles for a stay, the value of the miles can be as low as $12 (if you intend to use those miles toward a domestic free ticket that would otherwise cost $300) or as high as $100 (if you intend to use those miles toward a first-class international ticket that would otherwise cost $10,000). Refer to the calculation in the first paragraph of this section.
2. Redeeming frequent flyer miles for an air ticket that would otherwise be inexpensive is poor value. For example, using 25,000 frequent flyer miles when you can purchase a very cheap $200 roundtrip ticket does not make sense. Conversely, the greatest value lies in using your frequent flyer miles for international business- or first-class tickets that would otherwise be very expensive.

Become One of the Elite

Airlines reward their most prolific frequent flyers with what is known as "elite" status within their frequent flyer program. The elite status may grant such perks as:

- Bonus frequent flyer miles
- Inexpensive or free upgrade opportunities for travel within North America, and sometimes international travel, for passengers who fly 75,000 to 100,000 miles or more on the same airline during the same calendar year, achieving the highest level elite status
- A special reservations phone number
- Separate baggage check-in—usually with business- or first-class passengers
- Discounted, or occasionally free, use of the airline's lounge facilities

The major U.S. airlines typically have three levels of elite status for their frequent flyers, based on the number of miles flown in the prior year from January 1 through December 31:

- **Highest Level.** This is the top echelon conferred on those who travel at least 100,000 miles in a calendar year. (Certain airlines may have a lower threshold—for example, Continental and Northwest Airlines require 75,000 miles, while Alaska Airlines requires just 40,000 miles since it flies shorter distances than most other airlines.) Perks include at least 100 percent mileage bonuses (that is, double miles when flying) and top priority for domestic upgrades confirmed at least ninety-six hours prior to departure. On some airlines, such as United and American, this group of extraordinarily loyal customers may receive a significant number of domestic and up to eight international/Hawaii upgrade certificates that can be confirmed even with discounted tickets at the time of purchase no matter when reservations are booked.

- **Intermediate Level.** This is the middle stratum of the elite hierarchy, bestowed on those who reach 50,000 miles in a calendar year (some airlines may have a lower threshold). They receive 50 to 100 percent mileage bonuses and secondary priority for domestic upgrades confirmed seventy-two hours prior to departure.

- **Lowest Level.** This is the minimum entry point for elite status and usually requires 25,000 miles in a calendar year. (Again, some airlines may have a lower threshold; for example, Alaska Airlines requires just 20,000 miles since it flies shorter distances than most other airlines.) At this level, travelers receive just 25 percent of mileage bonuses when flying and the lowest priority for domestic upgrades confirmed twenty-four hours prior to departure.

Most airlines will offer "matching" elite status if you provide proof of having achieved the corresponding level in a competitor's program. Check out the Web site *Flyertalk.com* for information on all the different airlines' current activities in this regard. Travelers who may not have met the threshold number of miles in the prior year on any airline may request complimentary elite status if they will likely be traveling a significant number of miles in the forthcoming six- to eighteen-month period. Requesting complimentary elite status requires that the traveler write a letter to an airline's frequent flyer program, stating he or she will be a frequent traveler for the remainder of that year or the following year, and specifying the approximate mileage that will be attained on the airline.

For example, American Airlines offers the AAdvantage Challenge program, which has two levels.

1. The "Gold Challenge" to achieve the lowest level AAdvantage status is awarded to passengers who fly 5,000 full-coach-fare miles—or 10,000 if flying on a discounted ticket—within the ensuing ninety days. But there are no perks while participating in the challenge.
2. The "Platinum Challenge" to achieve intermediate level AAdvantage status is awarded to those travelers accumulating 10,000 full-coach-fare miles—or 20,000 if flying on a discounted ticket—within the ensuing ninety days.

To enroll in the AAdvantage Challenge, contact AAdvantage at 800-882-8880 and ask for the customer service department, since the program is not advertised. Challenges begun in the first half of the calendar year (January to June) will give you elite status to the end of the current membership year only, which ends in February. That means your status the following year will depend on the miles you fly during the year you accept the challenge. Challenges started in the latter half of the calendar year (July to December) will earn you elite status for the remainder of the current membership year as well as for the following membership year. You must, however, fly the requisite number of miles (100,000, 50,000, 25,000 for the respective elite levels described earlier in this section) within the following year to qualify for the year after that.

TIP

To learn more about the intricacies of American Airlines' elite program, visit the Web site "Unofficial Guide To AAdvantage" at *http://members.shaw.ca/fewmiles/AA/index2.html*, which is run by a fanatic AAdvantage customer eager to share years of accumulated knowledge!

Grab a Partner

As a savvy world traveler, you no doubt choose to fly on your preferred airline, where you have already attained, or aspire to attain, elite status. If you need to travel where your preferred carrier does not fly, check whether your preferred airline has a partner airline that flies to your destination, which you can do by:

- Going online to your preferred airline's Web site; the frequent flyer section will include detailed information about partners.
- Calling the frequent flyer desk for this information.
- Reviewing a complimentary copy of the in-flight magazine (either when on board or by calling the customer service desk and requesting a copy), which will also provide details of your preferred airline's partner relationships.

However, when flying on a partner airline outside North America, the savvy world traveler will want to consider two important mileage issues (both discussed in more detail in Chapter 12):

1. Whether frequent flyer miles will be earned on your ticket (certain discounted tickets on partner airlines may not be eligible to accrue miles)
2. If frequent flyer miles are earned, whether they will count toward retaining your level of elite status on your preferred airline the following year

The rules for earning miles when flying on discounted international fares and whether miles earned from flying on your preferred airline's partner contribute to elite status are complex and may need clarification from your preferred airline's frequent flyer program desk.

TIP

Do not rely on reservations agents for information regarding which partner airlines will or will not earn miles and whether the earned miles will contribute to earning or maintaining elite status. They frequently do not know—but may not admit they do not know! You must contact the frequent flyer desk, where agents deal exclusively with frequent flyer issues. And document everything you are told, including the name of the staff person and date you spoke to him.

Keep Track of Those Miles

It is exclusively *your* responsibility to track your earned frequent flyer miles, including miles earned other than by flying. The smart traveler will keep a "tickler" file for storing documentation of earned miles, including tickets and boarding cards from the airline itself as well as its partner airlines, hotel and car rental receipts, and so on. These receipts must then be submitted, usually within six months, to your preferred airline's frequent flyer program if mileage credit fails to appear on your regular update summaries. When seeking flight credit after-the-fact, mail in a copy of your ticket—keeping the original in your file—or boarding passes with the number of your airline ticket (boarding cards alone without reference to the ticket number are not sufficient since they may be from a free award ticket).

Frequent flyer mileage update summaries traditionally have been mailed every two to three months (or less frequently if there has been no mileage earning or redemption activity). Most airlines now encourage members to opt for monthly updates by e-mail, with rapid access to details on the Web. You may also review your frequent flyer statements by going online to the airline's frequent flyer Web site any time you want.

Web sites are also available to help you track your miles. Check out:

- *Mileagemanager.com* ($15 per year) is owned by frequent flyer guru Randy Petersen. Once you input each of your frequent flyer numbers with associated PIN number or password, it takes just one to two days' processing time to set up your account, which will automatically update your miles and points with more than forty airline and hotel programs. Once you have registered, all you have to remember is a single user name and PIN number. The site goes further than simple tracking, however, enabling you to see what destinations and classes of service you may redeem with your current balance, as well as blackout dates, if applicable. Members can also access information about supported programs, compare award schedules, and track missing miles or points. You can even receive e-mail updates when an account is updated, the balance reaches a certain threshold, or the miles are about to expire. Security is paramount, and the site offers a written guarantee of coverage should losses be incurred because of a security breach.
- *Maxmiles.com* ($30 per year—a three-month trial period is available) provides your updated balances for forty loyalty programs (the majority by far being airlines), analyzes current award offerings, and will keep you updated with regular e-mail reports.
- *Myairmiles.com* (free) tracks frequent flyer miles on only eight airlines, and no hotels. It is extremely simple to use. A unique capability is its "Ask Bob" feature, which answers selected questions on a weekly basis.
- *Yodlee.com* (free) tracks more than seventy frequent flyer mile and hotel programs as part of a broader operation, including bank and credit card consolidation, etc. It is technically the most complex of the mileage managers, and will, for example, enable you to program an e-mail notification when a preselected amount reaches a certain

threshold level. Like *Mileagemanager.com*, *Yodlee.com* will cover any losses due to breaches in security.

Other services worth checking out are *Milepro.com*, *Miletracker.com*, and *Totalmiles.com*.

You Don't Have to Take Flight to Earn Miles

The secret is out! Even though major airlines have lost tens of billions of dollars since the turn of this century, one component of their business is consistently profitable: the sale of frequent flyer miles. The options for earning frequent flyer miles have soared over the past decade, as the major U.S. airlines have sought new revenue streams. It has even been proposed that frequent flyer miles constitute the second currency of the United States! For airlines, selling miles to companies for distribution to customers and employees has been a revenue bonanza. They receive payment far in advance of the free trips being redeemed, often for frequent flyer miles that are never even used.

Your frequent flyer miles typically never expire as long as you have at least one mileage transaction posting to your account every three years.

Let's review the most important ways that you as a world traveler or road warrior can boost your frequent flyer miles in ways other than flying:

- **Credit Cards.** Paying for everything with airline affinity cards is by far the easiest and potentially most lucrative source of frequent flyer miles without flying. (Affinity cards provide some payback or bonus in direct proportion to the cardholder's spending, such as cash back, frequent flyer miles, donations to a not-for-profit organization or charity, and so on. Refer to Chapter 18 for more details.) Each and every world traveler and road warrior should have at least one mileage-earning charge or credit card that he uses everywhere the card is accepted. Mileage-earning credit cards almost always offer a superior payback to other affinity credit cards, especially if you use your earned miles for premium-class seats.

- **Hotels.** Most upscale hotel chains that cater to business travelers offer frequent flyer miles (typically a maximum of 500 miles per stay) or points toward their own frequent-stay program (refer to Chapter 15 for more information about hotel loyalty programs). The exception is Hilton Hotels' loyalty program, HHONORS, for which stays may receive both frequent flyer miles and hotel points (known as "double-dipping"). When travelers have to choose between accruing points in an airline's program or a hotel's program, choosing frequent flyer miles is usually the superior choice unless:

1. Your hotel stay will be two or more nights.
2. You have lots of frequent flyer miles and now need hotel points to ensure free accommodations when you use your award miles.

More important is to select the hotel that offers the best balance of quality, location, and price. Mileage- or point-earning opportunities from hotel stays should be much lower down on the list of hotel selection criteria, since earning 500 miles has a value of around $8 (refer to calculation method covered earlier in this chapter), while hotel points earned per stay may sometimes be worth even less!

■ **Car Rentals.** Choosing car rental companies that offer frequent flyer miles in your primary airline's program has become an increasingly futile exercise, as mileage accrual opportunities from car rental agencies have diminished considerably since 1998. Typically, car rental companies may offer just 50 miles per day for each rental, which is worth less than a dollar if you use these miles for advance-purchase domestic award trips! In general, the primary determining factor should be getting the best price; even a rare bonus mileage opportunity that gets you 1,000 miles may only be worth about $16! Watch out for special promotions that offer extra bonus miles, which are usually listed in the frequent flyer magazine *Inside Flyer* or its Web site *Webflyer.com*.

■ **Long-Distance Phone Service.** (Refer to example in the opening story of this chapter.) As with car rentals, frequent flyer miles offered by long-distance phone companies have declined over the past few years, not least because the industry's prices have been driven down by cutthroat competition and the bankruptcy of MCI's parent, Worldcom, in 2002. A typical sign-on bonus when you switch to a long-distance phone company may be 2,000 miles, with an additional five miles per dollar spent on long-distance calls. But keep a watch out for special bonus offers—almost always limited to new customers—which will be reported in *Inside Flyer* magazine or your regular airline frequent flyer newsletters. Such an offer might even arrive in the mail looking like any other piece of junk mail you receive! Resolute world travelers might switch long-distance service as often as two to three times a year to collect a new sign-on bonus. Before switching, however, make sure your new long-distance pricing plan is competitive.

■ **Merchandise.** Certain retailers—including those that are Web-based—may offer miles for purchases. Be sure you are getting the best price to avoid paying much more for the sake of a few hundred miles. In general, the bonus miles earning opportunity is miniscule!

- **Dining-for-Miles Programs.** Typically, you will earn ten miles per dollar spent when eating out at participating upscale restaurants. Enroll online at your favorite airline's Web site (frequent flyer section) or *Idine.com.*

- **Purchasing Frequent Flyer Miles.** If you want more frequent flyer miles (and who doesn't?), buy them from virtually any frequent flyer program's Web site! Each airline has a maximum annual purchase limit. And take advantage of mileage purchase promotions where the miles are being offered at a fraction of the retail cost, typically around $28 for 1,000 miles—$25 to $30 for 1,000 miles, plus 7.5 percent tax, plus a transaction fee of $1 for every 1,000 miles. More details are discussed later in this chapter.

TIP

To visit a Web site that helps you discover the "latest and greatest" ways to earn bonus miles, mainly from opportunities other than flying, point your browser to *Traveltactics.com, Mileage workshop.com,* or *Webflyer .com* (click on "deal watch"). *Flyertalk.com* is a free site where road warriors post questions and share ideas about any and every angle related to airline frequent flyer and hotel loyalty programs.

Watch for Airline Frequent Flyer Mile Specials

Any traveler who is committed to maximizing mileage must at least scan the regular newsletter from his frequent flyer program(s) carefully to benefit from special bonus-earning opportunities. For example, bonus miles may be offered to travelers flying a new route following entry of a new competitor or during slow months (typically January through March).

To be informed of the best frequent flyer opportunities as they occur, sign up for a free weekly e-zine at *Traveltactics.com.* For travelers serious about the nuances of earning frequent flyer miles, the monthly magazine *Inside Flyer* provides in-depth analysis of various programs and issues pertinent to frequent flyers, as well as detailed information regarding bonus opportunities and partners for every major program. Annual subscriptions cost $45 to $60 for 12 monthly editions. To subscribe, call 719-597-8880 or 800-767-8896, or visit their Web site at *Webflyer.com.* New subscribers are frequently eligible for bonus frequent flyer miles, so be sure to ask about mileage-earning promotions when you subscribe.

To be eligible for certain bonus mileage specials, you may have to register by calling a special toll-free number or by going online as instructed in the promotional information. Fail to do so and you will not receive the bonus.

If you want to keep abreast of major frequent flyer happenings without getting into the detail provided by *Inside Flyer,* go to *Frequentflier.com* and provide your e-mail address to receive regular e-mail updates in the form of its free newsletter, *The FrequentFlier Crier.*

Flyertalk.com was founded by frequent flyer guru Randy Petersen and has become the premier community forum for frequent travelers. The site combines elements of a chat room and bulletin board where novice and veteran travelers alike ask questions and share opinions about every aspect of airline and hotel frequency programs and levels of service. Each airline and hotel program has a separate module, and within each of these modules are submodules that focus on specific issues, such as elite status, getting upgraded, and mileage runs (the practice of extensive flying without any specific destination in mind, either to take advantage of a big promotional mileage bonus or to accrue sufficient miles near the end of a calendar year to earn or retain elite frequent flyer status). Although any visitor can review the comments, participation in the forum requires registration. There is no charge to visit the site, become a member, or participate online.

Purchase Frequent Flyer Miles Regularly

Purchasing frequent flyer miles is the most effective strategy for assuring confirmed upgrades at a fraction of the retail business- or first-class fares. For example, if a first-class ticket to Europe costs $8,000 or redemption of 100,000 miles, purchasing the miles at $30 per 1,000 will save over $5,000. That's a guerrilla-sized savings of 65 percent!

The world traveler who wants to fly in luxury regularly can do so by systematically purchasing miles from not just one but many airlines. This strategy works much like a savings plan, ensuring a large payoff for the frequent flyer who consistently purchases the maximum amount of miles allowed to his account. Frequent flyer miles may be purchased at "retail" prices from the airlines as:

- "Personal Miles"—with a cap on the amount that can be bought each year.
- "Gift Miles"—for example, your spouse can buy miles to give to you, and you can reciprocate.
- "Top-Off Miles"—select airlines offer the ability to deposit miles into your frequent flyer account that is a few thousand miles deficient for redeeming a specific reward.

American Express allows the primary cardholder enrolled in Membership Miles to purchase up to 500,000 miles per year. These can be transferred into frequent flyer mile accounts such as Delta, Continental, Hawaiian, and Virgin Atlantic.

Finally, the savvy traveler is always on the lookout for special promotions that allow the frequent flyer to accrue miles at a price lower than the retail cost of approximately $30 for 1,000 miles, for example, by switching long-distance phone carrier, getting a new affinity credit card, or subscribing to a magazine.

Beware of Mileage-Earning Opportunities That May Be Overpriced

In the vast array of opportunities for obtaining frequent flyer miles you may encounter, it's up to you to be smart about which ones are a good deal—or not. Using the mileage value calculation outlined earlier in this chapter (see "Just How Valuable Are Those Miles?"), you can easily analyze whether you can find an alternative nonmileage-earning opportunity at a considerably lower price.

Some of the possible offerings include:

- Investment funds or brokerage houses that offer participants miles when money is placed in select financial securities or mutual funds. Be sure you are purchasing highly rated investment vehicles. After all, what good is a few hundred frequent flyer miles when you have lost your shirt?
- Miles-for-Mortgages, where mileage that is accrued may be associated with higher interest rates or origination fees.
- Cruises, where select offerings may enable one to earn a significant frequent flyer mile bonus. However, in our experience, any cruise promotion that offers miles is overpriced! Check out offerings from cruise consolidators that offer great cruise prices—sans frequent flyer miles.

What About Frequent Flyer Programs with Low-Cost Airlines?

It is not simple to compare the frequent flyer programs of the major airlines with those of their low-fare value brethren, not least since major airlines offer frequent flyer miles whereas most low-cost airlines provide points or segments toward earning free trips. The two low-cost airline exceptions are:

1. America West, which was originally a major airline but switched its fare model to one resembling a low-cost airline while still retaining its original frequent flyer program
2. Frontier, which offers frequent flyer miles and has a program that quite closely resembles those of the major airlines

The following highlights the key differences associated with the low-cost airlines' programs:

- **Limited Award Coverage.** Low-cost airlines do not fly to Hawaii or abroad, so eliminate those possibilities. The two possible exceptions may be America West, which has partnerships with Hawaiian Airlines and British Airways that will get you to paradise and beyond with a free ticket; and Frontier, whose alliance with Virgin has enabled award travel to destinations abroad. Some low-cost airlines have limited route networks, but AirTran has enabled frequent flyers to fly anywhere on the mainland United States by purchasing tickets on other carriers as an award option.
- **Differences in Point Accrual and Redemption.** Low-cost airlines typically differ from majors in the unit of earning (miles versus points/segments); they also differ significantly from each other both in earning and redeeming awards. For example, with Southwest, travelers earn 1 credit per segment (one segment is one takeoff and one landing)—with 16 credits required for one roundtrip. Southwest may also offer online booking bonuses. JetBlue awards 2, 4, or 6 points for short, intermediate, and long-distance flights (and sometimes double if booked online); and offers a free roundtrip in exchange for 100 points. Bottom line—it is easier to earn a free trip with Southwest. In fact, just four roundtrips (each with 4 segments, meaning 1 stop with change of plane both ways), irrespective of distance, will give the Southwest frequent flyer one free trip. That is typically a faster rate of earning a free ticket than any major airline will provide! However, just five nonstop cross-country roundtrips on a major airline will earn a free ticket, with only 2.5 cross-country roundtrips required if you are an elite flyer who earns double frequent flyer miles.
- **Partners.** America West, Southwest, and to a lesser extent Frontier have a reasonable number of partners (such as hotels, car rentals, and credit card tie-ins) the traveler can use to earn credits or miles from sources other than flying. All other low-cost airlines have very limited or no partners.
- **Point/Mile Expiration.** Earnings for awards expire in one year with all low-cost airlines except America West and Frontier (which impose no expiration of miles provided you travel at least once every three years).

We suggest you base your decision whether to fly or not with a low-cost airline on factors other than the state of its frequent flyer program.

Southwest's Rapid Rewards frequent flyer program has received top award billing as the best frequent flyer program for several years in spite of its limitations, most likely because it delivers on its promises (no capacity controls, very easy to understand). JetBlue's TrueBlue frequent flyer program, on the other hand, received negative press when it was launched (one critic nicknamed the program "Boo Hoo"!), and it has received very little publicity since then. And America West's elite frequent flyer program earned top billing in the 2003 Freddie Awards ("loyalty program Oscars"), beating out all the other major airlines' elite offerings!

The Cream of the Frequent Flyer Crop

By now, you should recognize that there is no such thing as "The Best Frequent Flyer Program!" Determining the best frequent flyer program depends on the individual and on a significant number of possible variables. For example, if you live in a hub city for a particular airline, that will be a powerful reason to focus your business on that airline because of the greater range of nonstop options—and that will be the best frequent flyer program for you.

But if you're not locked into one particular airline, you might consider a number of factors. You might like American for its focus on "more room throughout coach" on most of its flights, more opportunities for earning nonflight miles than any other airline, and its extensive number of alliance partners that can get you anywhere in the world. Reasons NOT to consider a frequent flyer program may be that its mileage awards expire in one year or it won't get you to Hawaii or abroad—both drawbacks of Southwest's program. Some may eliminate Continental from consideration because it is virtually impossible to get an international premium-class award on that airline or because discounted tickets only earn half credit toward elite status—and it is very difficult to redeem frequent flyer miles for most standard awards.

In Summary

- When it comes to airlines and flying, frequent flyer miles can be earned in many ways. Flight miles are earned by the actual miles you fly and are the miles applied toward earning elite status for the following year. Additional miles that can be earned when flying include Elite Bonus miles once elite status has been earned (usually 25 to 100 percent of flight miles), Class of Service miles when flying on a paid business- or first-class ticket (25 to 50 percent of flight miles), and Promotional or Special Route Bonus miles for flying on new routes or on routes that are being heavily promoted. Paying for your ticket with a credit card that is affiliated with the airline you have chosen to fly may earn double credit card miles.

- There are numerous ways to boost your frequent flyer miles without flying. The most important factor in taking advantage of these opportunities is knowing the value of the miles you receive.
- Elite status is by far the most important way for frequent flyers to maximize earning of miles. One must usually fly at least 25,000 miles in a calendar year to earn elite status. Benefits associated with elite status include bonus miles for flying, a special reservations phone number, priority check-in with business or first class, and free or inexpensive upgrade opportunities.
- Use your favorite carrier's partner airlines if you need to fly somewhere your preferred carrier does not, preferably one on which earned miles will count toward retaining your elite status if that is what you are seeking to attain.
- It is up to you to ensure that your earned mileage from all sources (flight and nonflight) or hotel points actually appear on your statement of activity. Keep a tickler file with proof of earned mileage or hotel stays in case you need to provide documentation of missing frequent flyer miles or hotel points.
- When you wish to redeem your frequent flyer miles for a free ticket, always consider other potential uses of those miles by calculating the value of 1,000 miles for each alternative.
- The easiest and potentially most lucrative nonflight mileage-accruing opportunity can be found in affinity credit cards or charge cards.
- Purchasing frequent flyer miles can significantly enhance your frequent flyer account, and should be seriously considered if you find promotions selling miles at a discount to the $25 to $30 retail price for 1,000 miles.
- Hotels, car rentals, long-distance phone carriers, and dining-for-miles offer frequent travelers additional mileage-earning opportunities.
- Certain mileage-earning offers, including cruises, merchandise, retail shopping, and investment vehicles and mortgages, may be a poor value or overpriced when compared to nonmileage-earning options.
- The most important ways of being regularly informed about special mileage-earning promotions is to read your airline frequent flyer newsletters, to register for a weekly e-zine at *Traveltactics.com*, and to subscribe to *Inside Flyer* magazine.

- *Flyertalk.com* provides a forum for you to learn the intricacies of all frequent flyer and hotel loyalty programs, with no membership fee charged for contributing or reviewing comments. Participation in discussions does, however, require that you register.
- Low-cost airlines' frequent flyer programs are quite different from those of the major airlines, not least since they typically offer points or segments rather than miles. In most instances, awards from low-cost airlines will not take you to Hawaii or abroad, and earned credits or segments expire within one year.

CHAPTER ELEVEN

Getting the Most Mileage Out of Frequent Flyer Awards

Milan, Madrid, and Malaga in the South of Spain—those were the romantic cities our family of four planned to visit during the summer 2002 vacation, using frequent flyer miles we had accrued. Cashing in those miles for the flights we needed would be a simple, straightforward task, or so I thought. What I found, however, was that while accruing frequent flyer miles might be relatively easy, actually using them can be a bit more challenging.

For our trip, I started with Continental Airlines, where I had earned 150,000 miles and could use an additional 50,000 miles available from my wife's account. Unfortunately, Continental is the most difficult of the major U.S. airlines for actually getting award seats, whether traveling to domestic or international destinations. Not surprisingly, there were no seats on Continental for the dates I wanted. Next I tried Continental's partners. Nothing available on Air France or Northwest/KLM—but then I found success with Alitalia!

Once I had the carrier, I had to bone up on the rules of the frequent flyer program. Since the rules for most major airlines will permit award tickets to a destination beyond their hub city—as long as there is a stop in that hub—I booked Los Angeles to Madrid with a stopover in Milan, which is Alitalia's hub. All that was left was to purchase tickets from Madrid to Malaga, which I did at the European travel Web site *Opodo.com* for $229 per person.

While frequent flyer miles offer the traveler a tremendous opportunity to fly for free, cashing in on that benefit can be difficult and frustrating, given such factors as a lack of available seats and restrictions that may apply. Knowing how to get the most out of your frequent flyer miles takes a bit of experience and know-how.

Although you can use several tactics to help your cause, keep in mind these three keys to securing award tickets:

1. Book well in advance.
2. Check availability on airline partners on which you can use your awards.
3. Be persistent.

The following are the most successful strategies we've used to cash in frequent flyer awards time and again. They will work for you too.

Calculate the Value of the Miles to Be Used

When we started out looking at ways to increase accrual of frequent flyer miles in the previous chapter, we emphasized the critical need for you to understand the value of miles you may *earn* from any offer. The exact same logic applies to maximizing *use* of your frequent flyer miles—you must understand what your use of miles is costing so that you can ensure optimal value for your redemptions.

For example, the domestic traveler who uses a 25,000-mile award to fly nonstop coast-to-coast is obtaining a free ticket to avoid a purchase that would cost either of the following:

- An average of $400 if purchased in advance with a Saturday stayover
- $800 to $2,000 for a last-minute ticket purchase

In the former scenario, where use of 25,000 miles saves $400, 1,000 miles provides a value of $400 divided by 25, or $16. In the last-minute travel scenario, 1,000 miles provides a value of $800 to $2,000 divided by 25, or $32 to $80! So mileage value is driven by potential use.

Frequent travelers are often frustrated by how difficult it is to use their hard-earned miles, and publications regularly relate tales of angry travelers unable to redeem an award. While it is usually easier for leisure travelers to use miles for vacations because they may have longer planning horizons than business travelers, there some basic principles that can help road warriors and world travelers.

Why Using Frequent Flyer Miles Is More Important Than Ever for All Travelers

As will be discussed in this chapter, using frequent flyer miles has had the greatest value for travelers seeking to travel for less in business or first class or who need to travel at the last minute. However, using frequent flyer miles also offers significant benefits for travelers who use advance-purchase nonrefundable tickets on major airlines:

1. Nonrefundable (revenue) tickets are worthless if not used within one year of the date of purchase. If you need to cancel or change your ticketed schedule, you must do so prior to the initial flight's scheduled departure time. When rebooking—either with the same or a different itinerary—a $100 change fee (higher for international or if booking through a travel agent) will apply. However, if you decide to cancel an award ticket and will not fly within a year, you simply redeposit the miles into your account for a fee that is almost always less than $100, and then can rebook anytime in the future. Some airlines allow you to change dates and times on an award ticket without charge if you will still be flying to the same destination as originally ticketed.
2. With frequent flyer tickets, the traveler will usually have one year to complete travel from the date the award ticket was issued (though some airlines only require that travel *commence* within one year, giving one additional year to *complete* travel). Contrast this flexibility with nonrefundable discount tickets that typically allow you to be away for no more than thirty days.

Plan Ahead

I look forward every year to traveling abroad with my family on a summer vacation. Because I know we will go somewhere each year, planning and booking one year in advance has become a routine activity. In fact, while we're on one vacation, we usually begin talking about the next year's destination. Because we plan ahead, we have been able to use awards to fly free within the United States as well as to Hawaii, Australia, Fiji, Europe, Asia, South America, Africa, and the Seychelles during peak holiday periods.

> **TIP**
>
> **Some airlines will allow you to hold award seats in reserve for a few days before ticketing so you can check out hotel options before the frequent flyer miles are subtracted from your account. Once ticketed, you will be charged if you want to return the miles to your account. Some airlines now charge a fee to change dates once tickets are issued.**

Planning as far in advance as possible is almost always the best strategy, especially if you want to travel during peak periods, such as around Thanksgiving or the Christmas holidays. Ideally, you want to book award air travel about 330 days in advance of your desired travel date—that's the day seats for flights go into most major airlines' computer systems. Leisure travelers can easily book in advance since public holidays and school vacations are known well ahead of time.

Business travelers can use this strategy when they travel to annual trade association meetings or conventions, which are often scheduled at least a year prior to their actual date.

Some airlines (such as American, United, and Northwest) have eliminated blackout dates for award travel. However, very few seats are allocated for award travel on peak travel dates, so booking as far in advance as possible is your best strategy for snagging one (or more) of these precious seats.

Jump on the Waitlist

If you cannot get the exact time or date you want, make a definite reservation for the closest available date and ask the reservations agent to place you on the waitlist, which can automatically put you into seats on the flight you want should they become available. Not all airlines have this option, but be sure to ask. If the airline does not have a waitlist process in place, call every other week or at least once each month to see if award seats have opened up for your preferred date. The worst that can happen is you will either fly on the closest available date you booked or postpone using the award and buy a ticket. If you select the former strategy, you still have the option of going standby on your desired date, as long as that date is *prior* to the date of your confirmed booking. (Refer to Chapter 2 for details regarding standby flying and to the section "Go Standby" later in this chapter.)

Some airlines do not permit standby status on international routes, regardless of whether you are using a revenue (paid) or award (free) ticket. Be sure to check with the airline if you wish to try using this strategy.

Hop on Board at the Last Minute

The last-minute strategy is the polar opposite of the advance-planning concept—an attempt to book a free seat close to the departure date. In the week or month before a flight's departure, airlines do release unsold seats for frequent flyer redemption in the case of cancellations or if regular passenger demand has fallen below their projections.

Best Days/Worst Days

If you can't find the flights you want on your requested date and can be flexible on your dates, ask the reservations agent whether the computer system can scan for the nearest available open days, either before or after your specified date(s). Since many airlines now enable online booking of award reservations, you can try doing this yourself. Refer to Chapter 2 for more information regarding the best and worst days to fly.

Travel in the Off-Season

Another valuable strategy for using frequent flyer miles is to travel out of season. For example, besides Christmas through New Year, the Caribbean's peak travel season runs February through May—the time of year East Coasters and Midwesterners typically flee their freezing weather—so award seats are much easier to obtain for the Caribbean from June through mid-December. There can be other benefits to traveling off-peak as well: Hotel rates are much cheaper, room availability is better, crowds are smaller, and so on. Most Caribbean islands experience good weather year round, with the exception of the rare threat of a hurricane from July to October.

Search Different Routings and Departure Times

When making your award reservation, ask the airline reservations agent to try every possible routing as well as different departure times. For example, the traveler wishing to fly from San Francisco to Boston on United should ask not only for nonstops, but for routings with a stopover in Los Angeles, Denver, Chicago, or Washington, D.C., as well. The traveler who is able to obtain an award reservation with one or two stops can usually "go standby" for a nonstop or one-stop flight at the airport. (Refer to the section "Go Standby" later in this chapter.)

TIP

Don't rely on the airline reservations agent to suggest variations on and options for flight routing. You must take the initiative and request that the agent search the spectrum of award alternatives.

Fly into Alternative Airports

Checking availability into or out of nearby airports can have dramatic effects on award availability. Also, remember that award tickets do allow "open jaw" routings, which means that you might fly into one airport, but return from another—such as arriving into Washington Dulles but departing out of Baltimore–Washington International. Or you may be able to fly out of Oakland, and return to San Francisco. Of course, if you parked your car in Oakland, that SFO return might present a bit of a problem, so keep all aspects of your trip in mind!

Cash in a Premium (Double Miles) or Upgraded (Business- or First-Class) Award

Most frequent flyers redeem what are called standard coach awards—usually 25,000 miles for a domestic coach free ticket and 40,000 to 75,000 miles for an international coach award ticket. However, most frequent flyer programs have premium coach awards, usually requiring double miles—50,000 for a domestic coach award ticket and 80,000 to 120,000 miles for an international coach award ticket—that does not have any capacity controls—meaning the number of seats available for redemption with this award is not restricted. If there's just one seat left, it's yours! Remember to calculate the value of your premium mileage ticket, which doubles the cost versus a saver award.

Similarly, check out whether a standard business- or first-class seat is available. That can be excellent value, and frequently requires the same or fewer miles than a premium coach-class award! For most U.S. airlines, a domestic saver frequent flyer award usually requires 25,000 miles, while a premium award with no capacity controls may cost 50,000 miles. However, a business- or first-class saver award seat may be yours for just 40,000 to 50,000 miles. As an additional example, a United international coach saver award to Australia may require 60,000 miles, while a premium coach award with no capacity controls costs 100,000 miles. However, a business- or first-class saver award seat may be yours for just 90,000 and 120,000 miles, respectively.

Trailblaze a New Route

If the airline with which you have miles is introducing a new route, consider gearing your plans to travel on that route. For example, if a route is opened to a specific Caribbean island, consider making that your vacation destination if seats are readily available. In such instances, you will generally find fewer paying passengers, giving you a better chance to use your award to travel when you want. Be sure to check out what it will cost for a revenue ticket, since new routes may be associated with promotional fares that make it worthwhile earning rather than using your precious miles.

Seek Out Helpful Info

Airline frequent flyer programs will sometimes publish information in their regular newsletter or on their Web site outlining those destinations less likely to be chosen for award travel. Holders of the American Airlines AAdvantage Platinum credit card from Citibank receive periodic notification of destinations available for reduced mileage.

Choose a Partner Airline—Especially for International Travel

Try cashing in your award for a seat on a partner or codeshare airline. Partnering opens up many more options for you to use your miles. Say you want to fly to Paris, and American Airlines, with whom you have sufficient miles, does not have available seats. You can try using your American miles on a partner, such as Aer Lingus, Finnair, or Iberia.

But don't expect a reservations agent to proactively look for partner airline opportunities; be ready to request the search and to know which alternative airline partners may be options. Partner airline information may be obtained from the airline's frequent flyer materials sent to you upon enrollment, in the airline's in-flight magazine, at the airline's Web site, or by calling the frequent flyer desk. Refer to Chapter 12 for details about airline partners and alliances.

Try Redeeming an Award on Another Airline

Before you transfer any miles from a credit card account, first check whether your preferred airline or any of its partner airlines can get you the award space you need. However, some airlines will not allow you to make a reservation unless you have all the necessary miles in your frequent flyer account, but they will check an award availability. In such instances, the risk is that the award seat will have vanished once your mileage transfer is accomplished. With Starwood, American Express, and Diners Club, you may in certain circumstances request an expedited transfer of miles for a nominal fee (typically about $35), which will complete the transfer in one to two days rather than several weeks. Be sure to ask about the process.

This is one situation where accruing miles on different airlines can help you out. If your first choice of airline can't accommodate you, try a different airline on which you have racked up frequent flyer miles. If you don't have enough miles with another airline, consider other places you could access more miles, such as transferring miles banked with American Express or Diners Club charge cards, or from your Starwood hotel account. You can also purchase additional miles, for example, up to 500,000 miles per year from American Express Membership miles, or direct from the airline (refer to Chapter 10). This can greatly expand the range of choices on U.S. airlines or their partners.

Go Standby

As a last resort, go standby for the date you want, provided the airline rules permit standby (be sure to check). For example, if you want to fly out on Monday, but award seats are only available on Tuesday, show up for the flight you want on Monday. If you should be lucky enough to get on, you will not incur a penalty, as there is usually no charge for changing dates or times of travel on award tickets. Note that some airlines do not permit standby with international tickets—be sure to check.

You can only do this at the gate, usually twenty minutes before departure time once they know how many "no shows" there will be. If they have an available seat, you can board, in which case your baggage can be gate-checked or boarded the traditional way if tagged "standby" at regular baggage check-in. Better yet, travel light with carry-on baggage only.

When making the reservation—and again, one or two days before you plan to go standby—ask how full the flight is for which you wish to stand by. If it's relatively open, your chances of succeeding on a standby basis are greatly enhanced.

Don't forget to keep calling at least once every thirty days after you make your reservation to see if award seats have opened up on your ideal date.

Hotel Program Awards on Airlines

If you have an abundance of hotel points in the Hilton HHONORS hotel loyalty program, you may redeem your points for domestic and international airline awards, as well as combined air and hotel reservations. Coach-class awards to Hawaii start at approximately 100,000 points, while international coach-class awards start at around 150,000 points. Check the Hilton Hotel HHONORS program brochure, which is updated every few years, for complete details (or point your browser to *Hiltonhhonors.com*). In addition, you can transfer frequent flyer miles from American and some smaller airlines such as Hawaiian into the Hilton awards program at a transfer ratio of one mile to two Hilton points to get a free ticket.

If you stay at hotels within the Marriott chain frequently, you will want to look into the Marriott Hotel's Guest Rewards program, which also offers air and hotel packages. For example, 250,000 Marriott points will get you seven nights at a top-of-the line property and up to 120,000 frequent miles (depending on your destination). Check for details at *Marriott rewards.com*.

While the Hilton and Marriott programs offer the chance to convert hotel points into frequent flyer miles with most major U.S. airlines, the significant depreciation in value makes this a poor choice. Conversely, Starwood points convert to most airlines at a favorable 1:1 ratio, and add 5,000 bonus miles when transferring in 20,000 mile increments. Check out details at *Starwood.com*.

Use Those Miles on the Ground—At Your Own Risk

You don't have to fly anywhere to cash in your frequent flyer miles. Some airlines will periodically offer merchandise redemption in exchange for frequent flyer miles. In addition, Web sites such as *Milepoint.com* enable you to use your miles to purchase merchandise. Similarly, American Express Membership Rewards and Diners Club Rewards allow the use of banked miles toward purchase of a huge variety of retail goods. However, the value of your miles is almost always much less when applied to merchandise rather than flights—especially if you usually apply your miles towards first- or business-class tickets that would otherwise be very expensive.

Use the examples in Chapter 10 to calculate whether use of frequent flyer miles for merchandise is worthwhile, using prices you would otherwise pay for the merchandise in comparison to your best value use of those miles when applied toward flights.

In Summary

- Traditionally, using frequent flyer miles has held the best value for travelers seeking to travel for less in business- or first-class. In addition, using frequent flyer miles obviates the challenges associated with possibly canceling nonrefundable tickets that lose their value if not used within one year of purchase.
- The most important strategy for obtaining award tickets is to book as far in advance as possible—up to 330 days ahead of your desired travel date, when airline seats are loaded into the airlines' computer systems. Advance planning is especially important if you want to find free seats for travel over peak dates. Several major airlines have eliminated blackout dates for travel over peak holiday periods—but few award seats are allocated for redemption on those days. If you subsequently need to cancel your award reservation, simply return the frequent flyer miles to your account for a fee that rarely exceeds $100 per ticket.
- When speaking to a reservations agent or searching on the Web, if you cannot find a match to your ideal date, try:
  - Different dates
  - Alternative airports
  - Different routings
  - Using premium (often double) mileage rather than saver awards
  - Business- or first-class seating
  - Partner airlines
- Another option is to ticket for a "second best" date as close as possible to—and preferably after—your desired date, and waitlist for your preference if the airline you are booking offers the option. You can then go standby if your waitlist does not come through (note that standby may not be permitted with international flights). Contact the airline at least once every thirty days to see if award space for your desired date(s) has become available. You should also consider contacting other airlines if you have diversified and accumulated sufficient miles with more than one airline, or try using Marriott or Hilton hotel points for free flights or award air and

hotel packages if you have stayed in either hotel chain a significant number of nights.

- If you can focus your travel on off-season or days less traveled, your chances of success may increase significantly.
- Check out airline newsletters that accompany your frequent flyer statements or Web sites to find destinations with less demand. Destinations having greater award availability are likely to be experiencing their off-season. Selecting such locations may make your search much simpler and enhance your chances of getting hotel rooms at a reduced price—or even free if you're using hotel award space.
- Do NOT use your hard-earned miles for merchandise, since the value is considerably less than if you use your miles toward free flights.

CHAPTER TWELVE

The Many Benefits of Airline Alliances

A few years back, my wife and son and I visited Barcelona, where I had been invited to speak at an international pharmaceutical meeting. We flew from Boston to Amsterdam on Northwest, where we connected to KLM for a short flight to Barcelona. The price for the roundtrip ticket for Los Angeles to Barcelona was reasonable: just over $600 per adult, and $400 for my son, thanks to the 33 percent discounts for children on international routes. We arrived in Barcelona without a hitch—and, magically, so did our baggage.

International travel wasn't always this easy, however. In fact, in the old days, it could be downright tricky—and expensive. To reach a foreign destination may have required coupling a U.S. domestic flight with one or more flights on foreign airlines, just as it does today. But in years past, travelers routinely found themselves contending with conflicting flight schedules, paying exorbitant prices, and living in fear of the ever-present possibility that their luggage would follow a different itinerary than they did.

Northwest and KLM pioneered the concept of global alliances between international airlines, and did so with such success that they paved the way for several more. Today, the majority of major U.S. airlines flying international routes have formed global alliances with foreign carriers to increase their reach and the number of cities they serve. Alliance partners will readily:

- Offer favorable pricing if you are using more than one partner airline as part of the same itinerary.
- Coordinate schedules, which can be beneficial when you are connecting and transferring from one airline to its partner.
- Transfer baggage from one airline to another when you are traveling on more than one alliance partner.

- Enable accrual of frequent flyer miles to any partner airline you choose—and allow you to redeem awards on different partner airlines (sometimes flying on more than one partner airline within a single itinerary).

For example, while U.S. carriers do not fly to any countries within Africa, U.S. carriers can seamlessly transport loyal U.S. travelers to African destinations through their alliance partners. Consider travelers who want to travel to Nairobi, Kenya. Their choices of carrier could include:

Flying on one or more non-aligned airline partners to one or several destination cities can send the ticket price sky-high!

- United and Lufthansa
- American and British Airways
- Delta and either Air France or South African Airways
- Northwest or Continental and KLM

Of all the international alliances, perhaps the most sophisticated is United's Star Alliance, which has more partners than any other, giving travelers more opportunities for accruing and using United frequent flyer miles than on any of its multiple alliance partners, regardless of one's destination. A close second is American Airline's One World alliance, although some of its partners, such as British Airways, will not award frequent flyer miles when certain discounted fares are used. Delta, Northwest, and Continental are part of the Skyteam alliance, which also includes Air France, KLM, Aeromexico, and Korean Air.

TIP

The practice of codesharing may provide a significant fare-busting opportunity for all classes of service, most notably for international flights operated by two (or more) codeshare partners. For example, if you are flying to South Africa, check fares from codeshare partners Delta and South African Airways (SAA). While the flights are actually on South African Airways' aircraft, Delta also sells seats on these flights under the Delta umbrella. Not infrequently, the fares may be cheaper if purchased from the lesser-known SAA rather than Delta.

Formal domestic or bilateral alliances have historically been less common than international or global alliances because of overlapping route systems. However, some domestic alliance partnerships have provided similar benefits as the international partnerships, with the strongest being between Continental, Northwest, and Delta. Baggage is transferred efficiently between airlines, and frequent flyer miles can both be earned and redeemed on whichever airline you prefer.

Codesharing Arrangements

In a codesharing arrangement, airlines sell tickets to passengers who will fly one or more segments of their trip on a partner airline, or may even travel entirely on the partner airline. The airline that sells the ticket and the partner on whose aircraft the passenger flies split the ticket revenue, while the passenger may elect to receive miles from either airline. The key difference between alliances and codesharing is that under the former arrangement, the partner airlines have been granted antitrust immunity by governmental agencies. This relaxation of antitrust regulations allows partner airlines in an alliance to share sensitive competitive pricing information and to co-market to corporate clients; codeshare partners without a formal alliance do not enjoy this benefit.

Codesharing arrangements allow partner airlines to use other airlines outside their formal global alliances. For example, American and Alaska Airlines have entered into a codesharing arrangement whereby American purchases a certain number of seats from Alaska on several of its flights that will then have both Alaska and American flight numbers, which are coordinated to connect with actual American flights. Taking advantage of such an arrangement, a traveler going from Fort Lauderdale to Seattle with a ticket purchased from American Airlines may fly on what appears to be two American flights—the first from Fort Lauderdale to Los Angeles and connecting to another from Los Angeles to Seattle. Even though the latter flight will actually be on an Alaska Airlines aircraft, baggage is easily transferred between the two airlines and mileage is accrued entirely on American or Alaska Airlines. However, Alaska Airlines is not a member of American's One World Alliance.

Domestic codesharing arrangements include Alaska's tie-in with American; United with Aloha; and Northwest and Continental with Hawaiian. An example of international codesharing is American with Air Pacific (to Fiji) and Air Tahiti Nui. Note the absence of any major airlines aligning with low-cost airlines; the major airlines seem to pretend that the low-fare carriers don't exist!

Earning Frequent Flyer Miles with Codeshare and Alliance Partners

When flying on an airline partner within North America, you will almost always be eligible to earn frequent flyer miles in your preferred program (actual or partner airline) unless your ticket was purchased from a consolidator. However, the rules for earning frequent flyer miles when flying on an international partner are complex. (Refer to Chapter 10 for details regarding earning frequent flyer miles when flying with an international partner.)

On routes outside North America, miles earned on a non-U.S. partner airline will frequently not be eligible for frequent flyer miles or bonus miles if you purchased a discounted nonrefundable ticket, unless the ticket reservation was made with your preferred airline, which purchases a certain portion of seats on the partner's aircraft in a codesharing arrangement. Given the complexity of alliance and codeshare rules, we recommend a careful review of your preferred frequent flyer program's "fine print" in the most recent membership brochure, as rules and redemption opportunities may change from year to year. Or call your preferred airline's frequent flyer help desk for detailed clarifications to avoid forfeiting miles on long-distance trips!

When flying abroad, you might encounter any one of several scenarios for earning miles with alliance partners, including:

ALERT

Whenever you receive information from an airline customer service representative, repeat your understanding of what you have been told. Then ask for the person's first and last names and in what city he or she is based, and document both the date and time you called. If the person refuses to provide a last name, ask for his or her employee number. If a problem arises in the future, such as not receiving the miles you were promised, you will have documentation to support your claim.

- You may earn no frequent flyer miles, especially when traveling on certain discounted nonrefundable airfares or tickets purchased from a consolidator.
- You accrue frequent flyer miles on a discounted ticket, but only 25 to 50 percent of the actual amount of miles traveled is earned.
- Frequent flyer miles are earned, but do not count toward your qualifying for elite status on your preferred airline the following year.
- One hundred percent of flown miles are credited and all frequent flyer miles earned *do* count toward your qualifying for elite status on your preferred airline the following year—naturally the ideal result for the frequent flyer! A good example of this optimum outcome is earning American miles when flying on any of its One World Alliance partners (except British Airways transatlantic flights) or on Alaska Airlines.
- Frequent flyer miles earned *do* count toward your qualifying for elite status on your preferred airline the following year—but only if the ticket was purchased from your preferred airline. A good example is earning American miles when flying nonstop to Fiji on its partner, Air Pacific Airlines, which requires that your ticket be pur-

chased direct from American rather than Air Pacific, and may cost considerably more.

In Summary

- Codeshare or alliance partners allow you to fly on other partner airlines while still earning or using frequent flyer miles with your preferred carrier.
- By purchasing seats on their partner airlines and selling these seats associated with their own flight numbers, airlines can use their alliances and codeshare arrangements to expand their geographic reach without actually flying their own aircraft.
- Alliance partners are typically allowed (by regulation or law) to coordinate pricing, while codeshare partners without a formal alliance may be prohibited from doing so (frequently because of antitrust concerns). Because two or more airlines are selling seats on one of the airline's aircraft, quoted prices may differ! Be sure to check each of the partner's prices for your desired flight separately, especially for international routes.
- When using two different airlines with a stopover, alliances and codesharing allow for coordination of pricing to produce one integrated lower fare rather than two "split" fares, which can often be considerably higher if one uses two or more unaffiliated airlines with a single ticket. Schedules are coordinated, and travelers do not have to worry about their baggage, which is transferred between flights by the airlines.
- Because frequent flyer accrual rules vary greatly among airline alliances and codesharing arrangements, you must check whether you will accrue frequent flyer miles on your itinerary—preferably before you pay for your ticket. If you are planning to apply frequent flyer miles earned when flying with a partner airline toward elite status, be sure to check eligibility for a flight you have in mind by contacting your preferred airline's frequent flyer desk.

CHAPTER THIRTEEN

How to Capture the Best Price at the Best Hotel

All the service at half the price—that's the guerrilla way to travel.

The Ritz Barcelona is ideally located in the middle of downtown, near Las Ramblas, the bustling pedestrian arcade where locals and tourists alike come to eat, drink, relax, and shop. I was attending a convention in the city, and my wife and two-year-old son had come along to enjoy this vibrant Spanish city.

As we approached the registration desk, the staff person greeted me.

"Welcome, Dr. Brandt-Sarif."

Amazed, I asked how he knew who I was.

"Why, Doctor, you are the only guest checking in today with a young child."

And it gets better . . .

The elevators, which sat three steps above lobby level, posed a bit of a challenge for my wife, who wheeled our son around in his stroller while I attended meetings. Yet, whenever she had to negotiate those stairs on her own, a Ritz staff person would magically emerge to help her lift the stroller up the steps.

Another nice touch . . .

Each evening a clean, white mat was set by the bedside to protect our pampered feet from the magnificent wood floor.

The best is yet to come . . .

I so liked the unique complimentary bottle of men's cologne that I took it home and reserved it for special occasions. Two years later, when the bottle had finally run dry, I wrote the hotel asking where I could purchase more. Four weeks later, a package arrived in the mail with not one, but ten bottles of my favorite fragrance . . . compliments of the general manager at the Ritz Barcelona.

You might say this sort of service is to be expected considering what the Ritz charges. However, I had snagged an excellent rate simply by faxing my standard rate-request letter to the hotel, even though my visit occurred during peak convention and tourist season in a traditionally expensive city. With my *Entertainment Directory* 50 percent discount, the room cost just $182 per night, far below posted rates—and we loved every last minute of opulent service.

What Guerrilla Travelers Need to Know

Hotels expect business travelers—their prime source of revenue—to be relatively price-insensitive. Traditionally, upscale last-minute business travelers don't put much energy into searching out hotel discounts.

Conversely, some companies increasingly demand that their road warriors downgrade from upscale to midlevel hotels. Wary about losing road warriors who may be pressured to direct their business to cheaper midscale accommodations, upscale hotels (unlike airlines) will readily negotiate prices the closer it gets to check-in time, especially if the hotel is unlikely to achieve full occupancy for the night.

Travel agents can't usually help much when looking for great hotel rates because the deeply discounted rates are frequently not commissionable. While many travel agents belong to a consortium that arranges bulk purchases of reduced rate hotel rooms, the discount is invariably less than any guerrilla traveler can obtain using the process we'll outline for you.

This chapter will give you a detailed overview of the best ways to capture great hotel rates. In the next chapter, we'll describe the specific discounts you should ask for when using the process we set out.

Where to Get the Most for Your Money: Our Favorite Upscale Hotel Chains

The Grand Hyatt in San Diego has a magnificent lobby reminiscent of the finest hotels of Italy. Because I have periodically enjoyed Diamond Elite status, the highest level of Hyatt's Gold Passport loyalty program, I was offered free access to the very elegant concierge lounge—even though I was paying just $135 per night.

Hyatt hotels are known for innovative lobby architecture and comfortable rooms, with an excellent preferred member loyalty program that recalls prior preferences. Members of Hyatt's free Gold Passport program may enjoy accommodations on designated high floors, complimentary morning coffee, and, in certain Hyatt hotels abroad, free breakfast. Hyatt rewards its loyal customers. Westin hotels are known for their "heavenly" beds,

TIP

Concierge lounges can save savvy travelers significant amounts of money if they get the benefit for free or pay just a small amount extra. Complimentary breakfast and evening hors d'oeuvres are standard fare—with beverages and snacks offered throughout the day. When traveling with a family, the value of this option increases exponentially.

sleek room design, and other "divine" extras, such as comfy bathrobes and tasteful toiletries. They cater to the business traveler and offer all the amenities you could need.

Here are four reasons we prefer Hyatt and Westin when choosing an upscale hotel chain:

- **Consistency.** Hyatt and Westin hotels are typically rated "good," "very good," and "excellent" by such travel industry heavyweights as *Condé Nast Traveler* and *Business Traveler* magazines in their annual surveys. Sheraton and Hilton hotels are often inconsistent in the standard of properties they offer, many of which can hardly be considered upscale. Sheraton, which is owned by the same company as Westin hotels, is currently taking steps to upgrade the consistency of both its facilities and service.

TIP

Starwood owns several brands, including Luxury Collection and St. Regis (ultraluxury), Westin (upscale–luxury), W (chic), Sheraton (upscale but inconsistent standards), and Four Points (midlevel).

- **Luxury Properties Within the Same Corporate Family.** Westin's owner Starwood includes the plush St. Regis and Luxury Collection brands, while Hyatt's Park Hyatt properties in major cities offer magnificent accommodations in boutique-like settings. These luxury properties can be spectacular values when using hotel points earned at Hyatt and Westin hotels—or if you can enjoy them at discounted prices.

Marriott is one major chain that rarely offers discounts. During the years I have been a member of the Platinum-Elite level, the highest level of the Marriott Rewards loyalty program, I have found the rooms bland, with little to excite the senses, and perks inconsistent.

- **Availability.** There will inevitably be at least one or more Hyatt or Westin hotels in any major U.S. city and increasingly in large cities abroad.

- **Willingness to Discount.** Westin and Hyatt truly understand the meaning of "excess inventory," which makes them especially inviting to the price-sensitive world traveler.

Midscale and Extended-Stay Hotel Chains

I once attended a wedding in a Chicago suburb where the bride's family arranged for guests to stay in a nearby La Quinta Inn. I was quite satisfied by the plain functionality and cleanliness of our room. Availability of room service for a late night dinner—not on your life! But we did enjoy a good, complimentary continental breakfast.

Recently, hotel chains have focused on developing midscale properties catering to the budget-conscious business traveler. These include Hilton Garden Inn, Four Points by Sheraton, Courtyard by Marriott, Holiday Inn Select, Red Lion Hotels, La Quinta, Best Western, Comfort Inn, and Clarion hotels. Travelers can expect a clean room—sometimes even a larger room or suite—in a smaller hotel that does not offer restaurants or conference rooms. A free continental breakfast or buffet is often included in the standard room rate. Discounts off "rack rates"—the published price for a specific room—will be much smaller at midscale hotels; you can expect 10 to 20 percent at best. But the published prices will often beat out the discounted rates at major upscale hotels. These no-frills midscale accommodations may be an appropriate choice for some price-sensitive small business travelers.

Extended-Stay Accommodations

While on a consulting assignment, I spent a year in a Homewood Suites by Hilton extended-stay hotel, enjoying a bedroom, separate living area, kitchen, and bathroom with large dressing area. Having a discounted "residential rate" payable every night—even when I was back home or on vacation—meant that I never had to deal with the inconvenience of packing my bags to check out (or unpacking them when moving back in!). Great buffet breakfasts—but no room service. And the general manager was readily accessible to address any problem.

Extended-stay hotels offer lower rates (typically $45 to $120 per night, but there may be a five-night minimum) by eliminating restaurants, bars, and personnel (which sometimes means no daily maid service). You are much more likely to find coin-operated laundry machines than valet service. They are almost always found in suburban locations to reduce real estate costs. Examples include Extended StayAmerica, Homewood Suites by Hilton, Residence Inn By Marriott, Sierra Suites, Staybridge Suites, Hawthorne Suites (at which you earn Hyatt points), and TownPlace Suites.

Timing—What a Difference a Day (or the Season) Makes

I once attended a seminar in glitzy Las Vegas that ran from Friday through Sunday. At the spectacular Paris Hotel, I captured a fabulously low rate of $99 for the Thursday night before the seminar. I loved my huge room with trimmings befitting royalty. However, for the Friday and Saturday nights, the rate soared to $245 per night to take advantage of the gamblers pouring into the city. As a guerrilla traveler, I had to consider other alternatives. I found a brand new Hyatt resort about twenty miles off the strip offering me a $99 introductory rate for the two weekend nights, so I moved hotels on the Friday morning and saved $290 as "compensation" for the inconvenience. Yes, I did have to rent a car, which reduced my savings to $210!

Bottom line—I relocated to take advantage of a much lower rate elsewhere, a strategy discussed later on in this chapter.

Monday through Thursday nights will typically be more expensive in business-oriented cities, while they may be cheaper in hotels or resorts catering to weekend traffic. Las Vegas is a perfect example of the latter. Business-oriented hotels offer considerably reduced rates over Friday, Saturday, and Sunday nights, and sometimes on weekdays during the off-season (such as during the July–August summer vacation period when business travel slows down). In Anaheim, California—the home of Disneyland—hotels will be more expensive during summer vacation months and cheaper in the winter, especially while schools are in full swing. The exact opposite may be true in greater Los Angeles or San Diego, as they host more travelers during the winter months.

Guerrilla rates are the most difficult to capture during large conventions when rooms are scarce in the major hotels. This is an important point to keep in mind when traveling to the most common cities for large conventions: In the United States, these include Atlanta, Boston, Chicago, Denver, New York, Las Vegas, Los Angeles, Orlando, Philadelphia, San Diego, San Francisco, and Washington, D.C. In Canada, Toronto, Montreal, and Vancouver are major convention cities. We'll discuss more about how to jump that hurdle in subsequent sections.

The Web Factor

Start with the Web to find a standard rate for a hotel or hotels in which you are interested, refer to Chapter 16 for details, and then call or fax to see if you can beat that rate.

Web browsing may sometimes identify great values that eliminate the need for any future efforts. There are a huge number of sites that provide information about hotels, and they seem to be increasing daily. A good starting point is to check out prices at "neutral" sites such as *Orbitz.com*, *Expedia.com*, and *Travelocity.com*. In addition, *Travelweb.com*, which is owned by a variety of major hotel chains, provides prices for a variety of hotels in major centers—but with few significant discounts. *Travelaxe.com* is a free comparison-shopping program that displays prices for hotels in a limited number of cities side-by-side, including taxes and miscellaneous fees. However, you do need to download a software program to use its well-organized search capability. Also see what benchmark lowest price you can get for a four-star property at *Hotwire.com*, which sells "distressed inventory" at a discount by offering you a price for the grade of hotel you

Check multiple sources for a great room rate since many hotels offer different prices through different points of contact.

have requested, but reveals the name of the property only after your credit card has been charged. Once this is done, you're locked in; no refunds or changes allowed. Check out *Tripadvisor.com*, *Globapost.com*, and *Epinions.com* to peruse reviews of destinations and hotels.

Finally, most major hotel chains such as Starwood, Marriott, Intercontinental, Hyatt, and Hilton guarantee that they will beat the price of any Web site other than their own, including hotel consolidators. Call their central numbers to implement the guarantee. The downside regarding the guarantee is that the required steps can be time-consuming.

To Book with Central Reservations or the Hotel Direct? That Is the Question . . .

The Hyatt Web site gave me a lowest rate of $175 per night for four nights in Chicago, but a direct call to the hotel's reservations department got me a 50 percent discount off the $250 per night rack rate. Over the four days, paying $125 per night versus the $175 Web site rate totaled a savings of $200. A $200 savings that cost just ten minutes of my time making a toll-free phone call!

Most of us would prefer to access the Web or call the hotel chain's central reservation 800 number and avoid additional phone charges. However, we assume that the savvy world traveler will have a low-cost long-distance rate of ten cents a minute or less, or will use a cell phone's free long-distance capability to call the hotel direct, so this expense should be minimal.

Over 50 percent of the time, you'll get different prices from central reservations than from the hotel's reservation desk. In 80 to 90 percent of instances where there is a difference, the hotel's direct price will be cheaper, especially if you're calling within one to two weeks of the proposed check-in date. Ideally, you should try both methods for contacting hotels so you can compare. However, if you want to choose just one strategy, contact the hotel directly.

Finally—when calling the hotel direct, be sure that you have not automatically been connected to central reservations, perhaps because you are calling during the local reservations staff person's lunch break or after hours.

Fax (or E-Mail) Your Way to the Lowest Prices Possible

By far the most efficient way of effectively reaching hotel reservations departments is with the fax machine. (To find fax numbers for hotels, either call the central reservations line toll-free number and ask for the fax number; or type the specific hotel name [such as Westin Chicago] into a search engine, which will get you information about the hotel, usually including the fax number.) Some of the benefits of faxing include:

- **It's less expensive than phoning direct, domestically or internationally.** The long-distance charges are even lower if you fax at non-peak times.
- **It's convenient.** Sending faxes to multiple hotels is fast and easy, especially if your computer can be programmed to autofax via a modem without you or a staff person standing at the machine.
- **It's practical.** When contacting hotels in non-English-speaking countries, you don't have to worry if the switchboard operator or the reservations clerk doesn't speak English—or wait while he tries to find someone who does! Once your fax is received, the hotel has ample time to translate, without you incurring long-distance costs and wasting valuable time.
- **It's less intimidating.** For shy individuals or those who do not enjoy person-to-person haggling, the fax method offers a nonconfrontational method for negotiating price. It is, in effect, a silent auction between several hotels.
- **It's clear proof of the agreed rate.** Unlike phone verification, a fax confirmation page with printed rate information is indisputable evidence of the details of your reservation. It provides a much greater margin of safety at check-in or check-out if the bill reflects a higher rate than you agreed to.

Response rates when faxing requests to several hotels within a city are typically 70 percent within 24 hours and 90 percent within 72 hours. If you have a particular hotel that hasn't responded, you can always write a note on the original fax document and send it again: "Second Request—Please have the COURTESY to respond." You will inevitably get a rapid answer!

Here is an example of a generic rate request letter:

JOHN SMITH
9108 HILLSBORO LANE
ATLANTA, GA 40034
PHONE (410) 555-5678
FAX (410) 555-1234
E-MAIL JSmith@earthlink.com

ATTN: RESERVATIONS

September 8, 2004

Dear Sir/Madam:

Please advise the availability of one nonsmoking room for *one adult*, with two doubles or one king-size bed for one (1) night, Friday, November 13, 2004.

I am eligible for the weekend rate, Entertainment or Quest 50 percent discount, AAA rate, or any other value rate you may have.

Please fax your response as soon as possible to (410) 555-1234.

With thanks,

John Smith

Finally, e-mail isn't yet a perfectly effective method for finding out about hotel availability and rates. Hotel e-mail addresses aren't easy to get and responses are inconsistent. Therefore, phone and fax remain the best ways of contacting hotels directly. You may be successful, however, by typing in the hotel property's name at a search engine, for example, "Sheraton Los Cabos." If the hotel has its own Web site, it may offer a "contact us by e-mail" option, which you can use to obtain a rate quote—simply follow the exact same steps described in this section for faxing.

Know Where to Find the Hotel Contact Information You Need

The Four Seasons in Philadelphia and London. The Park Hyatt in Chicago and Tokyo. The Ritz in Barcelona and Singapore. I have stayed in some incredibly luxurious hotels and resorts during my extensive travels. Finding the right hotel sometimes requires a little detective work, and like any good detective, I have my "sources."

Web sites can rapidly help you find "the perfect hotel" (refer to Chapter 16 for more details). For example:

- *Tripadvisor.com* provides rapid links to booking sites and online information from destination book publishers, as well as feedback from upscale travelers who have visited a hotel you may be interested in. Also click on the travel section of *Epinions.com* to check out reviews of all kinds of travel products, including hotels. Check out *Globapost.com* for reviews from travelers and site staff.

- Search engines, such as *Google.com* or *Yahoo.com*, can be checked by typing in "Hotels" and the city you want—for example, "Hotels Denver." Or if you prefer a certain chain, type in the hotel chain's name and city—"Hyatt Denver." Or simply visit your favorite hotel chain's Web site, and select the city you will be visiting on the home page. Hotel and other travel agent Web sites will describe the property's attributes and sometimes provide photographs to give you a flavor of its best features.

- Guidebooks, such as those published by Frommer, Fodor's, Fielding, or Michelin, are another cost-effective way to get detailed information on hotel quality and phone and fax numbers for international destinations. You're better off buying the books (or perusing them in the bookstore), not least since those available at public libraries are usually several years out of date. These guides will have one or more chapters devoted to accommodations, typically dividing hotels into categories such as Very Expensive, Expensive, Moderate, and Budget. Each hotel description will provide details of location, amenities, and phone and fax numbers.

■ The annual *Resorts and Great Hotels* book sells for a mere $15 and can be purchased by calling 805-745-7100 or by going online at *Resorts greathotels.com*. Each yearly edition features glossy color pictures of some of the world's most stunning hotels and resorts. It's a must-have item for any serious traveler looking for spectacular upscale and deluxe hotels. While none of the featured hotels are in the bargain category, every hotel's rack rates are provided, so the savvy world traveler can try to negotiate rates that are at least 40 to 50 percent lower than the published price.

■ Monthly travel magazines such as *Condé Nast Traveler*, *Travel and Leisure*, and *Business Traveler* feature regular articles about destinations and hotels, and conduct reader surveys reporting the results as "Best of" each year.

Plan Ahead

Four nights at the Ritz in Barcelona for $182 per night. One free week in a three-bedroom Marriott vacation villa in the south of Spain. Four nights in a one-bedroom suite at the Hilton Noga in Cannes for $160 per night. Free nights at Park Hyatt hotels in Madrid, Paris, Tokyo, and London. My family and I enjoyed all of these spectacular values using earned hotel points—all during peak summer vacation seasons, and for one very good reason: Every booking was made at least six to twelve months in advance.

If you want to be in a highly desirable hotel or vacation resort during a major convention or over a peak holiday period, the possibilities for reduced rates are lessened. Without advance reservation of at least six to twelve months, reduced rates are almost impossible.

One of the most powerful tools for obtaining exceptional travel values is advance planning. Just as airline reservations can be made up to 330 days before the date of travel, hotel reservations can frequently be made at least one year in advance of arrival. Savvy world travelers and road warriors will frequently find an abundance of discount opportunities six to twelve months ahead of their travel dates. If you know you'll be seeking Thanksgiving accommodations for a family reunion in a beach resort area, act as far in advance as possible to grab the best deal in the house!

What If You Have to Cancel?

Any time you make a hotel reservation and guarantee the room with your credit card, record the hotel's cancellation policy so that you can be sure to cancel if you're not going to show up. A few years ago I made a reservation at an Intercontinental hotel, and when my plans changed, I forgot to call the hotel. As is standard in the industry, I was charged for one night's stay at $105. Not a mistake I care to repeat!

Typically, you'll be asked for your credit card number to guarantee a hotel room, especially if you'll be arriving late. If you don't arrive on the specified date and don't cancel before the deadline, you'll be charged for one night. In rare instances, the hotel policy may be to charge you for the entire stay. Ask for the hotel's cancellation policy when you make the reservation. If you don't want to provide a credit card number when making your reservation, the room won't be guaranteed and could be offered to someone else if the hotel is oversold.

TIP

Be sure to notify a hotel where you have made a reservation ahead of time if your length of stay will be reduced. Failure to notify the hotel about your change of plans at least twenty-four hours prior to check-in (or at latest when checking in) could mean being charged for the originally booked length of stay.

Unlike most budget airline tickets, hotel reservations are rarely fully paid for in advance and are usually fully refundable. This feature should allow you to make a reservation for a hotel and hold it, knowing that you may cancel the reservation without penalty if you should uncover an even better rate at the same or a different hotel any time before your scheduled stay, or your plans change and you need to cancel the reservation.

The most common cancellation policy offers no penalty, provided the reservation is canceled by a specified time on the scheduled day of arrival. That time varies from hotel to hotel, and is typically 6 PM on date of scheduled arrival at most major chain hotels catering to business travelers (but may be as early as noon). It's less common that cancellations must be made within 24, 48, or 72 hours—and even more rarely within 1 to 2 weeks—before your scheduled arrival. It's always safer to ask in advance and keep a record of the cancellation time and hotel phone number with your travel papers.

TIP

If you're a road warrior whose plans change often, keep a tickler file exclusively for recording cancellation numbers!

Conversely, some hotels—especially resorts—require full credit card payment at the time the reservation is made, but the amount will be refunded if you cancel before the specified deadline. In some instances, especially when booking online, the entire reservation may be completely nonrefundable from the time you provide a credit card number. This is especially true if you make reservations with a hotel consolidator such as *Hotels.com*, but you may find nonrefundable specials at retail sites such as *Travelocity.com* or *Expedia.com*, and even at hotel chains' own Internet sites. Just be aware of the terms of your reservation before you provide your credit card number.

Booking a deeply discounted hotel room online may sometimes be nonrefundable; be sure to check the "fine print."

Split-Rate Reservations

I was scheduled to be in Chicago for two nights—Thursday and Friday—and inquired about the 50 percent discount rate that was available for both nights. Most travelers would have been happy to secure a rate of $130 per night at a beautiful Westin hotel. But as a savvy world traveler, I recognized that Fridays are often slow nights for business hotels, so I asked about the weekend rate. It was $79! The hotel was quite happy to offer me one night at the $130 discounted rate for the Thursday and the second at the lower $79 weekend rate for the Friday. The advantages of a split-rate reservation may apply anywhere, anytime. It pays to just ask!

For stays of two or more nights, you'll sometimes be able to obtain superior discounts by asking for the best rates for *each* night separately. For example, a two-night Sunday–Monday hotel stay may offer the lowest rates by selecting a *50 percent discount rate* on Monday (a weekday night, typically more expensive in business-oriented hotels), and the *weekend rate* for Sunday night. Negotiating this kind of split-rate reservation usually needs to be done ahead of time over the phone—not when checking in at reception—and demands some degree of patience, persistence, and creativity! Increasingly, Web sites may offer this automatically, providing different prices for each of the nights you have specified.

Occasionally you may run into resistance in trying to arrange the split-rate reservation when speaking to a staff person on the phone, especially when an unimaginative reservationist cites that ubiquitous excuse: "Our computer system simply can't do that." As a savvy world traveler, however, you will be prepared. Tell the booking agent to make two or more separate reservations with separate confirmation codes, if need be. If the agent isn't helpful, call back as often as necessary until you find an agent who will work with you. There's no law that says you can't check into a hotel with more than one reservation for successive nights!

In the next chapter, we'll look at what discounts you should be asking for.

Consider a Nearby Location

I was challenged to find an excellent rate at an upscale hotel in Boston for three nights. My business was downtown, but a convention in the city had rates soaring to around $250 (and higher) at city hotels. I found a Crowne Plaza in the suburbs at $99 per night, with breakfast included. Boston has an excellent subway system, with rapid transit into the city for just a few dollars. My savings over three nights amounted to at least $400 and then some!

If you want to find the ideal quality accommodation at a great price in your preferred location, consider staying in an alternative nearby location, especially if you will have a rental car, taxicab rates are reasonable, or there is good public transportation. For example, if your place of business is downtown, check out hotels in the suburbs, and *vice versa*.

A Booking Checklist

When making a reservation, you want to be sure you have obtained the following information:

- If location is important, do you know where the hotel is on a map?
- What is the rate? What extra charges will there be (taxes, surcharges, gratuities, miscellaneous fees)? If quoted in foreign currency, what is the dollar equivalent?
- Did you leave a credit card number to guarantee your room, especially if you will be a late arrival?
- What is the cancellation policy?
- Is breakfast included?
- Did the hotel request your preferred bed type and note your (strong) preference for smoking or nonsmoking?
- Did you clarify facilities or special needs you may have, such as a gym, a swimming pool, or wheelchair access?

Getting an Ideal Room

If you are an elite member of a hotel loyalty program or will be checking into the hotel for some special occasion, fax the hotel's reservations manager one to two days in advance of your arrival. In your communication, mention your status or reason for your forthcoming stay and ask for extras such as an upgrade and complimentary breakfast. Sixty to seventy percent of the time, you will receive something you would not otherwise have gotten.

TIP

Before you check in, ask the bellman helping you with your baggage which are the choice rooms. It's worth a couple of dollars (additional) tip asking him which rooms he would choose for himself if he were checking in with his spouse or significant other for some special occasion.

Getting Around the Astronomical Cost of Phone Calls When Abroad

A Seattle-based company called Kallback is the originator of a unique telephone innovation called "callback" that provides low-cost U.S. international long-distance rates when calling from countries outside the United States. A customer simply dials the Kallback U.S. "trigger number," lets it ring once, and hangs up before it answers. Within seconds, the Kallback computer rings back the caller with a U.S. dial tone. Then, the caller dials out as usual, using this U.S line to call any country he chooses. Kallback bills at rates far cheaper than most every other country's long-distance service. Get more information at *Kallback .com* or by calling 800-338-0225.

Beware of Other Hidden Hotel Costs

During times when hotel revenues have declined, guests have been hit with a range of surcharges that are not always disclosed ahead of time. Watch out for:

- Service charges for housekeepers and bellmen that have traditionally been accounted for by optional tips.
- Room service delivery fees and administrative charges, in addition to automatic 15 to 20 percent gratuities.
- Minibar restocking fees, that may add as much as 20 percent to the price of the already expensive items.
- Phone charges just for dialing—even if your call is not connected. And don't be surprised if you see per-minute charges for local calls.
- Amenity fees at resorts for access to swimming pools, tennis courts, and so on—even if you don't use them.

A Warning About Handing Over a Credit or Debit Card at Check-In

ALERT

One of the biggest scams in travel is the "pay $495 and become a travel agent" opportunity. The major airlines and hotels are wise to this scam and will only provide discounted hotels or first-class upgrades to bona fide travel agents who have earned IATA credentials by achieving a critical threshold of sales. Don't waste your money on this—or any other scam that seems too good to be true!

You unsuspectingly hand your credit or debit card at check-in, unaware that a hotel may occasionally block out an amount up to $3,000 or even more—just in case you destroy the room, max out on the minibar, or run up massive phone charges. If you handed over a credit card with a finite credit limit, you may have no remaining spending power until you check out and the blocked high amount is reversed. Even worse is if you hand over an ATM or debit card, and the checks you wrote are returned NSF!

To prevent such eventualities, use a card with "unlimited" spending power, such as an American Express or Diners Club card, at check-in. If you want to close out your bill with a credit or debit card, you can then ask the front desk staff person to destroy the American Express or Diners Club invoice. At least you will have not allowed your credit card or checking account to be maxed out in the interim.

In Summary

- While airfares typically increase as one gets closer to the date of travel, a hotel will usually be open to discounting literally till the point of check-in if not all rooms have been filled. But travelers must seek out discounts independently since travel agents earn very little or nothing on significantly discounted hotel rates.
- Upscale hotels are more likely than budget or midlevel hotels to provide discounts up to 50 percent, with Starwood and Hyatt the most amenable to providing lower rates among the major chains with a significant U.S. presence. Conversely, Marriott is the least likely to discount its rates. Midlevel and extended-stay hotels such as Four Points by Sheraton, Homewood Suites by Hilton, or Courtyard by Marriott will rarely discount by more than 20 percent, but their base or rack rates are lower and breakfast is often included.
- In most major business cities, major hotel rates are cheaper on weekends, while the opposite holds true on weekdays. Conversely, hotels in vacation areas will be more expensive over the weekends, with reduced rates available during the week. Rates at resorts and vacation hotels will inevitably be cheaper out-of-season, which frequently coincides with periods outside school holidays and less favorable seasons. Be aware that seasonality can also work to your advantage. For example, in the Caribbean, where the weather is quite consistent throughout the year (except for the rare threat of hurricanes between July and October), peak season is January to May because of colder weather on the U.S. mainland during those months. So visit the Caribbean in June or November to get the lowest rates, without any threat of hurricanes.
- The Internet is an excellent starting point for obtaining information about accommodation options as well as standard or benchmark rates for hotels. *Tripadvisor.com* links you to major reservations sites and provides traveler reviews of hotels. However, "old-fashioned" strategies other than using the Internet described in this chapter will help you obtain more favorable rates almost every time.
- Many hotel reservations Web sites now include photographs to give you an idea of the key features of the hotel. Destination books from Frommer, Fodor's, Fielding, and Michelin can also be helpful and may be reviewed free in your local bookstore or in your library (but they are frequently out of date in libraries).
- Use Internet travel agent sites as well as hotels' own Web sites to get benchmark rates. However, contact the hotel direct by fax or

phone, which will typically get you the best rate. Another option is to call the central reservations number, although going centrally may not open up as many discount opportunities as the direct route.

- Planning as far ahead as possible is a very important part of obtaining the best possible hotel rates (or free accommodations using earned hotel points), especially if you are seeking accommodations in highly desirable venues during conventions or peak holiday season. Most hotels allow you to book one year ahead of arrival date. Since it is unusual that a conventional hotel reservation is nonrefundable, there is no risk of booking far in advance, even if you may need to cancel. The most notable exceptions to nonrefundable and nonchangeable hotel reservations come when purchasing from *Priceline.com*, *Hotwire.com*, or from some hotel consolidators such as *Hotels.com* (see next chapter). Be aware that hotel and retail travel agency Internet sites may offer deeply discounted rates that are nonrefundable and nonchangeable.
- When booking more than a single hotel night on the phone, don't accept the same price for every night of your reservation without checking whether other better discounts may be available on certain nights, known as the "split reservation." For example, the best price for a Thursday–Saturday reservation may be $120 (50 percent off) for the Thursday and $79 (weekend rate) for the Friday. Be sure to ask rather than accepting a $120 price for both nights!
- If you cannot find an ideal hotel in the exact location you want to be, consider an alternative location. For example, if your business meeting is downtown and hotel rates are too high, consider an airport or suburban hotel—and *vice versa*.
- Fax the front desk manager one to two days ahead of your arrival if you are an elite member of the hotel's loyalty program or are checking in for a special occasion. Ask for an upgrade and complimentary breakfast.
- Kallback is a Seattle-based company with a pioneering strategy that can save the international traveler on calls from abroad. Check out *Kallback.com* for details.
- When checking in, do not hand over a debit or credit card with a relatively low spending limit. To prevent maxing out your checking account, savings, or credit line, use an American Express or Diners Club card with "unlimited" spending power, in case the hotel blocks off a high charge to cover exorbitant incidentals or damage to the hotel room.

CHAPTER FOURTEEN

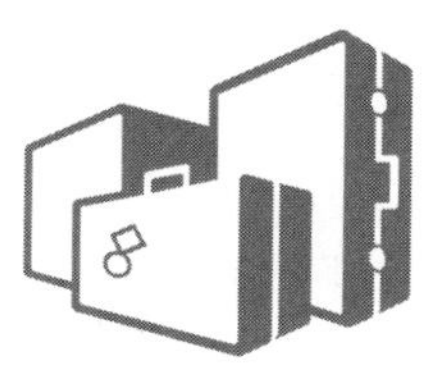

Ten Best Discount Rates to Request When Making a Hotel Reservation

I have stayed in all kinds of hotels around the world, always seeking out the best possible rate. For many years, one of my favorite discount opportunities was using certificates for 50 percent off from United Airlines' frequent flyer program. I would receive one certificate each time I redeemed a free ticket; and Hyatt, Westin, Sheraton, and Hilton hotels would readily accept the certificates worldwide. Then United stopped the hotel certificate program—but I was able to deploy a host of alternative opportunities described later on in this chapter.

I can instantly think of so many examples where I used some discount opportunity to significantly decrease the price of my hotel accommodation—enough to fill a book! Since travelers have often complained about high prices in the most desirable hotels abroad, let me tell you about some of my experiences in many of Europe's most beautiful locations . . .

Our stay at the Hotel De La Gavina on Spain's Costa Brava qualifies as a memorable one. A three-hour drive north of Barcelona and just south of Spain's border with France, this magnificent hotel is located in a gorgeous setting and is designated as one of the leading hotels of the world. I obtained the *Entertainment Directory* hotel discount of 50 percent, which gave us a rate of $197 per night, and have never forgotten:

- Our superb dinner in the hotel's award-winning restaurant where my wife and I sat with our two year-old-son on his best behavior
- One of the most magnificent runs I have ever taken, alongside the ocean and spectacular mansions where the wealthiest Barcelona residents spend their weekends

Then there was our stay at the Sheraton Towers Hotel in Stockholm, with a room overlooking one of the hundreds of lakes on which the city is built.

I used my Starwood discount certificate for 50 percent off (mailed faithfully each year when I renew my Starwood American Express card) to snare a $199 rate during the city's peak season. The Internet rate was $317—and was completely nonrefundable once booked with a credit card. This is an outstanding hotel for business travelers, well-located and offering all the amenities any executive could want.

These are just two of hundreds of instances where I have used a discount opportunity that could never be obtained over the Internet. Yes, the Web has countless sites offering access to online reservations for hotels around the world. Yet, with occasional exceptions, Internet booking sites do not facilitate inquiring about or taking advantage of the best discount rates—which leaves me wondering why millions of travelers book their accommodations online. Sure, it may be quick and easy, two attractive reasons, but the Web is not typically the road to big savings on hotels . . . .

If world travelers and road warriors who are price-sensitive yet discriminating take a few extra minutes to seek out enhanced pricing, they will be rewarded with big dividends in the form of extraordinary savings. And even if that first phone call to a central hotel reservation center or a hotel direct or even a travel agent yields only the inflated rack (or full-price) rate, it still provides a starting point and an opportunity to whittle away the price by pursuing possible discounts.

To be consistently effective at obtaining significant discounts—meaning at least 40 percent—when contacting upscale hotels worldwide, you need to know which discounts offer the greatest yield and broadest acceptability and whether any of these discounts is available. Since no single discount works in every situation, you want to be able to draw upon a range of alternatives. The following hotel discount opportunities are by far the most accepted on a national and worldwide basis.

50 Percent Discount Programs

Typically, the best available rates for hotels will be a 50 percent discount rate, especially on weeknights (Monday through Thursday) at business hotels and weekends (Friday through Sunday) at vacation hotels and resorts. While that discount is almost always applied to the rack rate, which is the full price rarely charged except when the hotel has very high occupancy, the savings can be significant.

The best-known and most widely accepted 50 percent discount program is the *Entertainment Directory*, which has far more hotels throughout the United States and abroad contracted to offer a half-price discount (whenever the hotel occupancy is 80 percent or less) than any other hotel discount program. The directory can be purchased for your home city or the city you will be visiting, including major U.S. and Canadian cities. The advantage of purchasing a directory for your destination city is the potential to use discount coupons for restaurants, fast food, movies, and theme parks at your destination. But hotel discounts apply to any destination city worldwide, regardless of which *Entertainment Directory* you purchase. Each year, the updated annual edition can be obtained soon after Labor Day from various charities, by calling 800-445-4137 or going to the Web site *Entertainment.com*. The price for each directory ranges from $25 to $45.

Consumer Reports has periodically analyzed at least eight major half-price hotel programs, and the *Entertainment Directory* program has consistently come out on top in terms of widespread hotel acceptance in the United States and abroad. There are other half-price hotel programs such as Encore (*Virtual-encore.com*), but none has the global recognition or variety of additional coupons and discount opportunities as the *Entertainment Directory*.

For members of the Starwood hotel frequent-stay program, a discount certificate for 50 percent off hotel rack rates valid for up to four nights may be obtained by redeeming just 1,500 Starwood points. While Starwood enables free nights when redeeming points without capacity controls or blackout dates, these restrictions do apply to use of the 50 percent discount award. Given that 1,500 miles is worth just $30 when used toward a free domestic coach airline ticket, this discount certificate's value can be staggering if it saves you over $100 per night for up to four nights. Another way to get 50 percent off rack rates at Starwood is to apply for the American Express Starwood credit card. You receive one certificate for a discount of 50 percent off when you pay your renewal fee each year.

Weekend or Holiday Rate

Beautiful San Diego: Warm sunshine 330 days per year. Deep blue ocean and pristine beaches. Superb children's activities, including one of the best zoos in the United States. We love visiting the IMAX theater where an audiovisual sensation takes you to places like the Galapagos, Mount Everest, and into virtual orbit aboard the Space Shuttle. Our weekend minivacations involve little more than a tank of gas, as we drive down from Los Angeles and stay in one of three Hyatts in the city's best locations. With weekend or holiday nights of just $99 to $125 per room (or up to 65 percent off the rack rate), it's a very inexpensive way to decompress and recover from life's stresses.

Typically, the best rates for hotels in business locations, especially on weeknights (Monday through Thursday nights), will be discounted 50 percent as outlined in the previous section. However, over weekends (Friday, Saturday, and Sunday nights) or holidays (such as Thanksgiving, Labor

Day, and Memorial Day), the weekend or holiday rate will frequently be less than the 50 percent discount rate. Conversely, hotels in entertainment or resort areas such as Las Vegas and Palm Springs experience much greater demand over weekends and holidays, and will therefore offer lower rates during the week.

If you will be requiring hotel accommodations over a weeknight and weekend (such as Thursday and Friday or Sunday and Monday), be sure to request two separate rates. (Refer to Chapter 13 for more information on split rates.)

Association or Affiliation Rates

By far the most recognized discounts in this category are the AAA and AARP rates, which can provide 20 to 50 percent discounts off the rack rate. The American Automobile Association (AAA) offers annual membership for about $50, depending on which state you live in, and is strongly recommended for all automobile owners because of the auto-assistance program and excellent range of travel discounts. The American Association of Retired Persons (AARP) provides benefits to those who are fifty and older for around $20 each year. Several hotel chain Web sites now enable you to request the AAA or AARP discount when making a reservation online.

In the United States, there are 26,000 trade associations (such as American Medical Association for physicians, Meeting Planners International for meeting planners, and so on) that are membership networks for people of similar professions, trades, or hobbies. Those with larger membership ranks may establish a preferred discount for their members (typically available year-round provided the hotel is not close to capacity for the nights you request), but the discounts are usually less than 50 percent.

(Negotiated) Corporate Discount Versus Corporate Rate

Medium- and large-size companies with significant travel volume are eligible to negotiate special rates for their traveling employees and receive volume discounts. Typically, the negotiated corporate discounts are 35 percent off the rack rate. In some instances, the agreement governing a negotiated corporate discount requires that the special rate be made available even if the hotel is close to or at sell-out, in which case the "less than 80 percent occupancy rule" for providing a discount does not apply. In addition, companies sometimes negotiate rates at one or more hotels in their headquarters city for employees, consultants, and suppliers visiting corporate headquarters. If you are working in some way with a major company, do not hesitate to ask for details so you can take advantage of the negotiated hotel rates.

In contrast, almost anybody is eligible for the corporate rate—all you usually need is a business card! But the discount is usually just 10 to15 percent, so only request the corporate rate if you must stay at the hotel and no other more favorable discount is available. And beware—sometimes the corporate rate is more expensive than the regular rate!

ALERT

Employees of companies with a negotiated rate should not try to book anything other than this rate without permission from the travel department. Since contractually negotiated rates depend on certain annual volume being met, the travel department may prefer that the special rate be selected, even if you have identified a cheaper alternative.

Convention Rate

As mentioned previously in this chapter, there are 26,000 trade associations in the United States, many of which hold regional and national meetings in major business cities on a regular basis. In fact, any well-organized trade fair, convention, or meeting that invites participation from out-of-town attendees will arrange hotel discounts—sometimes at a single hotel where the meeting will be held. Discounts will on occasion be offered for several hotels, especially for meetings where expected attendance exceeds the capacity of one hotel. These specially negotiated hotel rates are typically referred to as "convention rates," and stating your attendance at a specific convention should get you this reduced rate.

There are several occasions where I have enrolled "late" for a convention or meeting, and the special convention or meeting rate saved me a significant amount. In many instances, the convention rate may be the lowest available.

Meeting attendees provided with a specific discounted hotel rate who reserve their accommodation independently may increase the risk of penalties being levied on the meeting organizers, who receive free or discounted meeting facilities in return for a guaranteed room reservation volume.

Introductory or Renovation Rate

In the first year of a new hotel's life, an enticing introductory rate will frequently be offered, especially if the new hotel is an independent entity lacking the brand recognition associated with a chain affiliation. Sometimes this great rate will be published, but even if it's not, ask for it. The probability of being successful obtaining a favorable introductory rate is probably greater if you state that you are a frequent guest at a nearby competitor hotel in that city, but are very open to trying out a new alternative.

To attract loyal and new customers following refurbishment, a recently renovated hotel may offer significant discounts, especially if the entire hotel was closed during the renovation. In addition, you may on occasion arrive at a hotel undergoing refurbishment, with some construction-related inconveniences, such as closed-off public facilities, restaurant, bar, and so on. If you ever are faced with this challenge, feel free to ask for an additional discount over and above the discount you may have agreed to when making your reservation as compensation for the inconveniences.

A Suite Rate (One of the Best-Kept Secrets)

I was planning a trip to the Caribbean and noticed that Hyatt Hotels had a resort on Grand Cayman. One of Hyatt's frequent-stay program awards is a suite upgrade for up to four nights when redeeming just 6,000 points if the guest pays rack rate for a standard room. Better yet, this option is offered at any Hyatt or Park Hyatt property, regardless of the hotel's grade (or level of quality).

So for $325 per night, we had a beachfront suite that would normally go for $500 per night or higher! Over the course of four nights, we realized a $700 (or 35 percent) savings. Another option is to redeem 3,000 points for a Regency Club upgrade up to four nights, which offers standard rooms in the best locations as well as access to the concierge lounge for complimentary continental breakfast and hors d'oeuvres.

Refer to the next chapter for more details about how to earn and redeem points in hotel loyalty programs.

"Any Other" Great Rate (or Additional Amenities for the Same Rate!)

On another weekend getaway with my family to San Diego, I called the Hilton, which has a magnificent resort in the center of the city's attractions. I asked for various possible discounts, and the weekend rate at $109 per night seemed to be the most attractive. But, before hanging up, as always, I asked, "Do you, by any chance, have an even better rate?" I was rewarded with an offer of something called the "bounceback" rate, which brought the rate down to $79 per night, including breakfast!

When calling or faxing for a hotel reservation, your job is never complete until you have asked the reservations staff person about "any other great rate" the hotel may have, even if you believe you have snagged a rock-bottom discount! You will occasionally be amazed when you are told about an even better rate with some obscure name—such as the above-mentioned "bounceback" rate, designed for couples seeking a weekend stress-reduction vacation—or perhaps another discount at the same rate that also includes breakfast.

A variation on this strategy is to simply tell the reservations agent, "My budget is just $80. Do you have a promotion that can accommodate my budget—or not?"

Hotel Consolidators

I once enrolled to attend an Internet travel conference in Chicago at the last minute, which presented a challenge, as this conference was just one of many in Chicago during that period. The convention rate for participants of the meeting I was attending had expired several weeks prior. After struggling to find reasonable rates at an upscale hotel in the downtown area, I called some hotel consolidators and snagged a room at the Omni for $109 per night. As it happened, I checked in around midnight, and by that time all standard rooms had been allocated. So I received a huge upgraded suite, with separate sitting and dining areas apart from the bedroom, even though I must have been the lowest-paying customer!

If you have not succeeded in getting a great rate at a hotel after trying to obtain the above-described discounts, there may well be one or several conventions going on in the city. You may want to contact some hotel consolidators (a detailed list is provided in Appendix G), or consider staying in a nearby location. (Refer to Chapter 13 for more information.)

Hotel consolidators are brokers that sell hotel rooms at a predetermined discount by doing one or both of the following:

1. Buying blocks of rooms at volume discounts in certain major cities each night
2. Distributing "excess rooms" offered by hotels not anticipating full occupancy

The key advantage of booking a hotel night through a hotel consolidator is that just one call (or one Web site visit) can get you a room at a reduced price; however, prices are not negotiable. The principal disadvantages with using a hotel consolidator are:

1. The discounts will not usually be 50 percent off, but more typically 20 to 35 percent off the rack rate.
2. More commonly, independent hotels—where standards of quality may be unpredictable—rather than chains sell rooms through hotel consolidators. However, well-known chains may occasionally be included in offerings.
3. Cancellation or change fees may be significant, for example $50 within 48 hours of scheduled arrival or a full day plus tax if less

than 48 hours. Be sure to ask if booking on the phone, or read the fine print if making your reservation online.

4. You may not be eligible to earn hotel loyalty points—be sure to check with the hotel frequent guest desk.
5. One of the least appealing rooms may be assigned to you.

There are at least twenty hotel consolidators operating within the United States, with a few large ones covering major cities within the United States and abroad, and some smaller outfits making reservations for a single city. One additional benefit of hotel consolidators may be that they have rooms available when all hotels are sold out during conventions, especially those that buy up blocks of rooms. However, when room availability is tight, discounts from consolidators may be much smaller or even nonexistent.

Free

Starwood hotels has offered seasonal promotions offering free weekend nights after the traveler stays a certain number of paid nights. One that caught my attention was "Stay five nights at any Starwood, and earn one free Friday night at any Starwood Hotel. Then stay another five nights, and earn a free Saturday night." Since I had some business in various cities that would require ten nights in hotels during the four-month qualifying period, I geared my accommodations toward Starwood hotels.

The reward was accommodations right out of a dream at the St. Regis. This hotel occupies the upper floors of Starwood's Essex Hotel right on Central Park in New York City. We enjoyed a huge suite, with living and dining area, separate bedroom, two marble bathrooms, plush furnishings, and a heavenly bed. Cost of our weekend stay in this dreamland—zero. Not even tax.

The key to using free nights you have earned is to redeem them when the price of a hotel night would otherwise be expensive (unless the free night offer is expiring—then just go for it!). Typically, free hotel nights are earned in four ways:

> **TIP**
>
> **Be sure to check the rules of programs regarding any expiration of earned points should you go for more than eighteen months with no account activity. Each program has subtle differences with respect to its rules (refer to Chapter 15 for more details).**

■ **Frequent-Stay Programs** (refer to Chapter 15 for more details). Similar in nature to frequent flyer programs, hotel frequent-stay programs reward several paid nights with a free night. In general, a traveler requires at least ten paid nights to earn a free night, and frequently fifteen to twenty or more nights to earn one free night at a hotel chain's most beautiful and prestigious properties. Naturally, concentrating your paid nights with just one hotel chain will speed up the chances of earning free nights, and points earned with most hotel chains do not expire as long as you have some activity (points in or out) every two to five years. Free nights from use of earned points can increasingly be redeemed at short notice since notification is typically sent electronically from hotel frequent guest service centers to a selected hotel.

- **Special Promotions.** Certain promotions may offer free nights, particularly to encourage business during low season. For example, Hyatt, Starwood, and Marriott Hotels have annual promotions during slower months, offering free nights following a certain number of stays or nights. (Refer to Chapter 15 for more details.)

- **Following a Letter of Complaint.** When things go wrong with a hotel stay, it may be appropriate to request compensation that will include one or more free nights—either at the same hotel or any hotel within the chain. (Refer to Chapter 19 for more details.)

- **As Part of a "Stay Three/Four/Five Nights, Get One Free" Promotion.** Such promotions are common and widely promoted in newspaper advertisements as well as newsletters sent to airline frequent flyers (most airlines have hotel partners) and hotel frequent-stay program participants. Since the paid nights are usually quoted at rack rate (full price), this promotion is nothing more than a discount of 33, 25, or 20 percent and should be avoided if other discount opportunities will get you a better overall rate for your stay.

A New Rate for Business—Will It Take Off?

Just as most airlines now offer special programs for small business, typically offering company points in addition to the individual traveler's frequent flyer miles, hotels may try to follow a similar path. Starwood was first with its Starwood Preferred Business program, which offers 10 to 40 percent off published corporate rates, room upgrades, and Starpoints that will accrue both to the company's and the individual traveler's accounts. Sign up at *Spg.com/bizenroll1*.

In Summary

- There are several discount opportunities for the world traveler to exploit when seeking upscale accommodations, even during peak periods. No one strategy works every time, in every circumstance. If a hotel is not offering one type of discount, ask about another. And even another. Be persistent.

- The Web is a great place to start your search, as you can obtain information and check out standard rates.
- Naturally, use free nights you may have earned if the hotel rate would otherwise be expensive.
- Be sure to ask for at least four to five possible rates, including 50 percent discounts (such as the *Entertainment Directory* rate or Starwood half-off discount by redeeming 1,500 points for up to four nights), weekend or holiday rate, AAA or AARP rate, negotiated corporate rate/corporate discount, introductory or renovation rate for new or refurbished properties, and the convention rate if you will be attending a meeting for which hotel rooms have been assigned.
- When calling a hotel, never end the call before asking about any other special or promotional rates—you may be surprised what other discounts are forthcoming!
- Hyatt offers members of its Gold Passport program the options of using 3,000 or 6,000 points to upgrade to Regency Club or Suite, respectively, for up to four nights, when paying the rack rate.
- If you still cannot find a great rate, contact hotel consolidators. Potential disadvantages include discounts that are usually less than if you contact hotels direct, a focus on independent rather than chain hotels, no hotel loyalty program points, the possibility of getting one of the least attractive rooms, and the likelihood of stiff fees if you cancel or change.

CHAPTER FIFTEEN

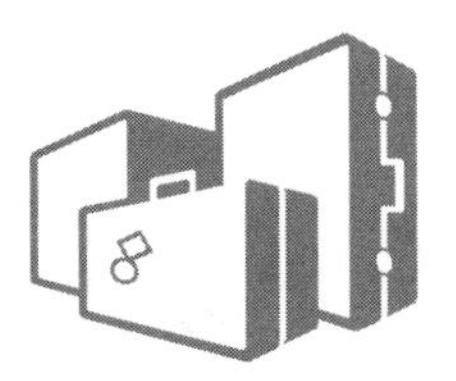

Hotel Loyalty Programs

Perks and Promotions Aplenty

The best free room I ever had? One that comes to mind is the six-night stay with my family at the Park Hyatt in Tokyo. Incredibly, there is no check-in desk. As we entered the hotel, we were ushered straight to our room on the fortieth floor by elevator, where we walked through the elegant lobby marveling at the spectacular views over Tokyo. Only after we were comfortably situated in our room did a staff person visit us. We signed the necessary paperwork in about thirty seconds—all from the luxury and comfort of the desk in our own room.

The amenities alone made the stay memorable. The huge bathroom greeted us with marble everywhere, while a giant tub invited us to sit, soak, and relax. Not only were the best shampoos, conditioners, and lotions provided each day, but also a new, top-of-the-line hairbrush *and* nailbrush. We lounged in complimentary silk kimonos and donned thick bathrobes after using the pool and spa—which was located a quick elevator ride away on the 52nd floor amid a dazzling 360-degree view of Tokyo.

For all of this, we paid absolutely nothing, not even a room tax. But, as we all know, there is no such thing as "free." It actually took twenty-one paid nights at Hyatt Hotels, using a promotional offer, to earn enough hotel points for that complimentary stay.

But here is the key point: When you accrue hotel points or intend to use some promotion toward free nights, make the most of what they offer! Just as you would redeem your frequent flyer miles for what would otherwise be the most expensive air tickets, use those free nights you earn *only* at hotels which would ordinarily be out of your budget.

The rates for the kind of accommodation we enjoyed at the Park Hyatt Tokyo would normally run at least $500 per night—a rate I'm not ready to pay. Yet, my family and I could still have this fabulous experience, thanks to the judicious use of my hotel points.

The Lowdown on Hotel Loyalty Programs

Almost all of the major hotel chains with a significant U.S. hotel presence have loyalty programs. Since joining hotel loyalty programs is almost always free, the savvy world traveler signs up with all the major ones. In addition to the perks mentioned above, members receive periodic information via mail or e-mail about special offers—such as discounts, bonus point promotions, or opportunities to stay free for fewer points.

You may sign up for hotel loyalty programs online or by calling the guest rewards phone number, which is usually toll-free. A list of phone numbers and Web sites is provided in Appendix F.

In some respects, hotel loyalty programs are very similar to airline frequent flyer programs, typically providing two key benefits:

- **Recognition.** This might mean simply offering the convenience of having your credit card on file when you call to make a reservation, or providing lavish elite perks for loyal customers who stay ten to seventy-five nights in a calendar year.

- **Free Nights.** Dollars spent earn points toward free nights as well as other travel or nontravel rewards.

ALERT

To decrease commissions paid to third-party Web sites, most major hotel chains no longer award loyalty points, credit toward elite status, or elite perks to guests who make reservations through online travel agents. On the plus side, hotel chains guarantee the lowest rates to guests who book at their own Web site or with the hotel direct.

Conversely, hotel loyalty programs are quite different from airline frequent flyer programs in the following ways:

- The amount of points you earn is almost always proportional to what you spend rather than the number of nights you stay (whereas airline frequent flyer earnings are mainly driven by mileage flown).

- Whereas one or one thousand miles are standard units of currency when speaking of frequent flyer miles, the value of hotel points is highly variable from one hotel chain to another, making comparisons virtually meaningless. For example, the major hotel chains reward three, five, or even ten points per dollar spent (before elite and other bonuses kick in).

- The ease of earning elite status is extremely variable between different chains. For example, the highest elite level is achieved by staying seventy-five nights within a calendar year at Marriott hotels—but just fifty nights or twenty-five stays with Hyatt.

Getting the Recognition You Deserve

There are essentially two levels of recognition: standard and elite.

The standard recognition program simply allows a hotel to serve you more efficiently. This is usually accomplished by collecting some data on your room preferences through a questionnaire; your responses are recorded and stored in the hotel's database until you make a booking at a hotel. This information might include:

- Your credit card number and expiration date, which can be automatically used to guarantee your room for late arrival when you call to make a reservation.
- A profile of your room preferences, including your choice of two doubles or a king-sized bed, a smoking or nonsmoking room, a room on a higher or lower floor, special requests such as hypoallergenic pillows, and so on.
- Your e-mail address, so you can receive information regarding special promotions that can save you money or get you more loyalty points for future stays. You may also elect to receive your updated point balances electronically rather than via regular mail.

How Hotels Treat Their Elite or Most Loyal Customers

Higher levels of recognition are given to those travelers who are more frequent guests at a particular hotel chain. As with airlines, hotel elite status is dependent on activity (number of nights or stays) at a chain's hotels within a calendar year, with the benefits typically offered for at least the following calendar year (and often into February of the following year while the hotel assesses who has made it into its elite program for the forthcoming year based on the prior year's activity).

Benefits that come with elite status include:

- Room upgrades, which may be into a room that is slightly larger and equipped with features especially useful to the business traveler. The highest-level elite hotel members may be eligible for upgrades to the concierge level, which is typically located on a high floor and offers a dedicated lounge with complimentary breakfast in the morning and hors d'oeuvres in the evening. The lounges are frequently staffed with a concierge available to provide tourist information and directions as well as implement special requests, such as booking a taxicab or limousine service and getting theater tickets. Upgrades into suites are the exception rather than the rule, but there is nothing to lose by asking at check-in, especially if you are a very loyal customer!

- Bonus hotel points for each stay, ranging from 20 to 50 percent.

While airlines typically have three levels of frequent flyer elite status, hotels may maintain just two levels that provide extra perks for their best customers—but there is much less uniformity across hotel programs than with major airlines. In general, the first level of hotel elite status is awarded at 25 nights or 10 stays in a calendar year, while the higher level requires 50 to 75 nights or 25 stays in a calendar year. But differences in achieving elite status can differ quite markedly, with Hilton requiring just 10 nights within a calendar year to achieve first-level Silver elite status, in contrast to Hyatt requiring 25 nights within a calendar year to achieve first-level Platinum status.

Elite status requirements for earning and redeeming points are also less uniform among various hotels than those observed across the different airlines.

Earning Hotel Elite Status Without Multiple Stays

A couple of hotel chains offer certain cardholders complimentary elite status:

- Starwood automatically offers American Express Platinum cardholders (annual fee $395) complimentary first-level Gold elite status that otherwise requires 25 nights or 10 stays in a calendar year. However, the Starwood American Express credit card does not offer this benefit.
- Marriott offers holders of the Marriott Visa affinity card (annual fee $45) complimentary first-level Silver Marriott Rewards elite status that otherwise requires 10 nights in a calendar year.

Finally—if you are an elite member of one hotel chain expecting to direct business toward a competitor, the competitor will frequently match status if you contact the customer service center.

What Loyalty Will Bring You

With each visit, most hotel programs offer their customers the option of earning points toward free hotel stays, or frequent flyer miles that are automatically transferred to the airline of the guest's choice. Hilton is unique in offering its guests the opportunity to earn both points and miles, known as "double-dipping." With such an attractive perk, Hilton would seem to be the savvy traveler's first choice, but its inconsistent level of quality—ranging from magnificent to mediocre and even poor—makes it difficult for us to recommend Hilton. Nor does Hilton have a strong global luxury brand hotel to offer for both earning and redeeming points, as do the other major chains. (Although the luxury Conrad group of hotels is part of the Hilton organization, it is only represented in a few cities.)

Starwood has been the favorite loyalty hotel program among frequent travelers for several years running for the following reasons:

- No capacity controls or blackout dates are imposed on the use of points for free hotel nights—a first among hotels. If there is just one room left, it's yours. This holds true even if you want accommodations during the peak Christmas–New Year season.
- Starwood points have a favorable 1:1 exchange ratio when converted to frequent flyer miles with most major U.S. airlines and British Airways. An additional 5,000-mile bonus is awarded if you transfer 20,000 miles at one time.
- Starwood owns many spectacular properties worldwide where points may be redeemed, including its St. Regis and Luxury Collection brands.

Not every hotel awards the same amount of points for each dollar spent. Starwood awards two points, Hyatt offers five points, and Marriott gives ten points. Note that higher earnings are naturally associated with higher thresholds for redeeming points toward free nights. Frequent guests who achieve elite status get bonus points for each stay, but again, the awards vary. For example, first-level elites will receive a 50 percent bonus when staying at Starwood, a 30 percent bonus when staying at Hyatt, and a 20 percent bonus when staying at Marriott.

Sound confusing? That's because it is.

To gauge which chain is providing the best possible deal, let's review the number of points required for a one-night stay in three of the chains' top-of-the-line brands. For our example, we'll assume that the guest has not qualified for elite status and is not earning bonus hotel points:

- For Starwood, the most luxurious hotels require redemption of 14,000 to 20,000 points per night, meaning a guest would have to spend $7,000 to $10,000 at an earning rate of 2 points per dollar.
- For Hyatt, one night in a room at its best hotels requires redemption of 15,000 points per night, which translates to spending $3,000 at an earning rate of 5 points per dollar.
- For Marriott and Hilton, the best hotels require redemption of at least 35,000 points per night, so $3,500 must be spent at an earning

rate of 10 points per dollar. However, Hilton also enables the traveler to earn frequent flyer miles in addition to hotel points.

Bottom line, Hyatt offers the least expensive pathway to award luxury in terms of a non-elite hotel customer seeking to earn a free night in a chain hotel's most luxurious accommodations. However, Hyatt has fewer properties worldwide than the other major chains with a significant U.S. presence, so earning points and claiming the award may prove to be more of a challenge. Conversely, Starwood trails the rest when it comes to earning free nights—yet its loyalty program has consistently been ranked number one by frequent travelers in the United States and abroad. In other words, other factors are coming into play—most likely Starwood's unique "no blackout dates, no capacity controls" policy and outstanding array of hotels of all grades worldwide.

Note that each of these major hotel companies includes midscale chains where points earned per night are usually fewer per dollar. (Refer to Chapter 13 for details.) For example, at Residence Inn Suites (a Marriott extended-stay hotel chain), guests earn only five points per dollar rather than the ten points earned at Marriott's full-service hotels. In contrast, guests at Hilton's Homewood Suites extended-stay chain earn a full ten points per dollar spent, comparable to earnings at Hilton's full-service brands.

But Wait—There's More!

Points accrued in all hotel loyalty programs can naturally be used for free hotel nights. However, some additional awards of note are as follows:

- Starwood: 1,500 Starwood points will get you a certificate for 50 percent off any Starwood hotel stay, which can be an outstanding value.
- Hilton: HHONORS offers a vast array of flight options beginning at the 40,000 to 70,000 point level or a land-only safari package in Kenya for around 250,000 points.
- Marriott: Marriott Guest Rewards also awards myriad choices of options, such as air and hotel packages for two beginning at the 225,000 point level (the air portion comes from frequent flyer miles deposited into your account) and seven-day cruises for under 400,000 points.

Points or Miles—Which Is the Better Choice?

Since major U.S. hotel chains typically offer either 500 frequent flyer miles or hotel points for each stay, which should you choose? Quite simply, you need to calculate which benefit will have greater value for you.

For example, assume you've chosen to stay at a Hyatt hotel, and one award option is 500 frequent flyer miles toward travel on the airline of your choice. Use the formula described in Chapter 10 to calculate what 500 miles is worth to you. (If 1,000 miles equals anywhere from $16 to $100, 500 miles would be the equivalent of $8 to $50.)

Then calculate the likely number of hotel points you will earn, should you select that option. If your room rate is $100 per night and the hotel offers five points per dollar, your one-night stay will net you 500 points. If you are targeting to earn 15,000 points for a free night in a luxury Park Hyatt room that would otherwise cost you $300, 500 points equals $10. (You can calculate that by dividing 500 points by 15,000 points, to get 1/30th; 1/30th of $300 = $10.) In this case, requesting the miles probably makes more sense, especially if you use your frequent flyer miles only for airline tickets that would otherwise be very expensive.

But staying two nights at the Hyatt, which earns you 1,000 points per night and is equivalent to $20, may be worth more than the $8 to $50 you will receive by choosing 500 frequent flyer miles, which do not increase with increased length of stay.

As a general rule of thumb, choose frequent flyer miles if your paid hotel night is less than $150 and one night in duration. For two or more nights, or one night with a room rate exceeding $150, choose to receive hotel points. And if you have more airline frequent flyer miles than you know what to do with, always select hotel points! With Hilton, you do not need to choose—"double-dipping" allows you the best of both worlds!

Only You Can Make Those Points Valuable

The same logic that applied to getting the most from your free airline tickets applies to redeeming free hotel nights: Don't waste free hotel awards for a stay that would otherwise be inexpensive. Since most hotels require that a greater number of points be used for more prestigious properties, calculate whether the amount of points you plan to use for a free room is a good deal compared to the best room price you can get using the strategies described in the previous two chapters.

Special Promotions

All hotel chains have special promotions offering free nights, typically to boost revenue during off-peak periods. Look for these specials, as they allow you to earn free nights without using your hotel points.

Here are a couple of recent examples of annual hotel promotions:

- Starwood's winter/spring promotion awards two free Friday nights at any Starwood property (except certain St. Regis ultraluxury brand hotels) with five paid nights. Pay for another five nights and earn two free Saturday nights.

- Hyatt's "Nights After Nights" rewards two stays or three paid nights with a free weekend night at almost any Hyatt or Park Hyatt property.

Note that many promotions require that you register online or by calling a toll-free number. If you fail to enroll, your free nights will not be awarded! And some promotions require that you pay for your nights with a specific credit card, which may be American Express, Visa, or MasterCard.

Once you join each chain's loyalty program, you will be informed about these promotions by mail or e-mail, and the most lucrative promotions are almost always advertised extensively in major daily newspapers. *Inside Flyer* magazine also lists hotel promotions, and you can receive e-mail notifications by signing up for weekly updates at *Traveltactics.com*.

Some Noteworthy Exceptions

The two largest ultraluxury hotel chains, Four Seasons and Ritz Carlton, do not have loyalty programs that offer points toward free nights. However, since Marriott owns Ritz Carlton, Marriott points may be redeemed at Ritz Carlton properties.

Wyndham is another major upscale U.S. chain that claims to offer its frequent guests better amenities while staying at its hotels, such as superior rooms and no charges for calling card phone use or Internet access. It also focuses on the specific needs of female travelers, providing entire floors "for women only." However, Wyndham does not offer points redeemable for future free stays.

TIP

Both Four Seasons and Ritz Carlton claim to have excellent databases that store key customer information and preferences, meaning that if you requested hypoallergenic pillows and comforters during one stay, that request will automatically be fulfilled on future stays. And to a significant extent, the promise is met.

In Summary

- Every world traveler and road warrior should join the loyalty programs for all the major hotel chains, as membership is always free! In return for your affiliation, you receive:
  - Recognition, as your guest preferences and credit card are kept in a database to simplify the reservations and check-in processes
  - Points that can be used toward free stays

- Information about special deals and promotions by regular or e-mail

- Hotel loyalty programs differ markedly from airline frequent flyer programs in that points toward free stays are earned almost exclusively in direct proportion to dollars spent.
- Hyatt has arguably the least expensive path toward earning free nights in a luxury hotel. Starwood points are easiest to use because the chain has no blackout dates or capacity controls and far more properties worldwide than Hyatt. Hilton hotels enable earning of both hotel points toward free stays and frequent flyer miles ("double-dipping"). However, your choice of programs should depend primarily on the availability of desirable hotels in the locations you are most likely to be.
- When deciding whether to opt for frequent flyer miles or hotel points for a hotel stay, a general rule of thumb is to choose hotel points if the rate for a single night exceeds $150 for stays of two or more nights, or if you have more frequent flyer miles than you know what to do with. Otherwise, choose frequent flyer miles.
- The best use of your earned points is usually for a free night that would otherwise cost more money than you are prepared to pay. If you're tempted to use your points for a regular hotel room, compare the lowest price available for that room to the value you would receive by redeeming your points at a luxury property in the future.
- To stimulate traffic during off-peak periods, hotels frequently have seasonal promotions offering free weekend nights after the guest has accrued a certain number of paid nights. Earning the free nights may require registration, which can be done online or by calling a toll-free number, and may require payment with a certain credit card, such as American Express, Visa, or MasterCard.
- Attaining elite status with hotels affords qualifications and benefits similar to those offered by the major airlines. The more often you stay at a particular hotel chain within a calendar year, the higher your status. The minimum is approximately 10 stays or 25 nights per year, but qualifications vary from chain to chain. The most valuable perks afforded to guests who achieve elite status are typically an upgraded room—which could mean it is larger, has more amenities, or sits on the concierge level—and the awarding of bonus points for each stay, usually at least 20 percent of the regular points earned. Complimentary first-level elite status may be earned without any stays by successfully applying for certain credit or charge

cards, including the Marriott Visa credit card for Marriott Hotels and the American Express Platinum (but not American Express Starwood) charge card for Starwood hotels.

- Two of the ultimate luxury hotel chains, Four Seasons and Ritz Carlton, do not offer any points for paid nights. But they do offer a relentless focus on excellence and a near-perfect experience time and again that, for many a discriminating traveler, override the absence of free night programs.
- Deciding which hotel loyalty program is the best is almost impossible because there is virtually no standard basis for comparison. Different hotel chains have different standards with regard to earning points, number of points required for free stays (or other rewards such as cruises), blackout dates, how elite status is earned, and the benefits associated with elite status.

CHAPTER SIXTEEN

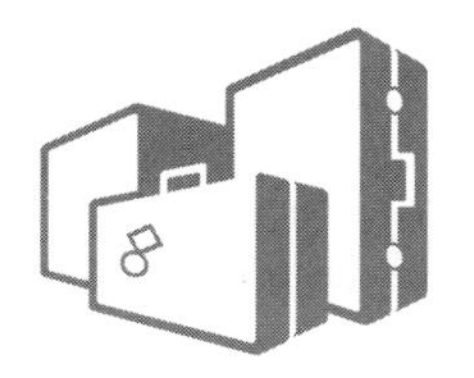

Hotel Internet

Where to Book Good Rooms at Great Rates Online

A three-day seminar in Las Vegas was just two weeks away when I decided to attend. Ordinarily such a small lead time might mean losing out on a good hotel room price, but since the meeting was midweek, I didn't worry. I felt confident I could obtain an excellent hotel rate, as Las Vegas hotels usually enjoy their peak occupancy over weekends when the gamblers come to town.

I sent out my faxes to every major hotel on the strip, but was taken by surprise when I received the responses. The first night presented no problem; I could get a good room at a good price just about anywhere. The second night was a different story: Some hotels were completely sold out, while others graciously offered me a room for $175-plus per night. Evidently, some major convention activity overlapped with my second night, and attendees had snapped up all the right-priced rooms.

I decided to give *Priceline.com* a try, which is famous for its airfare "bids"—but also offers hotels, car rentals, and packages at its site. I first bid $85 per night for two nights at a four-star property (the highest hotel rating on *Priceline.com*) on the strip, and my bid was refused. To bid again at a higher price, I had to change either my arrival date or desired location at my destination—a *Priceline.com* rule—so I simply bid for the *second night only*. My bid of $89 was accepted, my credit card duly charged, and I learned that I would be lodging at the newly constructed Paris Hotel. I then called the same hotel, asked for a range of possible discounts for the first night, and snagged the *Entertainment Directory* discount for $79.

When I checked into the Paris Hotel, I presented the first night reservation only and received an *upgraded* room simply by asking. The next day I showed my *Priceline.com* reservation to the front desk staff person and requested to stay in the same room for the second night. Since customers who reserve rooms through *Priceline.com* are usually given the worst rooms, the front desk staff person was not happy with my request to remain in an upgraded room, but agreed. What a great deal!

The strategy I used was certainly not conventional, but it illustrates one of my few successful uses of the Internet to obtain a rock-bottom hotel price. In general, Web sites do not allow the traveler to select a variety of discounts, other than AAA, government, AARP, or senior rates. What the Internet can and will do effectively is give the traveler a benchmark for hotel prices; the savvy world traveler will then contact the hotel direct and see if the rate can be beaten. Certain Internet sites can also give you a great idea about hotels' amenities and locations—sometimes even enabling you to take 360-degree tours of the property—helping you decide which ones will best suit your needs.

Hotels Online—Web Sites You Want to Visit

There are several different kinds of Web sites where you can research, view, and book hotel accommodations. Be aware that as advanced as Internet technology is, you will still encounter challenges; for example, Web sites may enable you to go through an entire booking process, only to be told when you enter your credit card number that rooms are sold out for the nights you specified!

This chapter reviews the most prominent Internet sites for obtaining hotel information and making reservations, organized by category.

Where Might You Want to Stay?

If you're going to a U.S. destination and have a specific address where you need to be, check out *Terrafly.com*. You simply input the address and then receive a list of hotels in the area with exact distances from the address you specified.

What Does Everyone Else Think?

It's always helpful to hear comments from other travelers who have "been there and done that." One of our favorite sites is *Tripadvisor.com*, which assembles articles about destinations and hotels from various travel publications and presents reviews from travelers. *Tripadvisor.com* also has links to major reservations sites and travel guides such as *Frommers.com*, *Fodors.com*, and *Concierge.com*, as well as a "hotel popularity index" that ranks hotels within a destination based on the quantity and quality of content in published resources (including guidebooks and newspaper reviews).

Epicurious.com compiles opinions given by "regular" people about anything and everything you can think of—including a variety of travel products. Click on "Travel" and you'll access opinions about airlines and hotels.

Globapost.com includes hotel and destination reviews from site users and its own staff.

Of course, information and opinions about an unusual hotel you're considering may be scarce or nonexistent, as expensive and exotic hotels are less accessible to the average traveler

To check photographs of a destination or hotel, go to *Google.com*. Input the name of the hotel or destination, and click on "images." *Google.com* will show you all available images found across the Internet.

Finally, when reading promotional material from hotels, be skeptical of descriptions you read—for example, check a map when you read "central downtown location" or "conveniently located to Mall Of America." If in doubt, call the hotel and ask the concierge for more details. Most upscale hotels will usually be glad to mail out a brochure in which you can see color photographs of rooms and amenities. Either call central reservations or the hotel direct.

Retail Travel Agency Web Sites

Check out hotel rates on the big three retail travel reservations sites: *Orbitz.com*, *Expedia.com*, and *Travelocity.com*. For global reservations, *All-hotels.com* includes a huge inventory of hotels in its database, including budget through five-star hotels worldwide.

Booking at Hotels' Own Proprietary Web Sites

The benefits of visiting hotel chains' own Web sites are that you can check out standard rates, and you may also be allowed to request government, AAA, AARP, or senior discounts. A listing of major brands belonging to hotel chains with several locations throughout the United States is listed in Appendix E.

A major emerging change is hotels trying to steer their customers away from third-party sites, to which they must pay a commission. As part of their attempt to get travelers to book online direct, most hotel chains including Starwood, Marriott, Hilton, Hyatt, and Intercontinental guarantee a rate at least as good as that found on any other Web site, such as a third-party agent site. Check each respective hotel Web site for details regarding the price guarantee. Furthermore, many hotel chains will now only provide loyalty points and elite amenities if your stay is booked at their own Web site, or by calling either central reservations or the hotel direct. Be sure to check if loyalty points are important to you (and they should be!).

Compare Hotel Rates Side by Side

"Site scrapers" such *Travelaxe.com* and *Sidestep.com* claim to scan vast numbers of travel Web sites to find the best hotel rates, providing a simple way to compare side by side. Each site has the capability to scan different sites, so none is able to access the entire universe. Both require that you download an application program onto your hard drive. *Travelaxe.com* focuses exclusively on hotels, and its well-organized search displays the total cost of the stay, including taxes and other surcharges.

Other Hotel Reservations Web Sites

- ***Travelweb.com*** is the hotel industry's equivalent to the airlines' *Orbitz.com*. This joint venture includes Hilton, Marriott, Starwood, Hyatt, and Six Continents (which is the parent company of Intercontinental and Holiday Inn), and fulfills a similar role for these major hotel chains as *Orbitz.com* does for the major U.S. airlines: permitting Internet distribution without paying commissions to a "middleman," that is, a travel agent. It is the ideal site for obtaining standard retail prices for all the major chain hotels that have a presence in your destination city—but don't expect much in the way of significant discounts. The site requires full prepayment at the time a reservation is made. Surprisingly, loyalty points or elite benefits may not be provided, even though this site is owned by the hotel chains rather than a third-party intermediary.
- ***Hotelbook.com*** lists over 5,000 hotels from the Utell reservations system. Like *Travelweb.com*, *Hotelbook.com* also requires full prepayment in advance.
- ***Lodging.com*** is the Web site for the travel company Cendant, which owns mainly budget-oriented hotels worldwide. The site also includes luxury and extended-stay options.
- ***Ase.net*** links you to multiple sites offering any hotel you request worldwide, enabling easy comparison shopping.
- ***Placestostay.com*** includes over 30,000 hotels worldwide, and also has a discount section for major cities.
- ***All-hotels.com*** includes over 100,000 hotels in its database and a selection the site claims you will not find anywhere else on the Web.
- ***Bookitcheap.com*** and ***Europcheapo.com*** are two sites that claim to have heavily discounted rates in the United States and Europe, respectively.
- ***Venere.com*** offers hotels in all major European countries.
- ***Laterooms.com*** is for hotels abroad.
- ***Bedandbreakfast.com*** is if you're interested in B&Bs.

Hotel Consolidators

The majority of hotel consolidators now have Web sites that enable online booking. The two largest are *Hotels.com* (now owned by the same company as *Expedia.com*), which has the largest U.S. inventory, and *Quickbook.com*, which has a smaller selection but higher quality inventory.

We avoid *Hotels.com* for three reasons:

1. It focuses on downscale properties.
2. Its prices are not especially low—sometimes just 25 to 40 percent off rack rates versus the possibility of a 50 percent or more discount if you contact a hotel direct. The rates may sometimes be higher than you can get by going to the hotel chain's own Web site or a travel agent Web site (such as *Orbitz.com*, *Expedia.com*, or *Travelocity.com*).
3. Once you guarantee your reservation with a credit card, it may be nonrefundable and nonchangeable; or if the reservation can be canceled, a $10 fee will be imposed.

Quickbook.com, on the other hand, has all the advantages missing from *Hotels.com*:

1. A good selection of well-known upscale properties that are screened by the Web site's staff.
2. Better prices than *Hotels.com*—although they are not necessarily the lowest, using this site can still save you lots of time.
3. Once you guarantee your reservation with a credit card, the cancellation policy established by your selected hotel usually applies—typically by 6 PM on day of arrival for a complete refund. In addition, *Quickbook.com* also includes rating information (hotel features, room features, service level, and business features) based on personal visits by its staff and a detailed survey of amenities for all hotels included within its system.

A list of hotel consolidators for domestic and international locations is included as Appendix G.

Our bottom-line advice: Try as many sites as possible—you never know which will come up best!

Auction Sites

1. ***Priceline.com*** (refer to the opening story of this chapter for an example of how to use this site). The well-known travel auction site *Priceline.com* pioneered the concept of bidding for airline seats, and subsequently for hotel rooms, car rentals, and packages. Visitors to the *Priceline.com* site can "name their price" for hotel rooms by location and by quality (following their one- to four-star rating system—sometimes including "resorts" as an additional option). Within fifteen minutes of submitting your bid, you'll receive an e-mail telling you whether or not your bid has been accepted. If your bid wasn't accepted, you will be asked to change the location, quality of desired hotel, or date of your request if you wish to resubmit another similar bid.

The major disadvantages of *Priceline.com* are:

- The operating model used by *Priceline.com* for hotels is also similar to the one it uses for airfares. Many major U.S. hotels participate by informing *Priceline.com* of the lowest rate they are prepared to accept on a specified date, which is stored in *Priceline.com*'s database. However, since the user has no idea what that lowest acceptable price is, he will often bid higher than necessary.
- The requirement to provide a credit card number without any advance knowledge of the prospective hotels in the system.
- The requirement to accept whatever hotel is offered on a nonrefundable and nonchangeable basis if your bid is successful.
- A questionable definition of hotel grading. For example, what *Priceline.com* considers a four-star hotel may not meet your definition of a four-star hotel.

To get an idea of which hotels are being offered by *Priceline.com*, check out a package option for your destination, where the specific hotel (but not the airline or schedule) is revealed before you bid.

Bottom line: The bidding process works fairly well for airline seats, which, as a travel product, are essentially all the same (although, as savvy world travelers, we would argue against this belief because time of departure, number of stops, and which airlines we fly *do* make a difference to us). Hotel rooms, however, can vary widely in quality of product, and choosing the "right" brand at the "right" location makes a huge difference to your comfort and convenience. As a general rule, we suggest using *Priceline.com* as a last resort, after exhausting all other methods for getting a great rate.

2. *Hotline.com's* hotel reservation system also follows a similar process to its air ticket reservation system. After you specify the area of town in which you need to be, *Hotline.com* offers details of several hotels, including their star rating, the neighborhood, and amenities. It also lists the price at which the room is available—provided you book within the next sixty minutes. The name of the hotel is revealed only after you accept an offer and pay with your credit card. As with airfares, this site is an excellent place to start a hotel rate search, since you can quickly ascertain what the hotels consider to be their rock-bottom, distressed-inventory price without being forced to commit to a nonrefundable/nonchangeable purchase.

3. ***Skyauction.com*** is a true auction site where prices can be bid up from "bargain basement." Check out "Last-Minute Getaways" for departures a month ahead.

TIP

Several Web sites now post information about successful bids from *Priceline.com.* These include *biddingfortravel.com,* which includes a community posting board through which travelers can exchange information and strategies. The site devotes a great deal of space to teaching you how to determine what your bid should be. Even though *Priceline.com* is barred from divulging any information about successful bids, it encourages use of these "secrets revealed" sites, since its profitability depends entirely on selling the available rooms by way of successful bids.

Discount Sites for Luxury Hotels

Deals at luxury hotels may be obtained through traditional retail Internet sites such as *Orbitz.com*, *Expedia.com*, or *Travelocity.com*. For example, we identified a Web-only, off-season special for the Ritz Carlton Jamaica ($182 per night) at *Expedia.com* versus best "normal" prices around $345.

Some luxury hotel chains distribute discounted rates exclusively through their own sites. Examples are Four Seasons (*Fourseasons.com*), Ritz Carlton (*Ritzcarlton.com*), and Peninsula (*Peninsula.com*). Four other sites to visit:

1. ***Luxurylink.com*** promotes itself as "the premier luxury travel resource, providing a searchable database of luxury travel properties worldwide, as well as special offers, exclusives, auctions, and additional information for travelers."

   The *Luxurylink.com* database contains thousands of products of interest to the sophisticated traveler—tours, cruises, specialty travel hotels, resorts, inns, lodges, yacht charters, villas, and spas. Visitors may click on "Exclusives" and "Best Buys" for savings on the most desirable hotel, tour, and cruise packages.

2. ***Allluxuryhotels.com*** claims to offer the lowest available rates at over one hundred destinations in the United States and abroad.

3. ***Find-luxury-hotels.com*** asserts that it has the best rates on four- and five-star hotels in select destinations worldwide.

4. ***Luxres.com*** represents Leading Hotels of the World—a consortium of more than 1,000 posh hotels worldwide. In select cases, dis-

counts of 15 to 40 percent may be offered. Sign up for its free e-mail newsletter.

Contacting Hotels Direct via E-Mail

E-mail isn't yet a universally effective method for finding out about hotel availability and rates. Hotel e-mail addresses aren't easy to get, and responses are inconsistent. Therefore, phone and fax remain the best ways of contacting hotels directly. You may be successful, however, by typing in the hotel property's name at a search engine—for example, "Sheraton Los Cabos." If the hotel has its own Web site, it may offer a "contact us" option, which you can use to obtain a rate quote.

I never underestimate the power of going direct. One experience of mine illustrates this point well. I needed three nights' accommodation while attending a meeting in Las Vegas. Through its online Web site, the Aladdin Hotel offered $75 for the first night, which was a weekday, and $139 for the two subsequent weekend nights. When I faxed the hotel, I obtained a rate of $69 per night for all three nights—a savings in excess of 40 percent!

A Final Word of Warning—Beware Cancellation and Change Policies!

Several online travel agents (such as *Expedia.com* and *Travelocity.com*) and hotel consolidator Web sites (such as *Hotels.com*) may charge stiff cancellation or change fees. For example, some sites will charge $10 to $25 to change or cancel more than 48 to 72 hours before your scheduled check-in date, but a full night plus tax for changes or cancellations within 48 to 72 hours of scheduled arrival. So be sure to read the fine print. Since booking with hotels direct will usually not incur any penalty if you cancel by 4 PM or 6 PM on the scheduled date of arrival, you can avoid onerous cancellation or change fees by calling with the hotel direct or booking at its own Web site if the prices are similar.

In Summary

- The more time you put in to finding a hotel, the more you will save. Because the range of options is enormous and you never know which Web site will offer the best accommodation at the lowest price, searching as many sites as possible increases your chances of getting what you want.
- The best uses of the Internet when seeking hotel accommodations are checking out "standard" prices, reviewing the range of the hotels' amenities, finding suitable locations by checking out *Terrafly*

.com, and viewing pictures of properties (for example, using *Google.com*'s "images" function).

- Go to *Hotwire.com* to find the bargain-basement fare for the standard of hotel room you want. Then check out the hotels' own Web sites.
- *Frommers.com*, *Fodors.com*, and *Concierge.com* are good starting places to decide where you may want to stay at your destination(s).
- Review the hotel offerings by the three major Internet travel agencies—*Orbitz.com*, *Expedia.com*, and *Travelocity.com*—to get a benchmark price for all the major chain hotels that have a presence in your selected destination. *Travelweb.com*, *Lodging.com*, *All-hotels .com*, and *Placestostay.com* may also be worth checking out.
- Go to *Luxurylink.com*, *Allluxuryhotels.com*, *Find-luxury-hotels.com*, and *Luxres.com* for top-of-the line properties.
- For regular travelers' opinions regarding hotels, visit *Tripadvisor .com*, *Epinions.com*, and *Globapost.com*.
- Cancellation and change fees when you book at certain sites can be stiff—sometimes up to one full night plus tax. Be sure to read the fine print before accepting a reservation with your credit card. Avoid the potential for onerous change or cancellation fees by booking with the hotel direct by phone or fax or at its Web site online.
- After checking online prices, check prices for a few hotels by fax or call the hotels' reservations departments, which will frequently beat online offerings.
- An alternative to faxing or calling a hotel direct may be e-mailing a hotel's reservations department. There is no directory of hotel e-mail addresses, so use a search engine to find the site of the hotel in question and click on the icon "contact us" if available.
- The authors' top ten hotel Web sites are:
    1. *Orbitz.com*
    2. *Travelocity.com*
    3. *Expedia.com*
    4. *Hotwire.com*
    5. *Quickbook.com*
    6. *LuxuryLink.com*

7. *Allluxuryhotels.com*
8. *Ase.net*
9. *Terrafly.com*
10. *Tripadvisor.com*

But don't forget to visit the hotel chains' own Web sites!

CHAPTER SEVENTEEN

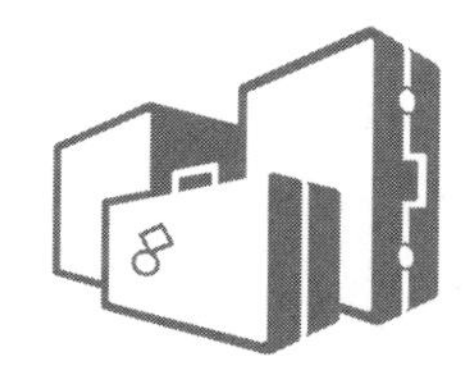

Car Rental Strategies

How to Put Those Savings in Overdrive

Recently, while driving a car I rented in the Boston area, I had to search for something I had left in the glove compartment. Among other things, I found the contract agreement from the prior occupant—and was amazed to see that he had paid $327 for his one week rental.

I was driving the same car, under the same conditions, for the same length of time—yet I was paying just $175 for a week—a whopping $152 less.

It seems to me that finding the best deal on a car rental has become a lost art, but it doesn't have to be for the savvy traveler. By following the strategies we outline in this chapter, you will consistently find the best deals on car rentals.

Since booking a car at home in the U.S. or in Canada can be a vastly different experience to renting abroad, we've divided the information into domestic and international car rentals.

Domestic

Who's the "fairest" of them all?

Avis, Hertz, and National usually rate among the higher-priced car rental companies, while Alamo, Budget, Dollar, and Thrifty are typically less expensive. National and Alamo have increasingly begun to link their operations since the two companies merged and declared bankruptcy soon after the turn of the twenty-first century, with National focusing on the business traveler and Alamo targeting the vacationer. Avis and Budget now fall under the same corporate umbrella, while Dollar and Thrifty also operate within a merged organization.

There are occasional exceptions to this rule that the "big three" can be found at the airport. For example, at the Orlando airport, Budget is within the airport terminal, while Hertz is located about two miles away.

The "big three" higher-priced companies are usually located adjacent to the airport terminal, while the lower-priced alternatives may sometimes be situated a short distance from the airport. Although not quite as convenient, off-location companies may offer customers the additional advantage of avoiding airport rental fees or taxes, which can be substantial.

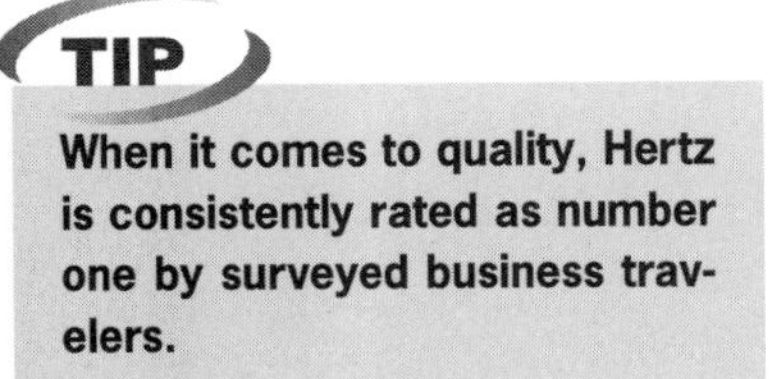

Enterprise is one major rental car company that has focused on suburban rather than airport locations. Although its prices may be similar to those of the other major car rental companies, it may not have a presence at major airports, so customers need to take a cab or get a ride, which will not only decrease the savings but take up valuable time.

Viva la Internet Revolution!

The one area of travel pricing that has unequivocally been revolutionized by the Internet to the consumer's advantage is car rentals. While consumers will not always get the best hotel rate on the Internet, just the opposite is true with car rentals. The Internet is the fastest, most effective way of finding the lowest car rental rates, especially if you are not seeking out any of the specific discounts we'll talk about later in this chapter. For the road warrior seeking speed and great value, the Internet is the epitome of one-stop shopping.

The best site to start for airport pick-ups is *Orbitz.com*. Once you input your arrive airport with your date of pick-up and drop-off, *Orbitz.com* will show you a detailed matrix with different-sized cars on the left and each major car rental company's options across the top. If you are interested in a certain size of car from a specific company, you simply click on that rate, and details regarding the rental, including taxes and any other charges (such as airport fees), are provided immediately. If you find a great rate online, complete your reservation by providing your name, contact information, and credit card, and then exit. You are done! If you subsequently need to cancel your *Orbitz.com* reservation, that can quickly be done online as well by clicking on the cancel icon within the car rental module. And if you register and visit again, the site will automatically remember prior information, thereby enabling faster repeat experiences.

The thorough traveler will check to see if he can find a better rate at other online travel agent sites such as *Travelocity.com*, *Expedia.com*, or *Onetravel.com*. Alternatively, each car rental company's own Web site must be checked if the pick-up location is other than at an airport.

Shop Around on Their Dime

An Internet site—whether it be the car rental company's proprietary site or a travel agency—will rarely allow the traveler to request a specific discount option. This must be done by talking to a real person, which is easily accomplished by calling a car rental company's toll-free number.

Before calling about a specific discount, be sure to first get a standard or benchmark price by checking *Orbitz.com*. Note that airport-based car rental agencies will rarely make reservations when called direct using their local number, but city or suburban car rental companies will be happy to quote a price and possibly negotiate.

TIP

For travelers who don't want to go online but can spare ten to fifteen minutes on the phone, calling at least two or three car rental companies can save significant amounts of money.

Hotwire and *Priceline*—Cyber Sites for Serious Savings

While we don't recommend *Hotwire.com* and *Priceline.com* for airfares unless you are the most price-sensitive and flexible traveler, we see little risk in making car rental reservations at these two Web sites.

Hotwire.com's car rental reservation system follows a similar process to that for booking flights. After you specify which airport you need a car rental, *Hotline.com* provides details for booking a car and a price which you must accept within sixty minutes. Only after you accept the offer and pay with your credit card are you provided the rental company's name.

Bidding for a car at *Priceline.com* also follows the model for air reservations. You name your price; if it's accepted, your credit card is charged and you're locked in.

ALERT

All car rental companies operating at certain airports are increasingly being relocated to a central off-site location. Getting to and from these locations can add fifteen to twenty minutes to your trip.

The main drawbacks with *Hotwire.com* and *Priceline.com* are:

1. If you need to change your plans, you're stuck, as your purchase is both nonrefundable and nonchangeable.
2. It's possible that the rental car location will be not just outside the main airport area, but actually off-site, perhaps a ten- to fifteen-minute ride away.
3. You probably will not earn any frequent flyer miles (but then, car rentals earn very few frequent flyer miles anyhow—up to fifty miles per day—and car rental companies increasingly charge for those miles!).

If you can live with these limitations, it may be worth checking out these two sites, as the discounts can be huge! Start with *Orbitz.com* to get your benchmark price. Next, try *Hotwire.com*, which has the benefit of providing you with a "rock bottom" price up front before you provide a credit card number—the only unknown being which car rental agency is making the offer and where it is located. Then go to *Priceline.com* and bid 50 percent of the best price you found at *Orbitz.com* or 65 to 75 percent of the price you obtained from *Hotwire.com*!

Watch Out for Those "Miscellaneous Charges"!

Car rental companies may impose a whole host of miscellaneous taxes and charges that can add up to 35 percent of a car rental cost. In some cases, the rental companies are not obliged to warn you in advance unless you specifically ask. My (least) favorite example of outrageous add-on costs is at Boston's Logan Airport, where the renter pays a 10 percent concession fee (that is, the cost of picking up a car from an on-site airport rental location) *plus* a 5 percent sales tax *plus* a $10 convention charge to fund building the new Boston Convention Center!

The "additional driver charge" is one of the biggest rip-offs in travel. Some car rental companies let your spouse or immediate family members drive without additional cost, while others charge extra for relatives who move into the driver's seat. Many more charge for each additional driver other than the spouse or immediate family member. There's no rational reason for an additional driver charge—except in the case of high-risk younger drivers. It's just another way to inflate your car rental bill. Still, if that is part of the rental car company's contract, don't try to fudge and let someone else drive without having paid that charge. If another driver is at the wheel during an accident, it is a violation of the contract that will almost certainly negate your insurance protection.

Let's summarize charges that may surprise you:

- Taxes, including those charged by the state and city
- State surcharges for improving transport infrastructure, such as to build highways or a convention center, which can be a single flat fee or a per-day charge
- Airport or concession fees to recoup costs of being located on-site at the airport, which can be 10 percent of your rental rate or higher
- Transportation fee (typically $5 to $12), which is especially common where car rental companies share a location and shuttle buses for vehicle pick-up
- Vehicle registration fee
- Additional driver charge—usually $3 to $5 per day

Although it may be impossible to avoid these charges if you need to pick up your car at the airport, it's still a good idea to ask about miscellaneous charges when you make your reservation (or check the fine print when booking on the Internet—some sites will detail the extra charges). If you can rent from a company that is a short distance from the airport, the cost of your rental may be significantly less, as you can save on airport fees or taxes.

Car Rental Insurance: What's on Offer?

The various insurance options available when renting a car are very expensive, potentially adding $10 to $25 to rental costs each day! The most common types of insurance are as follows:

- **Collision Damage Waiver (CDW) or Loss Damage Waiver (LDW).** This is usually priced at $10 to $25 per day and relieves you of responsibility for damage to the car, as well as theft or vandalism. Some coverage may only be for the first $500 to $3,000 damage, specifically intended to cover the deductible prior to your own personal insurance kicking in.
- **Supplemental Liability Insurance (SLI).** This is usually priced at $7 to $10 per day and relieves you of liability for causing injury or death to others, as well as damage to someone else's property—usually up to a maximum of $1 million. In almost every state within the United States, car rental companies have to provide some level of SLI coverage, but the amount (which varies by state) is usually insufficient for travelers with significant assets who could be sued for sums approaching or exceeding $1 million.
- **Personal Accident Insurance (PAI).** This is usually priced at $2 to $10 per day and covers you alone in case of injury or death. Most travelers are already covered under their own medical and term life insurance—and possibly under a travel insurance policy taken out for the specific trip.
- **Personal Effects Coverage (PEC).** This is usually priced at $2 to $4 per day and protects against theft or damage to personal items. However, these items are typically covered under your homeowner's or apartment renter's insurance policy. Furthermore, there are so many exclusions to PEC coverage as to make it virtually worthless.

Car Rental Insurance: To Buy or Not to Buy?

Before you sign up for any rental car insurance, check what coverage you might have through your personal auto insurance plan. In most cases, your policy will cover you while driving a rental car and you can decline the insurance offered. Your own car insurance policy will almost certainly cover you for collision damage (though you will still have to pay the deductible, just as you would if you damaged your own vehicle), while your liability coverage protects you if you are responsible for an accident that damages property or injures others. Health insurance policies will likely cover medical costs associated with injuries incurred in an accident. Basic theft from your vehicle may be covered by your homeowner's insurance minus your deductible, and unless you intend to transport valuable items, it's unlikely that your basic baggage will be worth the costs of insuring. As a smart traveler, you know to never leave valuables in your baggage or in a car (even if it's locked).

Employees of large corporations are often told not to accept any insurance offered by car rental companies because the company either has taken out such insurance (usually just CDW) or provides its own coverage (meaning that the company takes the risk). To protect yourself, be sure you understand exactly what is and is not covered—and under what conditions coverage may not apply.

Credit cards may cover you for collision-related damage—but not for any of the other types of coverage. Travelers who have the Diners Club Card (which will be discussed in detail in Chapter 18) are completely covered for *any* collision damage to the rented vehicle, known as *primary* collision coverage, for up to thirty-one days. This means that Diners Club will pay for any damages to the rental car in full, starting with the first dollar incurred to repair the damage, so you don't have to even pay a deductible. In fact, your insurance company is never contacted, meaning there is no risk to your driving record or car insurance premium. But certain luxury vehicles may be excluded from Diners collision coverage, so be sure to check with Diners Club in advance if you intend to rent a top-of-the-line vehicle. All other credit cards (including Gold or Platinum Visa, MasterCard, and American Express) provide only *secondary* collision coverage, meaning that the credit card company will only pay what your personal insurance will not cover. This gives the impression that they are providing a service, when in fact under this type of coverage they rarely have to pay anything—and you may still have to cover the deductible associated with your coverage.

If you do opt to take out insurance coverage from the car rental company, be sure you understand what *is* and *is not* covered. For example, standard car rental insurance contracts are deemed void if you drive off "standard" roads, are under the influence of alcohol, or have an unauthorized driver at the wheel. In addition, most companies will refuse to honor your coverage for a stolen car if the key was left in the ignition or the doors were not locked. Be sure to read the small print—and use common sense!

One final piece of advice: Drivers who do not have personal car insurance must be sure to take out supplemental car rental liability insurance, even if their credit card or charge card provides collision coverage in case of accidental injury or death. While state laws may require the car rental company to provide some minimum level of liability insurance, that coverage may fall short in case of a serious accident. If you rent often and don't own car or liability coverage on your own vehicle, check out nonowners insurance from a private insurance company. At $200 to $300 a year, it may be more cost-effective than having to take out insurance every time you rent a car.

One-Way Rentals and Drop-Off Charges

Travelers who wish to pick a car up in one city and return it to a different city will frequently be charged a drop-off fee, which can exceed $100. Some companies may not charge a drop-off fee, especially for renters requesting a negotiated corporate rate (see section below), but watch out for a higher per-day rate if the drop-off charge is waived. In many instances where pick-up and drop-off will be in different cities, the car rental company may charge a per-mile fee (in contrast to the usual "unlimited mileage" feature), which can add significantly to the cost of the rental for travelers who will be driving considerable distances. When faced with this circumstance, it definitely pays to shop around to find the best overall rental rate.

> **TIP**
>
> **Always check that the vehicle you are renting comes with "unlimited mileage." If not, you may pay substantial per-mile fees for exceeding a specified average number of miles per day (usually one hundred).**

A one-way car rental can sometimes work to your advantage if the rental company needs to move the vehicle from one location to another. An example might be picking up a car at a downtown location and returning it to the airport, in which case not only may the drop-off fee be waived, the car rental may be a less expensive rental. It pays to check!

The Joy of "Express Pickup"

> **TIP**
>
> **National's express program, known as Emerald Aisle, is unique in that it allows renters to choose their vehicles within the category they have reserved (such as compact, midsize, or fullsize). In our experience, however, the actual available choices are quite limited.**

Each of the major car rental companies has an "Express Pickup" program that expedites the pick-up process and allows the renter to bypass a counter. The traveler proactively completes an agreement as part of the enrollment package that includes preferred size of car, driver's license details, credit card information (which is revised periodically to account for updated card expiration dates), and a one-time indication of which insurance options will be accepted and declined.

In most instances, the traveler picks up the car rental company's shuttle bus outside baggage claim and is dropped off first at the area where the "Express Pickup" members' cars are parked. The renter goes straight to her car without stopping at the rental counter and can drive off since the key is already in the vehicle. She then drives to the checkout area where a gate attendant checks her driver's license. For this privilege, some car rental companies charge up to $50 for annual membership, but free membership can be obtained in a couple of ways:

1. By negotiating a corporate or small business rate (review "The Great Rate Chase" section below)
2. Through periodic offers to members of various frequent flyer programs—especially to those who have earned elite status

Does Size Matter?

Different car rental companies may classify the same car differently with respect to size, so don't assume that a fullsize is a fullsize is a fullsize without checking what specific models are included within a category. Most car rental companies have at least ten or even up to twenty different categories of car, from the smallest, usually known as "subcompact," all the way up to multipassenger vans. In fact, car rental companies' designation of size can be largely arbitrary—and is certainly not related to the actual length of the vehicle or engine's horsepower alone! Bottom line—if you have a preference for a certain size car, ask for examples of what models fall into that category. Better still, request a specific model—although availability cannot always be guaranteed.

When "Downsizing" Can Work to Your Advantage!

Don't assume. When calling to reserve a car—rather than booking on the Web where you can see several different prices simultaneously—be alert to the fact that smaller cars may occasionally be more expensive than larger ones! Check out the prices for each size of car offered by asking the phone representative the differences in price.

The tired cliché "less is more" actually has merit when it comes to renting cars.

If you want a midsize car, consider requesting a compact or subcompact; if it's a fullsize or luxury car you want, request a midsize.

Before you decide we've taken leave of our senses, let us assure you there is method to this madness. The reasons for downsizing your request are twofold:

1. If the rental agency has sold out of the requested size of vehicle, it will upgrade the car for free.

2. It almost always costs less to negotiate an upgrade at the counter as compared to reserving the size of car you actually want.

The Great Rate Chase

One book could never cover every possible rate out there, but we have compiled a focused list of those most likely to help you out on the next few pages. When you make your booking, you may be eligible for more than one kind of discounted rate, so make sure you check out which is most advantageous to you. In many cases, you are given a special rate or code number that must be provided when making a phone or Internet reservation.

Negotiated Corporate Discounts

There is power in numbers. Medium- and large-sized corporations with a significant volume of business travel will typically negotiate a corporate discount with one or two major car rental companies. These corporate rates are usually the best you can find for weekday rentals, which typically are more expensive than weekends because of increased demand by business travelers. In most cases, employees of these companies are mandated to use the special discount to track the amount of business generated as a basis for maintaining or even enhancing price breaks the following year.

But what if you're an entrepreneur or a professional with a relatively negligible car rental volume? Most car rental companies now offer a small business rate which, while not as good a rate as that of a larger company with a bigger volume of rentals, is still considerably cheaper than renting without any contract at all for weekday rentals. The small business agreement will typically guarantee a full-size car for around $45 to $50 a day just about anywhere within the United States.

There are typically no mandatory volume targets for obtaining a small business rate, and the package is frequently accompanied by free membership in "Express" programs that enable renters to bypass the counter when picking up their vehicle. (These include Hertz's Gold, Avis' Preferred, National's Emerald Aisle, Budget's Fastbreak, or Alamo's Quicksilver programs. Refer to details regarding "Express Pickup" programs above.) The experienced road warrior will set up small business preferred rate contracts with at least two car rental companies, which will provide a variety of choices and options.

AAA, AARP, and Other Important Abbreviations and Acronyms

Members of the American Automobile Association—known nationwide as AAA—may routinely obtain discounts that are 5 to 10 percent higher than

TIP

When making a car rental reservation over the Internet, follow up with a call to the car rental company. Have your confirmation number ready and ask if they will provide an additional AAA discount. While on the phone, ask about some of the other discounts specified in this section. Or, you can negotiate for additional discounts or (more likely) upgrades at the rental counter when you pick up your car.

other discounts, whether on weekday, weekend, or weekly rates. Members should always ask for the AAA rate when making a reservation by phone and have their membership on hand at all times for verification—not only for car rentals and for roadside service, but for discounts at hotels, fast food establishments, and tourist attractions.

If you belong to a significantly large trade association, be sure to ask whether your affiliated organization has negotiated a special discount. AARP is one of the largest and most successful groups when it comes to getting a special rate, so if you qualify—and don't let vanity stop you since you only have to be fifty years old to be a member—be sure to mention it.

Weekend or Holiday Specials

For travelers renting over a weekend, or where some of the rental days will include the weekend—such as Thursday at noon till Monday at noon—the weekend rate will frequently beat any other rate, including a negotiated corporate or small business rate. Similarly, rentals in major cities that occur over holidays such as Thanksgiving Day, Labor Day, or Memorial Day may also be eligible for a holiday rate.

When booking over the Internet, weekend rates will automatically be incorporated into the specified rate if your rental dates coincide with a weekend. However, if you book a combination of weekend and weekday rates over the Internet, check that you can obtain different rates for each to capture the lower weekend rate rather than one uniform high weekday rate for each rental day. You may have to make two separate reservations. If renting five days or more, check out the weekly rate, as explained in the next section.

Cheaper by the Week

Rentals of five, six, or seven days are eligible for the weekly rate, which will almost always be superior to renting by the day. There is no early drop-off penalty when requesting a weekly rate for a five- or six-day rental, provided you state upfront when making the reservation that you will only be renting for that time period. Conversely, if you state that your rental is for seven days and take advantage of the weekly rate, but return the car early (for example, after four days), you may incur an early drop-off penalty (or be charged by the day).

Combine the Fly with the Drive

If you make an airline reservation directly with the airlines, you will no doubt be asked whether you need a rental car. It never hurts to check out the rate offered. Who knows? You may luck into a special discount offered by the partner car rental company.

Similarly, airlines may offer packages that bundle air, hotel, and car, or just air and car. (This benefit may be advantageous to both leisure and business travelers, especially for last-minute trips. Check with the airlines' vacation package desk.)

Frequent Flyer Discounts

Car rental companies frequently offer discounts to members of various frequent flyer programs, though no proof of membership (such as frequent flyer number or card) is ever requested. The traveler doesn't even have to be flying in to the destination on the particular airline mentioned to qualify for the frequent flyer rate. Simply ask for the American, Continental, Delta, or even Southwest Airlines frequent flyer rate.

Even though you may not be flying on Southwest Airlines, requesting its frequent flyer rate will often provide the most significant frequent flyer program savings.

Noteworthy Newspaper Ads

Car rental companies will frequently advertise special discounts in the weekly travel sections of newspapers. The advertisement may require that you request a specific code number—mentioned in the ad—when calling to make your reservation. Discounts can be substantial. Pay attention to other stipulations; for example, such promotions occasionally require payment with a certain credit card or may be restricted by certain blackout dates.

Cash in Those Coupons

Car rental agencies provide many discount coupons through their airline and hotel partners, which are distributed with activity statements from airline frequent flyer and hotel frequent-stay programs. The *Entertainment Directory,* essentially a book of coupons, is especially useful for obtaining discounts on rentals from all major car rental companies. By far the most common discounts are for:

- Upgrades, typically requiring a minimum rental of three or more days
- One free day, usually applied to a rental of two or more weekend days or three or more weekdays

- A savings certificate, such as $15 off a weekend rental or $25 off a weekly rental

In most cases, these coupons cannot be used in conjunction with any of the discount rates, such as the AAA or AARP discounts described above, but always ask—you have nothing to lose. And the sales agent will often tell you which one is the best discount opportunity for you to use.

Prepaid Gas Option? Don't Even Think About It!

The shrewd traveler will never consider buying into the prepaid gas option, for a couple of reasons:

1. The offer is for a full tank of gas, so unless you return the car on dead-empty, you pay for more than you need.
2. The prepaid gas price is usually higher than the average price you can get from local gas stations.

Always Return Your Rental Car with a Full Tank of Gas

Presumably you have taken the advice of the previous section and not accepted the prepaid gas option. This means you will need to return your car with a full tank of gas. Failure to do so will incur an exorbitant gas fee (usually around two to three times the normal price). So add a few extra minutes before you return your car to fill up.

Erratic Service

Renters may find that car rental company service standards differ, especially when dealing with nonairport locations which may be:

- Privately owned and simply license the major car rental company name
- A franchise network—Thrifty is a good example
- Affiliated with subsidiaries abroad

If you experience problems with your rental car that the local affiliate does not resolve, be sure to contact headquarters.

Frequent Flyer Miles with Car Rentals

In the "good old days," generous amounts of frequent flyer miles were awarded to travelers for each car rental. Today, those generous rewards have disappeared for the most part, and most car rental companies impose a tax on the traveler for the small amount of frequent flyer miles awarded! At the time of writing this book, that penalty is restricted to travelers requesting frequent flyer miles and does not apply to those who request hotel points.

As far as we can tell, no car rental agency shines in awarding frequent flyer miles (usually a maximum of fifty miles per day, which is worth less than a dollar and for which you may be charged $0.50!), so shop around for the best price or remain loyal to the company that offers you the best service. Occasionally a car rental agency will have a special bonus offer, such as 500–1,500 miles with the rental, but you may be required to request a special code number when booking or present a certificate at the car rental counter when picking up the vehicle.

When Your Driving Record Isn't Spotless

If you have a black mark on your driving record, you may be in for a rude awakening when you check in at the car rental counter. Some companies wait until you show up to review your driving record, and if your driving record does not meet its standards, they have the right to turn you away. Since they are not required to give you any advance notice, this could put you on the spot, not only having to scramble to find another car, but having to do some embarrassing explaining if you are traveling with others.

Some car rental company Web sites warn potential renters about what their company considers to be unacceptable with respect to one's driving record. Your best bet is to check the company's policy if you're concerned your history might be questionable.

Most U.S. travelers should only consider renting a car in English-speaking countries, or European countries where driving is also on the right and rules of the road are similar to those in the United States. In those countries where English is not widely used, or where characters rather than letters compose the written language—such as in most Asian countries—the savvy traveler should select alternative methods of transportation.

Unique Twists and Turns When Driving Abroad

We're not in Kansas anymore.

As you might guess, renting a car in another country can be quite an adventure. Once again, covering all the myriad possibilities in this one chapter is an impossibility.

The following guidelines will help you navigate some tricky rental car waters when you travel outside the United States by telling you what to expect and where you can save money.

Look for the Best Overall Price

In planning a trip to Israel for a week, I followed my standard procedure of first checking out offerings on *Orbitz.com* for rates on a luxury vehicle.

A Thrifty car came up as cheapest, with Budget not far behind. However, on closer scrutiny, I found that Budget actually offered the lower *overall* price alternative, because Thrifty charged mandatory collision insurance coverage, while Budget would waive the charge if my credit card included such protection. (Of course, my trusty Diners card covered me for collision damage in full.)

Before I committed to the Budget car, I checked all the major car rental company sites, as well as the travel desk affiliated with my American Express Platinum card (for which I pay a hefty annual fee $395), but found that none could beat the *Orbitz.com* price.

The Best and the Worst Prices in Western Europe

As a general rule, car rental rates are least expensive in Germany and most expensive in Italy. Rates in the United Kingdom and France fall somewhere in between.

If you wish to drive through several countries in Europe, it makes sense to fly into Germany to pick up your car (provided, of course, you can get a competitive airfare!).

Those Inevitable "Other Charges"

In a prior section, we discuss additional charges unique to domestic rentals. Some examples of additional charges you may be forced to pay on rentals abroad include:

TIP

Any time you rent a car, you want to ask what the grand total price will be. So ask about *all* of the additional charges or taxes you will have to pay, because you can bet there will be some.

- Collision and theft insurance is mandatory in Italy
- VAT (value-added taxes) or city taxes can be significant in certain European countries, occasionally reaching 20 to 30 percent of your car rental charge
- A road tax may add $1 to $2.50 per day, while a highway user fee can add an additional $0.60
- Airport surcharges may be substantial—for example, 13 percent at Brussels airport
- A per-mile charge above a certain daily allowable (alternative is "unlimited miles," which is always preferable)

When you rent on the Internet, additional charges are usually itemized, so you shouldn't suffer any nasty surprises. If you make your reservations by phone, ask the car rental company about all additional add-on costs and request documentation of these costs by fax, e-mail, or regular mail with your confirmation.

One last precaution: Check your final credit card statement to be sure no additional surcharges have been added! If you notice any new and unapproved charges, call your credit card company and the rental car company to dispute them immediately.

Renters abroad have on occasion found that their final rental car credit card charge is much higher than expected, based on the car rental company stating that the returned vehicle had incurred significant damages. It is difficult to dispute such allegations, not least when you are thousands of miles away from the country making the assertion several weeks after returning the vehicle. Protect yourself by doing the following:

- **Ensure comprehensive insurance (by way of your personal policy or by paying with the Diners Club card or accepting applicable coverage from the car rental company).**
- **At drop off, have a car rental company staff person check the car's condition with you—then have him sign a statement that the car has been returned in perfect condition.**

Know Exactly What You're Renting

As always when you travel, the meanings of certain words and terms vary from country to country. This is an important concept to keep in mind when renting a car abroad.

A European subcompact or compact car may be significantly different from what we consider to be that size here in the United States—in fact, those cars can be downright tiny! For example, "intermediate" may actually refer to what we know as a "compact" rather than a midsize.

And then there's the little matter of what's considered to be standard features. Automatic transmission and air conditioning—which are expected with every car rented in the United States—are not always included on European cars, and may well carry a higher price tag, adding as much as $100 or more per week. If these features are important to you, make sure you stipulate their inclusion and ask that the price quote reflects this.

Watch Out for Drop-Off Charges

The drop-off charges when renting at one location and dropping off in another (even within the same country) can be significant. If this is your intention, it definitely pays to shop around.

The Power of the Advance Purchase

Some major U.S. rental companies offer discount rates within Europe when you request your rental from the United States as a 7-, 14-, or 21-day advance purchase. However, the car rental company may charge your credit card for the full price of the rental immediately, and the amount charged may in some cases be nonrefundable.

As always, it pays to shop around—and to make sure that you fully understand the terms of your contract before you provide your credit card number or sign on the dotted line.

When renting a car abroad, make sure you ask for all the details regarding the kind of car you will be getting within the category you've chosen, any restrictions or unforeseen add-ons, and the all-inclusive price.

When East Does Not Meet West

Renting a car in Eastern Europe can be very expensive. And driving a rental car from a western European country into Eastern Europe is often prohibited by the rules of the rental contract, mainly because of the higher risk of car theft in the Eastern Block countries. It's sometimes possible for renters intending to drive from Western into Eastern Europe to purchase insurance, although the price will probably be steep.

An Additional Caution About Insurance

All our advice about car rental insurance—as discussed in the section above—applies both to domestic and international car rentals. However, travelers should check that their personal car rental insurance covers them for international rentals *specifically* in the countries where they will be driving, especially when renting a car outside Western Europe. Some countries—Ireland is one example—may be excluded from routine policy coverage.

Certain kinds of insurance protection are required by car rental companies in some countries. For example, car rental companies in Israel may require that the traveler take out collision coverage, because the risks of theft or vandalism are high in that country. Although these kinds of stipulations should be mentioned at the time of booking, don't assume that you have all the information you need. It's your responsibility to make sure you know all the hidden costs, so you can compare equivalent rentals. Take the initiative and read the fine print of an Internet reservation agreement or ask for information on all costs—and what they're for—that will be applied to your rental contract. Only then can you effectively compare prices and prevent any nasty surprises when you pick up your car or—worse yet—when you get your bill!

One final caveat—even if you do take out collision damage insurance for your rental abroad, there may still be a deductible (typically $300 to $500). Be sure to check. There may be an extra fee you can pay to reduce or even eliminate this deductible.

Beware When Booking Abroad on the Web

If your car rental in another country is anything other than a simple airport pickup, with a drop-off at the same location, booking on the Web may not be the way to go (except at *AutoEurope.com*—see later section regarding car consolidators). European car rentals have subtleties not apparent on a typical Web site that could lead to some unwelcome surprises. For example, you might reach the site of a franchised local affiliate and find that all information is given in the native language—which you don't speak. If you had planned to pick up the car at a site other than an airport, or drop it off at a different location, you may find the procedure confusing or the cost prohibitive.

Disparity in car sizes, stipulations of the contract, hidden taxes, a variety of currency exchange rates—all of these variables make it worthwhile to call and speak to an agent in person when renting abroad to make sure you know what you're getting, how to get it, and what the cost will be.

Call from the United States to Make Your Car Rental Reservation Abroad

The rates for car rentals usually soar when you make the booking over the phone in a foreign country. If you don't book a car before you travel abroad, call a rental agency located in the United States—yes, even if you're calling from a foreign country—and book your car with them. The long-distance charge will pale in comparison to the money you'll spend booking a European car rental from within Europe. Better yet, go online to a U.S.-based Web site, considering the cautions mentioned in the previous section.

Car Rental Consolidators

In Europe, Kemwel, Europebycar, and AutoEurope act as lower-priced car rental companies or discount distribution channels for major car rental companies when they have excess inventory. Frequently, the traveler who has rented through one of these European companies will actually pick up his car at a major car rental company such as Hertz or Avis.

AutoEurope proves the exception to the rule about avoiding Web bookings for overseas rentals. It maintains an excellent Web site, where reservations can be made for rentals not only in Europe, but Australia and South Africa as well. Additional features include:

- The capability of obtaining a 5 percent discount for senior travelers
- A price guarantee regardless of currency fluctuations once your reservation is confirmed

- The potential to set up a lease agreement for a brand new Peugeot if you will be keeping the car for at least seventeen days (refer to the next section for details on leasing agreements in Europe)

Finally, click on AutoEurope's affiliate *DestinationsEurope.com* for low airfares from the United States to Europe.

AutoEurope	888-223-5555	(*www.autoeurope.com*)
Europebycar	800-223-1516	(*www.Europebycar.com*)
Kemwel	800-678-0678	(*www.kemwel.com*)
	877-820-0668	

Leasing

For travelers who will be renting in Europe for at least seventeen to twenty-one days, leasing a car will frequently provide the best value. The lease terminates when the renter returns the car on the prearranged date. Shop around for the best deal.

Like Your Car? Take It Home with You!

European luxury car manufacturers offer the world traveler the chance to purchase his vehicle at a discount below sticker price from the manufacturer's production facility, drive it around Europe, and then have it shipped home at no extra cost. Other travel perks may also be included in the package deal, such as air and hotel for reduced or no cost.

If this opportunity interests you, you can find more information from the following auto companies:

- Mercedes Benz (Germany) *Mbusa.com*
- BMW (Germany) *Mmwusa.com*
- Volvo (Sweden) *Volvousa.com*
- SAAB (Sweden) *Saabusa.com*

In Summary

- Car rentals are a frequently overlooked component of savings potential for world travelers and road warriors.
- The Internet has revolutionized the speed with which one can obtain a reservation and get an excellent rate. In particular, *Orbitz.com* will quickly compare prices for every category of car across all major car rental companies.

- Car rentals through *Priceline.com* and *Hotwire.com* offer the opportunity for excellent savings, with the greatest risk being that the rental car company may be at an off-airport location, usually no more than a fifteen-minute ride away. Try *Hotwire.com* first, then put in a bid at *Priceline.com* for 65 to 75 percent of the rate *Hotwire .com* offered!
- Designation of car size (such as midsize or fullsize) is not uniform across all car rental companies. For example, a Pontiac Grand Am may be a midsize at one company and fullsize at another. Ask for examples of vehicles available within a category you desire.
- Using affiliation rates such as AARP or AAA, trade association discounts, or coupons obtained from the *Entertainment Directory* or with frequent flyer statements will require that you contact each car rental company's toll-free number to check out special rates inaccessible over the Web.
- Small business travelers will set up an agreement with one or more car rental companies, enabling lower rates and free membership in "express programs." Employees of major corporations may be mandated to use the corporate discount negotiated with a car rental company. Employees who are requested not to take out insurance when renting a car for company business must check what is—and is not—covered.
- To thoroughly compare various car rental options, savvy world travelers and road warriors will check whether there are hidden costs such as taxes, airport fees (which can be high though unavoidable at certain airports), transportation or shuttle charges, or drop-off fees if returning the vehicle to a different airport from pick-up. Certain car rentals abroad may incur mandatory insurance coverage costs. Bottom line—ask what the *total* cost of the rental will be.
- Do not take out the prepaid gas purchase option since it is unusual that you will be able to return the car having used a complete tank of gas, that is, with the fuel gauge at empty. Always fill your vehicle at a gas station reasonably close to the airport before returning it or you will pay the car rental company to fill up at two to three times the normal price of gas.
- Travelers who have insurance on their own vehicle usually do not need to take out additional insurance coverage on domestic and most international rentals. (Check with your insurance company especially if going abroad.) Paying with a Diners Club charge card covers all domestic and most international rentals for pricey collision damage—including paying for all expenses incurred through an accident—whereas all other credit and charge cards provide only

secondary coverage, kicking in after your personal car insurance company's coverage. If you travel frequently but do not own a vehicle and hence have no car insurance coverage, consider purchasing a nonowner or umbrella liability policy, for which you can purchase up to $1 million coverage costing $200 to $300 per year.

- Be sure to check that your rental is "unlimited miles." The alternative is a per-mile charge if you exceed a specified average number of miles each day (usually one hundred), which will be expensive if you plan to drive significant distances.
- To avoid lines when picking up a rental car, savvy travelers join "Express Pickup" programs whenever they receive a promotion offering free membership. Entrepreneurs and professionals are eligible to join car rental companies' special small business programs that offer guaranteed discounts during the week (when rental rates can be higher) and membership in the car rental companies' express pickup programs, all available at no charge.
- Unique caveats for international travelers are to book from the United States and seek out cars for pick-up in countries that are typically cheaper (such as Germany) rather than expensive (such as Italy). The price for a vehicle with an automatic transmission and air conditioning may be considerably higher. Furthermore, watch out for extra unanticipated charges, such as value-added taxes (VAT), that may increase the cost of the rental substantially. Because car sizes are traditionally smaller in Europe, travelers should ask what the U.S. equivalent would be. Advance-purchase rates may offer huge savings, but are often completely nonrefundable.
- When returning a car abroad, have a staff person sign off that the vehicle is in pristine condition. This will prevent any subsequent unanticipated credit card charges based on alleged damage.
- Given the subtleties associated with car rentals abroad, Web bookings should be made with caution, especially if you are picking up the car in one country and dropping it off in another. Smart travelers will check whether there are any add-on costs at the time of booking and request that these charges be confirmed in writing, together with exact directions to pick up the vehicle if not at an airport location.
- European rentals over seventeen days may qualify for a leasing option. World travelers seeking to purchase a luxury European car may pick up their new vehicle at the factory as part of a special package that frequently includes a tour package, a discount on the sticker price, and free shipping of the car to the United States.

CHAPTER EIGHTEEN

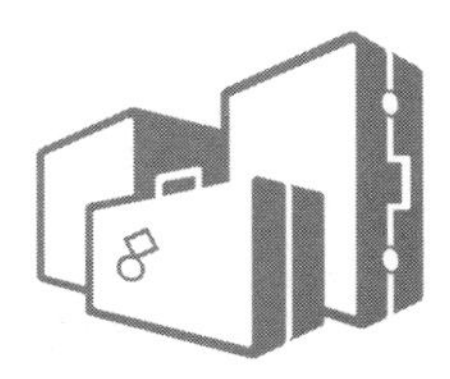

The Affinity Card Advantage

Why Smart Travelers Buy Now and Pay Later

The summer our family took our around-the-world trip, we were able to do it in style. We traveled first class across Japan on the bullet train, cruised Alaska on a luxury Princess-line ship, enjoyed a business-class roundtrip flight from Los Angeles to London and Nairobi . . .

Those four roundtrip business-class tickets on British Airways were all free, "courtesy" of Diners Club, which I use for all travel expenses and anything else I can. As an affinity card, Diners Club has had a standing annual promotion with British Airways in which earned miles—that is, those miles banked in a Diners Rewards account until needed—are doubled if converted into British Airways frequent flyer miles during the specified period.

Credit cards allow users to carry a balance that may be paid off over several years, while charge cards require complete payment within one to two months of each transaction. But beware! Carrying a balance on frequent flyer affinity credit cards can incur significant interest costs.

How Frequent Buyers Become Frequent Flyers—The Wonderful World of Affinity Cards

An affinity card is simply a credit or charge card that pays back the cardholder with a reward of some kind for its usage.

In general, for every dollar you spend with an airline affinity credit card, one frequent flyer mile is automatically deposited into your frequent flyer account, usually posting within four to eight weeks of your credit card statement date. Obtaining a MasterCard or Visa credit card that automatically earns miles or points can therefore boost your frequent flyer mile or hotel point balance considerably. Annual fees are typically higher than for nonmileage cards—usually ranging from $25 to $125, depending on

TIP

Like conventional (or nonaffinity) cards, credit cards that earn frequent flyer miles typically come in three varieties—Classic (or regular), Gold, and Platinum. Classic have the lowest annual fees, lowest credit limits, and highest interest rates. Platinum cards have the highest annual fees, highest credit limits, and lowest interest rates. Features for the Gold card fall in between the Classic and Platinum. When approved for a new affinity credit card, Classic will offer the lowest enrollment bonus, while Platinum will offer the highest. Gold falls somewhere in between—although several banks have now eliminated Gold cards.

whether you select a Classic (regular), Gold, or Platinum card. Credit card companies offer frequent flyer mile enrollment bonuses that typically range from 2,000 to 10,000 miles once you are approved for the card. However, for travelers who carry significant balances, exorbitantly high interest rates (15 to 19 percent is standard) charged by affinity credit cards can effectively wipe out the benefit of free travel. Therefore, travelers who carry large balances on their credit card will be much better served by giving up their affinity credit card in exchange for a credit card that carries a much lower interest rate (or do balance transfers from high affinity to low interest credit cards). Carrying a charge card (such as Diners Club or American Express) that mandates complete payment within thirty to sixty days can be another way for the overspender to enforce personal spending discipline—yet still earn frequent flyer miles.

When you first use your new affinity card, you may notice that bonus or earned miles or points may not appear in your original frequent flyer account. This commonly happens because, when you receive the affinity card, you also are assigned a new frequent flyer account, meaning that you have two accounts accruing miles. Once you receive your first statement from your new (second) account, simply call the credit card company to cancel the new account number and have all points credited to the original account number. Alternatively, see if the airline affiliated with your frequent flyer account will be willing to merge the new account into your original one, ensuring that all future miles earned post to your original account.

Doing a balance transfer or cash advance from an affinity card does not usually earn any frequent flyer miles. Given high interest rates, don't do it!

But Are Affinity Credit or Charge Cards Really Worth Their Annual Fees?

While affinity credit and charge cards are outstanding tools for earning frequent flyer miles, they do come at a price, usually an annual fee and higher interest charges for unpaid balances than ordinary cards. You want to make sure that the miles you earn are worth whatever the costs are for using that card.

Here's how to calculate whether it's cost-effective to use a credit card with an annual fee to accrue frequent flyer miles. Let's assume 1,000 frequent flyer miles is valued at $16 and that your annual credit card fee is $80. Using these numbers, you would have to earn 5,000 miles ($80 divided by $16 equals 5), which corresponds to $5,000 in spending to cover your annual fee. If you do not meet the minimum spending threshold, get a card with a low or no annual fee, and allocate your savings toward purchasing an airline ticket. Naturally, significant enrollment bonuses can decrease your needed threshold spending—at least for the first year.

Most airline affinity credit card companies now offer mileage-earning cards without an annual fee. The catch is that you only earn half a mile for each dollar charged.

Fantastic Plastic—Credit Card Bonuses

Because the credit card market is so competitive, some airline affinity cards will offer certain promotions to entice new customers. One is to offer approved applicants frequent flyer mile or hotel point bonuses; another is an introductory low interest rate for the initial six months on new or transferred balances. One of the most tantalizing is a certificate for a free companion ticket, typically for coach-class travel within the United States and Canada. Be sure to check what special promotional offers are available when applying on the Internet or by phone.

Delta is the only major U.S. airline for which an affinity Visa/MasterCard is not available. Rather, Delta has aligned with American Express, which distributes a Delta Skymiles credit card. Similarly, Starwood and Hilton hotels are aligned with American Express credit cards, although a Hilton Visa card is also available.

The Lowdown on Hotel Affinity Credit Cards

With the exception of the Starwood American Express card, which provides the traveler with one hotel point per dollar spent (more on this in the next section—refer to the fourth bullet point), the hotel credit card payback is not as lucrative when compared with frequent flyer miles earned from an airline affinity card. We therefore do not recommend any hotel affinity credit card other than the Starwood card—unless you have more frequent flyer miles than you know what to do with, and need some hotel points to ensure your free vacation! One other reason to sign up for a hotel affinity credit card is to take advantage of a lavish sign-up bonus. After that, however, lock the card in a drawer so you can continue using those other cards that provide you with more lucrative paybacks.

To find out about credit cards for your preferred airline, you can go to your airline's Web site and click on "credit cards" in the frequent flyer section, or using any search engine, type in the name of your preferred airline and "credit card." A list of airline credit cards is provided as Appendix I.

Three Airlines and a Hotel

The following credit and charge cards offer unique benefits that should be considered, especially by travelers who are unsure which airline credit card is the best choice for their unique circumstances.

- Miles earned from spending on the American AAdvantage MasterCard count toward million-mile status (lifetime Gold elite status) and two-million-mile status (lifetime Platinum elite status). And with AAdvantage's vast network of partner airlines, you can reach just about any destination on earth with your earned miles.

- The Alaska Airlines Visa card offers a unique benefit in that Alaska frequent flyer miles can be used for awards with that airline's unprecedented number of high-quality partners—American, Continental, Northwest, Hawaiian, British Airways, KLM, Qantas, and Lan Chile—in addition to free flights on Alaska.

- American Express's Delta credit card has been very popular with Delta and non-Delta frequent flyers, not least because it has offered double miles for all supermarket, gas, drugstore, hardware, U.S. postal service, and Delta ticket purchases—every time. Special promotions are frequent, including double miles for all purchases during a specified period or double miles for year-end taxes paid with the card. Finally, Delta Platinum cardholders receive a free companion certificate each year they renew, but this certificate may not be used with a deeply discounted ticket. The annual fee of $125 is reduced by $50 if you hold a personal American Express charge card. For all these reasons, carrying the Delta American Express card should be considered by every serious world traveler.

- Another outstanding credit card offering from American Express is the Starwood card. Although this is a hotel card, the "currency" of Starwood loyalty points can be used toward hotel stays throughout the Starwood system or transferred into most major airline frequent flyer programs on a 1:1 basis, with the minimum transfer usually being 2,500 points. (For Starwood Platinum Elite members who stay fifty nights or twenty-five stays per year in Starwood hotels, this minimum is waived.) Therein lies the power of the Starwood program—earnings may be used for free hotel stays *or* applied toward flights! One additional perk associated with the Starwood points program is that transferring 20,000 Starwood points into any airline earns an additional 5,000 points, effectively providing the cardholder a 25 percent bonus. Look for mileage transfers from Starwood to an airline to occur within thirty days. Furthermore, when Starwood points are used for free hotel nights, there are no blackout dates or capacity controls. That means you can redeem your award at any participating hotel, on any day of the year, as long as that hotel has space. And Starwood owns some superluxury brands, including St. Regis and Luxury Collection, which both feature extravagant properties worldwide. If you're wondering whether to use Starwood miles for free flights or hotel stays, just remember that the *value* of earned points will usually be higher when converting them to free flights rather than free hotel stays, especially if you will use your frequent flyer miles for premium-class (business- or first-class) award tickets.

Considerations When Selecting an Affinity Credit Card . . .

There is no clear-cut "best" airline or hotel credit card. Less frequent travelers may prefer to select an airline credit card that accrues miles with their favorite airline, supplementing miles earned from infrequent flying with other sources such as hotels, car rentals, and long-distance phone service. Alternatively, travelers loyal to one airline who travel extensively may prefer to obtain a credit card that accrues miles from another airline, which diversifies their redemption opportunities. The savviest world travelers acquire flexible cards (such as the Starwood American Express card) that enable mileage conversion into multiple airline programs!

Those who travel smart will almost always carry an affinity credit card, but charge cards must also be considered an important part of the tool set for maximizing frequent flyer miles, as we will discuss in the next section.

. . . Or an Affinity Charge Card?

As mentioned above, charge cards are similar to credit cards in all but one respect: The balance may not be carried from month to month, but must be paid in full, usually within twenty to sixty days. When it comes to earning frequent flyer miles, charge cards differ significantly from affinity credit cards. While affinity credit cards automatically post earned frequent flyer miles to the linked frequent flyer or hotel loyalty program within four to eight weeks of the statement date, charge cards store the earned miles indefinitely, allowing the cardholder to transfer as few or as many earned miles into a

Banked miles from a charge card become inactive if you cancel your account. Do not close your account until your mileage balance with the charge card is zero.

variety of participating airlines or hotels whenever he wants—or even to obtain merchandise.

American Express and Diners Club are the two major charge card companies. American Express is accepted at more places than Diners Club in the United States, while acceptance is about equal abroad. Both cards are accepted by all major airlines, hotels, car rental companies, cruise lines, and other travel suppliers.

American Express

American Express has long enjoyed a prestigious image in the area of personal and business charge cards. Until recently, the standard Green and Gold American Express cards did not automatically earn frequent flyer miles—the cardholder had to call Membership Rewards to enroll and pay an additional $35 annual fee to earn miles. For new members, American Express now automatically includes enrollment in membership miles, offering two options:

1. American Express Rewards (Green $65 per year; Gold $90), which only earns half a mile per dollar spent. Beware of misleading advertising that does not make the deficiencies of mileage earned on the Rewards card crystal clear to the consumer. We do not recommend this offering, given that an additional $45 per year for the preferred card gets you double the miles.

2. American Express Preferred Rewards (Green $110 per year; Gold $135), which earns one mile per dollar spent. We strongly recommend the American Express Preferred card for use on daily necessities, such as supermarket, drugstore, gas station, hardware, and U.S. post office purchases—all of which earn double miles that are banked without expiration, ready to transfer into over twenty airline frequent flyer programs as well as into hotel loyalty programs or for use toward free merchandise. The benefits of the Gold card include preferred seats for cultural and sporting events, as well as free shipping and handling on some mail order and Internet purchases.

Diners Club

The Diners Club is the best charge card for frequent travelers. Diners is superior to American Express in the key areas of:

- **Service.** We have found that service provided by American Express is marginally acceptable, whereas service from Diners Club is consistently excellent. Here's one example that will no doubt resonate with all of us: When you call Diners Club, a real live articulate person answers promptly, ready and willing to actually talk to you and help you with whatever you need. Call American Express, and you must follow a serious of recorded prompts, first entering your card number, then some additional information, such as your selected password, as a security precaution. After you've done this, a person comes on the line and grills you further, asking you to repeat your card number and then answer the same or different security question! After jumping through these hoops, you may get your problem taken care of, although even then you can't be sure. As compared with Diners Club, where a billing dispute is typically resolved quickly, disputes can go on indefinitely with American Express—and sometimes never be resolved to your satisfaction.

■ **Frequent Flyer Miles.** With both American Express Membership Miles associated with the Preferred card and Diners Club Rewards, each dollar charged earns one mile. (With Diners, each dollar actually earns two points—but still the equivalent of just one mile.) In both programs, miles are banked and never expire. However, Diners miles may be transferred into every major airline and hotel program to "top off" any account from which the traveler wishes to redeem an award. Note, however, that while transfers from Diners Club to an airline take about two to three weeks at a cost of $0.95 per 1,000 miles to offset the cost of taxes, you can expedite transfers to occur in one to two days for a fee of $35. In contrast, American Express miles cannot be transferred into at least four significant airline programs: United, American, Northwest, and British Airways. Another plus for Diners is that it frequently offers promotions for bonus miles, such as the double-miles promotion with British Airways featured in this chapter's opening story. Bonus miles promotions are rare and less lucrative with American Express.

■ **Car Rental Collision Insurance.** While driving a luxury BMW through Ireland during the summer of 2000, I found myself on one of that country's famous narrow bridges, forced to drive the extreme edge to let an oncoming car pass. Branches from a dense bush scratched the door of the car, requiring repairs—and Diners Club paid every cent of damages. Diners Club is the only credit card offering car renters *primary* collision coverage when car rental insurance is paid for with their card, which means any damage to a rental car is reimbursed by Diners in full, never involving the traveler's personal insurance. All other credit cards (including Gold and Platinum Visa and all American Express cards), offer *secondary* collision coverage, meaning that the card's insurance only covers what the traveler's personal vehicle insurance will not pay. With secondary coverage, the renter is eligible to pay his deductible, following which his personal car insurance policy must pay the covered amount. This means that the occurrence is documented on the driver's personal insurance record—which could contribute to an increase in personal insurance premiums.

- **Payment Grace Period.** Diners Club gives its members sixty days to pay; American Express allows just twenty to thirty days (and in some cases even less time). If an American Express cardholder is late with a payment, the earned miles are forfeited for that month unless the cardholder pays a $15 penalty fee.
- **Cash Withdrawal at ATMs.** With the Diners Club card, cash can be accessed from almost any ATM, with no special arrangements other than selecting a PIN. The transaction incurs a fee, just as any credit card cash advance would. In contrast, there are very few ATMs from which cash can be accessed with an American Express Rewards, Preferred, or Platinum card, and even then only after special forms have been filled out, submitted, and approved, enabling the cash advance to be drawn from the cardholder's personal checking account.
- **Airport Lounge Access.** Diners Club cardholders may use the eighty club lounges located at airports in most major international cities (and two in the United States). Only the American Express Platinum card offers a competitive package, allowing the traveler and up to two companions use of Delta, Continental, and Northwest lounges on the date of travel with any of these three airlines.

Finally, Diners Club recently made a credit card available to its customers. Called the "Diners Montage" card, it has many of the benefits associated with the Diners charge card. However, the most notable exclusion is primary car rental coverage. Customers may carry balances up to their credit limit, just like a regular credit card. The Montage card offers three types of benefits packages for annual fees of $0, $25, and $75. Since frequent flyer miles are only offered with the $75 option, this would be our suggested choice.

Is Premium Really Better Than Regular?

During the summer of 2000, we stayed at the Singapore Ritz Carlton in a luxurious four-room suite with spectacular views from every room for the incredible rate of $182 per night—a special rate we obtained through American Express Platinum's travel service. The unique benefit when paying with the prestigious American Express Platinum charge card is special recognition from affiliated hotels that may result in a space-available upgrade.

Diners Club Carte Blanche

Diners Club Carte Blanche card comes with an annual fee of $300. The best benefit it offers is one free companion ticket on British Airways per year, in any class of service, with one paid ticket. Golfing fanatics may value the added benefit of membership at three hundred prestigious golf courses worldwide (including St. Andrews and Gleneagles in Scotland). However, at $95 per year, the standard Diners Club card provides such outstanding services that this upgrade seems unnecessary for most world travelers and road warriors! However, if you consider the free companion ticket on British Airways to be an extraordinarily valuable perk (which it is!), go for it.

American Express Platinum Card

The American Express Platinum card has gained a reputation as an ideal card for jetsetters willing to pony up a $395 annual fee. The benefits include:

- Occasional hotel upgrades or other benefits—such as late checkout or a special welcome gift upon arrival—at luxury hotels booked through the Platinum desk's travel agency service, although the rates are often considerably higher than those you can get by applying the strategies outlined in this book
- A program offering one free companion roundtrip ticket with a paid business- or first-class ticket on at least fifteen domestic and international airlines
- An excellent high-end travel magazine, *Departures*, mailed six times per year
- "Free" access to Delta, Continental, and Northwest airlines' lounges when flying any of those airlines
- Travel emergency assistance around the world, including referrals to English-speaking medical and legal professionals, and, when necessary, provisions for emergency evacuation at no cost to the cardholder

However, standard American Express service (which translates to "mediocre"), is a travel agent service whose prices are usually much higher than you can obtain for yourself, and enrollment in its standard but below-par mileage-earning program make this card a substandard choice unless you see any of the benefits outlined above as especially useful.

We suggest that you use the American Express Platinum card if you fly Delta, Continental, or Northwest frequently and would like to visit their lounges (although access is granted only on the day of your flight), want to take advantage of hotel upgrades, or think you will benefit from the free premium companion airline tickets. Otherwise, pay with your regular

Diners card for all eligible purchases to benefit from Diners' enhanced mileage program and vastly superior service.

American Express Centurion Card

The Centurion card costs $1,000 per year, with an express invitation and charges exceeding $150,000 per year being prerequisites for obtaining this prestigious card. Additional benefits over and above those offered with the Platinum American Express card include elite-level membership in US Airways, Delta, and Continental Airlines, as well as with Hyatt and Starwood Hotels.

We suggest you acquire this card if your ego needs a boost. Better yet, save a grand and just frame the invitation to show your friends that you *could* have owned the card—and wisely resisted!

Other Bank Credit Cards That Offer a Free Ride

To profit from the frenzy associated with earning free travel from credit card use, several banks offer cards that promise the user a free airline ticket simply by reaching a certain threshold of dollars spent using that card. Novice or naive travelers are often enticed into accepting the offer based on promotions that advertise "any airline" and "no blackout dates." What they miss is the small print explaining that the bank will purchase a ticket on any airline for a specified amount, usually up to $400 or $500. To give the bank the opportunity to purchase a deeply discounted ticket, the award rules mandate at least twenty-one days' advance notice with a Saturday night stayover. Furthermore, if that ticket is to be used over a peak period, when airfares are higher than the $400 to $500 maximum allowed, the customer will pay the difference—which could amount to several hundred dollars. And, failure to reach the threshold spending within a defined period—often three years—may result in forfeiture of accrued points. Some cards offer earnings denominated in miles, which may be misleading, since these miles are not combinable with frequent flyer miles the consumer has in any airline accounts. On the plus side, these bank travel credit cards have lower annual fees—typically $0 to $50—with lower interest rates on balances, which can be as low as 10 percent or as high as 19 percent.

A new type of travel rewards credit card has emerged from travel agent Web sites such as *Orbitz.com* and *Travelocity.com*, designed for those who don't charge enough to earn sufficient miles for a free trip. For example, the cardholder can earn a $100 certificate toward an air ticket purchased online from the travel agent for spending just $7,500. Our principal objection to this reward earning capability is that $7,500 spent on a standard airline affinity credit card would traditionally get you 7,500 miles, worth at least $120 (assuming 1,000 miles is valued at $16). Furthermore, using an American Express card can rack up double miles for routine purchases, such as from supermarkets, drugstores, gas stations, and U.S. post offices.

Given that frequent flyer miles earned from debit and charge cards affiliated with major airlines never expire and can complement miles obtained from all other sources (such as flying, hotel stays, car rentals, and long-distance phone service), the savvy world traveler will toss these offers where they belong—in the "round file"!

Separating Business Expenses from Personal

I sat across the table from one of the world's greatest sculptors at lunch in a Sheraton hotel restaurant overlooking the ocean in Fiji. He explained how he uses a frequent flyer mile Visa card for personal expenses, and a nonaffiliated card that earns no miles for business expenses. His logic—an accountant told him to separate personal from business expenses.

There is a much simpler (and possibly cheaper) way to achieve his accounting goals—and earn frequent flyer miles from *all* purchases. Simply ask the bank that has issued your mileage-earning card for one or more additional cards, which will usually have a different number. There is typically a nominal or no extra charge for additional cards. Sometimes the issuing bank will offer a mileage bonus for requesting additional cards—I once received a 5,000-mile bonus simply for requesting an additional Delta Skymiles American Express Platinum card for my wife. Or simply get another frequent flyer mile credit card unrelated to the one you use for personal charges. For example, the Starwood American Express card is an outstanding choice, free the first year, and $35 each year thereafter.

What About Debit Cards?

A debit card acts like a Visa or MasterCard, providing all the convenience of a credit card anywhere in the world. However, since the amount you charge automatically comes out of your checking account, you can only spend what you already have, which makes this an ideal proposition for those who want to avoid or do not qualify for a credit card. While almost all airline affinity card banks also offer debit cards for an annual fee around $20 to $30, most earn only 0.5 miles per dollar spent. The exception is the Premium Citibank AAdvantage debit card (annual fee $65), which offers one mile per dollar spent.

In Summary

- Affinity cards allow you to earn airline miles or hotel points with purchases, typically at a ratio of one mile or one point per dollar spent. Credit cards allow you to carry a balance, but interest rates for affinity cards are extremely high. Charge cards must be paid in full within twenty to sixty days.

- Make sure you spend enough—and earn sufficient miles each year—to cover your annual fee. If the annual fee is $80, you must spend at least $5,000 and earn 5,000 miles each year, assuming 1,000 miles is valued at $16.
- Frequent flyer miles earned from credit cards automatically post to the linked frequent flyer account within four to eight weeks of your statement date. With charge cards, the earned miles are banked indefinitely without expiration as long as your account is active, until you call to have a transfer made to any of several participating airline frequent flyer or hotel loyalty program accounts. Transfers from a charge card to an airline or hotel program may take two to four weeks, although Diners Club can expedite the transfer in one to two days at a cost of $35.
- The best card for frequent travelers is the Diners Club charge card for a variety of reasons, including excellent service and the most lucrative and versatile frequent flyer program.
- The American Express Starwood credit card is second best, as it has some of the benefits associated with the Diners card (notably the flexible transfer of miles into most airlines), but lacks many of the Diners advantages, such as excellent service and primary collision rental car coverage. On the plus side, American Express is more widely accepted than Diners Club.
- The American Express Preferred credit card is an excellent choice for supermarket, drugstore, U.S. post office, and hardware purchases because of double miles accrued at these retail outlets. The Delta American Express card offers double miles at the same outlets, but the American Express Preferred card holds a distinct advantage since it enables transfer of earned miles into many airlines—including Delta.
- For places that only accept Visa or MasterCard, the American Airlines AAdvantage MasterCard or Alaska Airlines Visa card are the best choices.
- To separate personal from business credit card expenses, and earn frequent flyer miles without paying two annual fees, simply ask for an extra card or cards from your issuing bank. Each card may have a different number, simplifying the task of separating personal business expenses. There is either no charge or a nominal annual fee when you request additional cards that are itemized separately—

and be sure to ask if there is a frequent flyer mile bonus for requesting an additional card!

- Debit cards may be a good alternative for those who want to avoid or do not qualify for a credit card. Almost all debit cards, however, earn half a mile per dollar spent—with the exception of the Premium Citibank AAdvantage debit card (annual fee $65), which offers one American Airlines mile per dollar spent.

CHAPTER NINETEEN

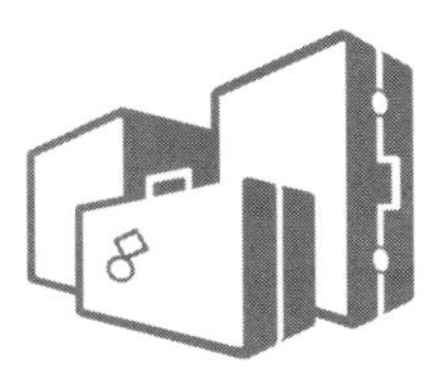

The Art of the Complaint

How to Make It Right When Things Go Wrong

If you travel, something is bound to go wrong, sometime, somewhere. The more you travel, the more legitimate complaints you will have with airlines in all classes of service, hotels of all grades, and car rental companies.

An Example of Great Customer Service

My wife and I, with our then one-year-old son, were staying at Chateau Lake Louise in the Banff area of the Canadian Rockies. This magnificent traditional hotel looks just like a castle out of a fairytale, with awe-inspiring views of the azure blue lake against a magnificent backdrop of Canadian Rockies.

Thanks to my guerrilla travel tactics, we were paying just $120—instead of the rack rate of $300—for our one-night stay at this breathtaking resort.

We settled into our comfy king-sized bed as our toddler son snuggled into his crib with his bottle. Before long we heard the empty bottle bouncing on the carpeted floor, our son's traditional way of saying he was ready to go to sleep. We all drifted off to dreamland, cozy and more than content in our luxurious accommodations.

In the middle of the night, my restful sleep was broken by a sharp elbow to the ribs from my wife.

"Theo, wake up. There's a mouse in the room!"

At first I thought I was dreaming—or that *she* was dreaming. A mouse in our room at this luxurious and prestigious landmark hotel? I didn't hear anything, but just in case she was right, I clapped my hands, intending to startle this rodent in the hope he would run off into the night.

The next morning, when my wife retrieved our son's bottle from under the crib, she got a surprise.

"Aha!" she shouted triumphantly. "Look at this!" She held up the bottle, and on its liner were tiny teeth marks, *indisputable* proof of our tiny rodent visitor.

We cleaned the liner and attached it to my letter addressed to the hotel's general manager at checkout. Of course, we received a full refund for our room, which attests to one of the reasons why this hotel has sustained its deservedly high rating.

Few topics give rise to as much passion among travelers as experiences with customer service. By far the majority of casual discussion about travel centers on the good and bad experiences themselves. But talk of how travel companies respond to complaints is much less common because travelers don't "fight back" nearly as often as they should.

The savvy world traveler knows when, how, and to whom to complain, making sure he or she receives the best possible product and service, every time. We'll break it down into the three time frames in which you might lodge a complaint: immediately, after the fact, and over the long term when you receive no response.

Complaining Right Away (or "On the Spot")

■ **Speak Up Now Instead of Later.** Addressing a problem you experience sooner rather than later enhances the probability the issue will be resolved to your satisfaction.

Take the example of my traveling on an American Airlines transcontinental flight one Friday afternoon. I had been guaranteed my favorite "upgrade"—an aisle seat at the rear of the plane with two guaranteed empty seats next to it. But storms in the New York area delayed departure by forty minutes, and while we waited at the gate, a new passenger came on board and took one of my promised seats. I immediately went to the flight purser, who simply told me there was nothing she could do. Not satisfied with this answer, I asked for a supervisor. It took the supervisor just ten seconds to devise a remedy, instructing the purser to move the new passenger to another open window seat.

If I hadn't spoken up, I would have lost the comfort and convenience I had been promised for that flight. No amount of complaining later would have changed that.

TIP

One important tactic we've learned is to be pleasant when first bringing our complaint to a staff person. We're more likely to get the solution we want and still enjoy the goodwill of the staff if we don't blame anyone in particular, but take the attitude that sometimes "things happen" and here's what we would like done about it. Trust us, it pays off!

On another occasion, my family and I checked into the beautiful Hyatt

Acapulco late at night, tired, and more than ready to enjoy a much-needed long weekend. Because I had given Hyatt a lot of business in the previous year, I had faxed the hotel in advance and requested an upgraded room for the duration of our four-day stay. When we reached our room, we found it to be small, with no view of the fabulously famous bay.

Next morning, I returned to reception and asked to talk to the general manager. He was most apologetic as he acknowledged my loyalty to Hyatt the prior year as well as the faxed request for a superior room. He immediately upgraded us to a huge suite with a view encompassing the entire magnificence that is Acapulco's bay—and threw in a complimentary breakfast each day to boot.

■ **Know How and Where to Take Your Complaint.** The very nature of travel dictates that things don't always happen the way you anticipate. Knowing how to complain—politely, firmly, effectively, and as soon as possible—will help you weather those little bumps in the road and get what you want, and maybe more.

A good rule of thumb is to start with the staff person who originally helped you, explaining your complaint and asking for the remedy you want. If you don't receive satisfaction, ask to speak to a manager or supervisor. Sometimes you must go directly to the top, as I did with the hotel room in Acapulco. Don't be afraid to go as high up in the managerial hierarchy as necessary to get what you believe is justified.

It doesn't matter whether it's the wrong room or a bad meal, an inadequate rental car or an undesirable airline seat. Don't accept the unacceptable; speak up as soon as possible and you'll be surprised at how successful you can be in getting what you want and deserve.

When You Have to Complain After the Fact

My wife and I had meticulously planned and organized a package tour of Scandinavia to coincide with business I had in Germany. The first night of our trip we were on our own, and planned to stay at the Radisson SAS, one of Copenhagen's premier hotels with views overlooking that city's world famous Tivoli Gardens. Using my guerrilla tactics for hotel savings, I had obtained the fantastic rate of $128 for a room with a published rack rate (the full price charged only when the hotel is at full occupancy) of $310.

As we entered this magnificent hotel, we were dazzled by the cascading waterfalls and coolly elegant marble that graced the hotel lobby. I remember walking up to the reception desk, confident—maybe even a bit smug—in knowing that I had confirmed my reservation and incredibly good rate at this five-star property just prior to departing the United States. You can imagine my dismay when the immaculately dressed woman behind the counter could not find our reservation! Because it was late and we were exhausted, we decided against taking the time and trouble to try and find something better somewhere else.

Since there was no qualified person on staff, such as a supervisor, who could unravel the snafu, I did the next best thing: I asked for a room with the best rate possible. The room we eventually stayed in cost about $200—$70 more than the one I had previously arranged—and it was lovely. My wife, who was pregnant at the time, still remembers the towels and bathrobe placed over heaters, and I found the furnishings so well appointed that I have been a fanatic for Scandinavian furniture ever since.

After we returned home, I decided to let Radisson know of their reservation glitch and to ask for the refund of the $70 extra we had to pay. I sent off a letter to the president of Radisson SAS Hotels in Europe, calmly explaining exactly what happened.

"We loved your hotel and had a marvelous stay," my letter said. "The only problem was that the reservation we made, having confirmation number XYZ *and* reconfirmed by me on such-and-such a date, did not exist in the hotel's computer system. We hope you shall be able to refund the difference between our confirmed rate and what we ultimately did pay."

Fast forward two months to an afternoon soon after our eldest child Trevor was born when I received a call at work from my wife.

"Guess who just called?" she quizzed me.

"Ed McMahon?" I asked optimistically.

"No, silly goose! The president of Radisson SAS in Europe. He was calling about that letter you sent, wanting to know if we're going to be back anytime soon so he can make it up to us."

"What did you tell him?" I asked.

"Well, Trevor was making quite a racket in the background, which he could hear. I just said, 'I don't think we'll be going anywhere for a while.' But he was very nice, apologized, and said he'd be sending us 'something' in the mail."

One week later, an envelope arrived with a letter of apology and a check—not for the $70 I requested, which would have been the difference between our confirmed rate and what we paid; not $200, which would have been a full refund; but for $400. Yes, you read correctly—a whopping $400: $200 as a full refund for the one night, *and* an additional $200 to welcome our newborn son to the world.

I would have been happy with the $70, which I thought was fair, given my advance planning and agreement with Radisson Hotel's central reservations. But the way in which my complaint was handled reinforced my original opinion that this was a top-rate, first-class organization.

Radisson also understood the value of a happy customer. I can't tell you how many times my wife and I have related this story to friends over dinner, or how many times I have told this story to large audiences at seminars and conferences around the world. Radisson SAS has received far more positive PR than $400 could ever buy—and they deserve it.

Of course, your attempt to resolve a problem right away as we discussed in the prior section may be unsuccessful. This is especially true of major U.S. airlines that have adopted the attitude "only he or she who shouts the loudest will get heard." If the issue is important enough to you, a letter of complaint may be your next step.

How to Write the Letter of Complaint

Writing the complaint letter that brings the results you want is not difficult, but it does require some organization and often a certain doggedness. Here are the key elements we've found that work for us time and again:

■ **Document the Facts as Soon as Possible.** Write down the key facts as soon as possible—preferably as the problem occurs or soon after it. Ask for names of people, and note the time, the place, and so on. Safeguard any tangible proof such as boarding cards or receipts. Take a photograph if your complaint relates to something visual, such as a stained carpet, torn drapes, or a hotel window overlooking a dumpster when you were promised an ocean view!

■ **Be Timely.** Send the correspondence within six weeks of the adverse occurrence—and preferably within two weeks if the problems were of a significant nature. Although issues can still be resolved as long as six months after they occur, the matter loses impact if addressed after a considerable time has elapsed.

■ **Word-Process Your Letter.** Although correspondence can be handwritten, you give yourself an edge with a printed letter. Use a word processor, taking advantage of the spell-check feature, and print out the letter on plain white paper. The more reader-friendly your letter is, the more likely it will be read and your request acted upon. And be sure to keep a copy for yourself, with all relevant documentation, which we'll discuss below.

■ **Personalize.** When writing any letter of complaint, address it to a specific person, preferably the chairman, president, or CEO of the company. This information is almost always available at the company Web site—check out "press releases" or "contact us." Your letter will frequently be referred to customer service for a response, but it will carry greater weight coming from the executive suite. When writing about a problem at a hotel, target the hotel's general manager. The name of the hotel general manager is usually on the first page of the "list of services" binder placed on the desk in your room—often as part of a welcome message.

■ **Be Brief and Businesslike.** Describe the problem as simply and logically as you can, so the reader can easily understand what went wrong and why you feel you should be compensated. Keep the letter to two pages at the most—one page is even better! No businessperson has the time or patience to deal with longer correspondence, and you're more likely to get the response you want if you can succinctly state your case.

■ **Describe the Context and Damages.** Introduce the complaint with an explanation as to why you were using that company's services. State your expectation and why it was important that it be met. And explain what kind of setback you suffered due to the problem: For example, did a delayed flight cause you to miss a business meeting? Was a memorable vacation spoiled? Did you pay more than you should have? Most important, if you are a regular customer who has attained elite status with that airline or hotel, emphasize your loyalty to position yourself as an especially valued customer this company does not want to lose.

■ **Attach Relevant Documentation.** Send along anything that might support your case. For complaints regarding a flight, attach a copy of your ticket or boarding card. When lodging a complaint about a hotel stay, send along a copy of your bill. For those problems that are visual in nature and can be photographed, remember that a picture speaks a thousand words. And wherever possible, always send copies, not the originals—keep those in your tickler file!

■ **Request Specific Yet Reasonable Compensation.** Perhaps the greatest omission from letters of complaint is a request for specific and satisfactory compensation, such as a partial or full refund, a voucher toward a future flight or hotel night, or bonus frequent flyer miles or hotel points. The request should be reasonable; asking for seven free nights because the air conditioning was faulty during a one-night stay will get you nowhere and devalue what otherwise might be a valid complaint. Again, by explaining what the problem cost you personally or professionally, you can request compensation that matches your loss and increases your chances of getting what you want.

TIP

You are much more likely to get compensated by way of free flights or nights than in cash—but don't hesitate to ask for either.

■ **Give an Ultimatum.** If you have some leverage to motivate the company to grant your request, by all means use it. Remember to keep your tone professional: You don't want to threaten the person or company you are writing to, but do want to suggest that inaction will bring about negative consequences. You can state that failure to resolve the matter to your satisfaction by a specific date will leave you no choice but to move your business to the competition or take the matter to small claims court. Don't be afraid to spell it out, politely but firmly.

■ **Use an Attention-Getting Envelope.** Mail your correspondence in a priority-mail envelope, which costs around four dollars anywhere within the United States. For a serious matter, consider sending your correspondence via Federal Express or another overnight mail service. Although more expensive, next-day delivery always gets attention! Federal Express also has a cheaper three-day delivery option—and the recipient has no idea whether you requested rush priority or not!

■ **Persist.** Keep a copy of your correspondence in a tickler file. If you have not received a response after six to eight weeks, send another copy. Handwrite across the top "*Second request—please have the courtesy to respond.*"

The Last Resort

When you've tried to remedy your problem on the spot with no success, and followed up with letters and documentation but still with no results, then you have to take more serious action. Here are four additional actions to take:

1. Dispute either a partial or complete amount of your credit card payment. (Savvy world travelers always pay for travel services with a credit or charge card for this reason.) But the charge must be disputed as quickly as possible—preferably within sixty days of the transaction.

2. Take the vendor to small claims court. As long as the vendor is a company doing business nationally, you have a right to sue in your local small claims court—but you need to identify a contact (with specific name and address) in a local office or subsidiary. For example, if your complaint is with a major airline, find out the name of the manager at the airport together with the mailing address.

3. Have your attorney write a letter—but this can be expensive. Or contact the Legal Advice Hotline (*Legaladvicehotline.com*/800-595-2948), which will write a legal letter for you for $49.95.

4. Submit your complaint to the ombudsman—a fancy word for "consumer advocate"—of a major travel magazine such as *Condé Nast Traveler*, or *National Geographic Travel Magazine*. If your dispute does come to the attention of an advocate—and only a few do—he or she will contact the company on your behalf, possibly including

the issue and company response in the publication. Sometimes just sending a copy of your request letter that has been submitted to an ombudsman can prompt the offending company to settle the problem to your satisfaction.

Knowing Your Rights

You can reach the Department of Transportation at *Airconsumer.ost.dot.gov,* or call 202-366-2220. This Web site enables you to document your complaint against an airline and publishes each airline's rules known as "Conditions of Carriage" (including policies regarding involuntary bumping and lost baggage), which can also be requested by writing to DOT, Consumer Protection Division, 400 Seventh Street SW, Washington, D.C. 20590.

Remember to Acknowledge the Good as Well as the Bad

Most U.S. surveys analyzing customer satisfaction—in all industries—note that levels of service have progressively deteriorated. However, occasionally you will experience excellence. When this happens to us, we ask those responsible for providing the superior service to provide their name and position, as well as their supervisor's name, along with the address of the company headquarters, so that we can mail a letter of commendation.

We do this for a number of reasons, but the most important one corresponds to our sense of what is fair and right. If we're going to complain when we do not receive an acceptable level of service or product, we should also acknowledge service that exceeds our expectations.

Smart businesses regard letters of complaint as an opportunity to find out what's not working and find a way to fix it. Conversely, complimentary letters can reinforce which processes and personnel are performing well, ensuring that the company keeps up the good work.

Everyone likes to know when he does a good job, and we are more than happy to give that acknowledgment.

In Summary

- When things go wrong, try to get the problem resolved immediately. Go to a manager or higher authority if your complaint is not satisfactorily resolved on the spot by the appropriate staff person.
- If your complaint can only be addressed after the fact, write down the details, including key names, to ensure accurate recall.
- Use a word processor to write and print out a brief businesslike letter to the most senior executive *by name*, preferably within six weeks of the event. Explain why you used the company's service,

what went wrong, the impact of the unfortunate experience, and what specific compensation will keep you happy. Don't forget to attach as much proof as possible (receipts, boarding pass, photograph). Keep copies of everything!

- If you don't receive a response within about two to three months, resend a copy of your original letter and documentation with a handwritten note in the top right-hand corner stating "Second request—please have the courtesy to respond!"
- Last resort strategies include disputing the charge on your credit or charge card, taking this issue to small claims court, having your attorney write a letter, or asking a travel magazine ombudsman to represent you.
- Check out *Airconsumer.ost.dot.gov* to document your complaint against an airline, as well as to obtain details of each airline's rules or "Conditions of Carriage."

CHAPTER TWENTY

The Last Word

A Quick and Easy Checklist of Ultimate Savings Strategies

Take a moment and answer this question: What would you consider to be your top ten most enjoyable and unforgettable memories?

If you're like most people, at least a couple of those fond memories will involve travel. It could be the family vacation where everything went right or a life-changing pilgrimage to your ancestors' homeland. But while research shows that over 90 percent of us include a trip we have taken among our most memorable life events, more than 80 percent of us don't believe we can afford to travel in the style we prefer as often as we would like to . . .

Of course, if you've been reading this book, you now see things differently. You know that you hold in your hands one of the most powerful tools for traveling in not just comfort but luxury—at a fraction of the retail cost. In fact, you may have already started *using* the strategies presented in this book to achieve your travel dreams . . . because you have discovered how you can afford to be a savvy world traveler and road warrior on any budget, at any age, right *now*!

Our goal has been to give you an accurate, efficient, and easy-to-utilize resource to help you realize your travel goals and fantasies. To that end, we'll use this final chapter to recap what we believe are the ten most important strategies for the road warrior and savvy world traveler. Master these strategies, and you'll be well on your way to excellent travel experiences, at a fraction of retail prices.

1. Plan as Far in Advance as Possible. Planning ahead is the single most important strategy you can use to consistently travel where you want, when you want, at the lowest possible price. Planning seven days in advance is better than nothing at all, planning a month out is better yet, planning a year ahead of time is ideal, especially if you want to use frequent flyer miles and hotel points. That's not to say you should purchase your air ticket or book your car rental one year in advance, but to simply start the wheels in motion. When you begin figuring out what you want to do well in advance of your travel date, you give yourself the opportunity to research various strategies and maximize your options.

2. Buy Your Airline Ticket at the Right Time. The best time to purchase a nonrefundable coach-class airline ticket is when the airlines are having a sale, which occurs at least six times each year. However, if you must purchase a ticket for travel less than one month out, you may not have the luxury of waiting for a sale: Your best bet then is to try for a fourteen- or twenty-one–day advance-purchase price. For travelers who intend to use an award for an air ticket for coach-, business-, or first-class travel, the best chance of obtaining a free seat on the preferred flight will generally be 330 days prior to the date of travel, when seats are loaded into the airlines' reservations systems. This is especially important for travel over a peak period, such as around Thanksgiving or the Christmas/New Year holidays, when standard frequent flyer mile award seats are quickly snapped up.

One final word of caution when purchasing a nonrefundable fare from a major airline: Understand the "use it or lose it" rules about changes. If you will not be using your nonrefundable ticket, be sure to call and cancel before the scheduled departure time for the outbound flight or else the entire ticket may become worthless! When you reschedule at the same time or at a later time (within one year of your ticket being issued), you will also have to pay a change fee (usually $100 but may be higher for international travel)—and any difference between what you paid for your original ticket and the current price (if higher).

3. Be Flexible. When you make flight reservations, flexibility can save you a considerable amount of money. Online capabilities at various travel sites can help you obtain a good fare or award seat, but you can also check each of these possibilities over the phone:

- Be prepared to *make a stop*—Everyone likes to fly nonstop, but if you can live with one or two stops *en route*, you may on occasion have a better chance of getting the fare or award seat you want.
- Travel during a *different time of day*—If you can widen your window of departure and arrival times, you may significantly increase your chances of getting a good fare.
- Check out *different dates* for your outbound or return flights—Changing your itinerary by just one or two days can sometimes reduce your fare by hundreds of dollars.

- Consider flying into or out of *alternative airports*—Most places you fly to will have at least one and maybe more airports within a one hundred–mile radius—and usually closer. It may be worthwhile flying into an airport other than your first choice. Consider, of course, what using an alternative airport will cost in terms of extra time and transport expense.

4. Go Online. The Internet has revolutionized the way we select travel services, and one of the best sites we've found is *Orbitz.com*. In spite of (or perhaps because of) the fact that *Orbitz.com* is owned by the major U.S. airlines, the airfares offered are frequently the lowest. And, again, if you can be flexible in your travel arrangements, *Orbitz.com* offers a dazzling array of options that also includes hotels and car rentals. With a simple click of the mouse, *Orbitz.com* will display fares for all major airlines (and some minor ones too) for your requested route, including such variables as:

- Zero, one, or two stops
- Alternative times
- Different departure and return dates
- Cities with airports within 25, 50, and 100 miles

Other useful retail Internet travel reservations sites include *Expedia.com* and *Travelocity.com*. Consolidator Web sites worth visiting include *Cheaptickets.com*, *Overstock.com*, and *Flights.com*. *Hotwire.com*, which is a distribution channel for distressed inventory, is an excellent site to get a price quote that will provide you with a benchmark on how low major airlines are willing to go for an airfare. *Bestfares.com*'s Quickfare Finder informs you about the best possible fares for a specified itinerary, including airfare code for each specific airline, advance-purchase requirements (such as seven or fourteen days), when the fare expires, blackout dates—and similar information for alternative airports and member-only prices if you book through *Bestfare.com*'s consolidator agency (but this requires paying a $60 annual membership fee).

Our favorite site for hotels is *Tripadvisor.com* since it presents articles, guidebook reviews, traveler feedback, and links to reservations for thousands of hotels worldwide. The simplest and most effective Web site to use for car rental reservations is *Orbitz.com*.

5. Achieve Airline and Hotel "Elite" Status. Whenever possible, road warriors travel on the same major airline—or its partners—to accrue 25,000 or more elite-qualifying miles within a calendar year and receive the coveted "elite" status that comes with that milestone. Be aware that the mileage threshold for achieving elite status may be lower for certain airlines, for example, 20,000 for Alaska Airlines. Conversely, Delta and Continental led the way to apply only 50 percent of flight miles toward elite status qualification the following year when traveling on a discounted ticket. Members of the elite class enjoy a variety of benefits, including baggage check-in at business- or first-class counters, bonus miles every time they travel, and the opportunity to receive upgrades on domestic flights, either free or for a nominal dollar amount. Hotels offer frequent-stay loyalty programs, which reward elite members who have stayed about ten or more nights during a calendar year with benefits such as room upgrades (often to the concierge level, especially for the highest elite levels) and bonus hotel points. First-level hotel status may also be obtained by acquiring certain credit cards such as Marriott Visa card or American Express Platinum card (for Starwood).

6. Use Frequent Flyer Miles and Hotel Points Wisely. Smart travelers know the value of their frequent flyer miles and never waste them on a ticket that can be easily purchased at a relatively inexpensive price. Instead, they get the highest return on those miles by redeeming them for premium travel—meaning business or first class—on international trips or for last-minute flights, which can be very expensive. The same goes for using hotel points.

Here's a quick example to illustrate this key point: Traveler A uses a 60,000-mile coach-class award to purchase a free ticket to Asia, which he could have bought for around $900, if purchased in advance with a minimum five-day stay. The value of his award can be found by dividing $900 by 60, which comes to $15 per 1,000 miles. Traveler B uses his 100,000-mile award for a first-class ticket to Asia that would otherwise cost $10,000. The value of his award—$10,000 divided by 100—comes to $100 per 1,000 miles, clearly a much better use of his hard-earned frequent flyer miles award.

7. Purchase Frequent Flyer Miles Regularly. Purchasing frequent flyer miles is the most effective strategy for assuring confirmed upgrades at a fraction of the retail business- or first-class fares. For example, if a first-class ticket to Europe costs $8,000 or redemption of 100,000 miles, purchasing the miles at $30 per 1,000 will save over $5,000. That's a guerrilla-sized savings of 65 percent!

The world traveler who wants to fly in luxury regularly can do so by systematically purchasing miles from not just one but many airlines. This strategy works much like a savings plan, ensuring a large payoff for the frequent flyer who consistently purchases the maximum amount of miles allowed to his account. Frequent flyer miles may be purchased at "retail" prices from the airlines as:

- **Personal Miles.** With a cap on the amount that can be bought each year.
- **Gift Miles.** For example, your spouse can buy miles to give to you, and you can reciprocate.
- **Top-Off Miles.** Select airlines allow you to deposit miles into your frequent flyer account if it is a few thousand miles deficient for redeeming a specific reward.

American Express allows the primary cardholder enrolled in Membership Miles to purchase up to 500,000 miles per year. These can be transferred into frequent flyer mile accounts such as Delta, Continental, Hawaiian, and Virgin Atlantic.

Finally, the savvy traveler is always on the lookout for special promotions that allow the frequent flyer to accrue miles at a price that is lower than the retail cost of approximately $30 per 1,000 miles—for example, by switching long-distance phone carrier, getting a new affinity credit card, or subscribing to a magazine.

8. Optimize Coach-Class Comfort. If you don't have a way to guarantee an upgrade on a flight, make sure you select an aisle or window seat when making your reservation. Ask the agent to check that the adjacent seat is open when making your reservation, and if you are an elite member of certain airlines' frequent flyer programs, ask if he will block that open adjacent seat (which means it won't be assigned unless the flight approaches capacity). If you and a companion are flying, ask for an aisle and window in a row where a middle seat is open. Your chances that the middle seat will stay open are greater if you select a row as far back as possible.

At check-in or at the gate, once again ask for your ideal seat, preferably with an open seat adjacent to you (or even an entire row!). If the flight does not appear to be full, and if you don't need overhead space for your carry-ons, you may want to get on last, taking any open row or seat to your liking. Or, if you are already seated, move to a better seat as soon as you hear the announcement that the door has been closed.

Bring your own gourmet food and snacks, which guarantees that you eat exactly what you want, precisely when you want it! And don't rely on the airlines for reading matter—bring your own newspapers, magazines, and books. Frequent travelers will do well to invest in a top-of-the-line noise-canceling headset.

9. Check Out Low-Cost Airlines. Southwest Airlines has revolutionized the U.S. travel landscape with its no-frills, reasonably priced product. No preassigned seating, no first-class cabin, seats tightly spaced, and a bag of peanuts—that's as good as it gets. If you prefer the frills, always check the prices of major carriers—they may match Southwest's prices in competing markets.

When flying Southwest, check in early to assure a low check-in number for early boarding if you don't want a middle seat. And, again, don't forget to bring your own food.

Other low-cost carriers have also emerged that offer some frills, including America West, JetBlue, America Trans Air (ATA), AirTran, Spirit, and Frontier. JetBlue, in particular, has emerged as a formidable competitor to Southwest, offering satellite television at every (leather) seat and assigned seating—at low prices. However, low-cost airlines do not offer elite status in their frequent flyer programs, and most do not offer first- or business-class cabins. America West is the closest U.S. carrier to being both a major airline and low-cost operator. It offers assigned seating, a first-class cabin, a traditional frequent flyer program, acclaimed elite status benefits, partners that will get you to Hawaii and abroad, and low fares!

10. Use Mileage-Earning Credit and Charge Cards. Every serious road warrior and world traveler will carry at least one mileage-earning affinity card. Best friend of the savvy world traveler is the Diners Card, indisputably the ultimate charge card for leisure and business travelers who spend at least $5,000 per year on travel purchases. The annual cost is just $95, but the service vastly exceeds that of the prestigious American Express Platinum card, which costs $395 per year. All airlines, hotels, and car rental companies accept the card, and you have sixty days to pay off the balance. The Diners Club card is the only one to offer travelers primary collision car rental coverage, meaning that Diners Club will pay every cent of damage incurred in an accident. As with regular American Express cards, miles are accumulated in your Diners account at a rate of one mile per dollar spent. However, unlike accumulated American Express miles, Diners miles are transferable to almost every airline you can think of! And Diners Club regularly has promotions that significantly boost the value of your transferred miles. Request your Diners Club card by calling 800-2DINERS or visiting *Diners.com*.

Our second favorite affinity card is the American Express Starwood credit card (free first year and $35 per annum thereafter). The card is widely accepted. Accumulated points may be redeemed for free stays at Starwood's various hotel brands or transferred into virtually all major airlines' frequent flyer programs. An ideal strategy for the road warrior may be to use Diners card for all business travel expenses, and the Starwood American Express card for all personal charges.

So there you have it. The bottom line is: You need to take action. The most important point we hope you have learned from this book is that you don't have to work all your life to travel in luxury. Because the more you travel, the better you will become at experiencing the worldly things we have. These are all skills that feed on themselves.

Don't wait. If you start using these strategies, you have the power to achieve your travel goals and dreams. You can go anywhere your heart desires or your business takes you. In style. Bon Voyage.

APPENDIX A

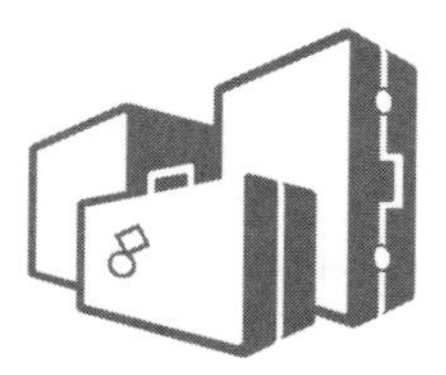

Major U.S. Airlines

Airline	Web Site	Reservation Phone #	Frequent Flyer Plan Name & Phone #
Alaska Airlines	www.alaskaair.com	800-426-0333	Mileage Plan 800-654-5669
Aloha Airlines	www.alohaair.com	800-367-5250	Aloha Pass 808-486-7277
American Airlines	www.aa.com	800-433-7300	AAdvantage 800-882-8880
Continental Airlines	www.continental.com	800-525-0280	One Pass 800-621-7467
Delta	www.delta.com	800-221-1212	Sky Miles 800-323-2323
Hawaiian Airlines	www.hawaiianair.com	800-367-5320	Hawaiian Miles 877-426-4537
Midwest	www.midwestexpress.com	800-452-2022	Midwest Miles (No direct phone number. Select as an option from main phone number.)
Northwest Airlines	www.nwa.com	800-225-2525	World Perks 800-447-3757
United Airlines	www.united.com	800-241-6522	Mileage Plus 800-421-4655
US Airways	www.usairways.com	800-428-4322	Dividend Miles (Select as an option from main phone number.)

APPENDIX B

International Airlines and Their Frequent Flyer Programs

Airline	Web Site	Reservation Phone #	Frequent Flyer Plan Name & Phone #
Aer Lingus	www.aerlingus.com	800-474-7424	Travel Award Bonus*
Aeroflot	www.aeroflot.com	888-340-6400	Aeroflot Bonus Program +7-095-723-82-60
Aeromexico	www.aeromexico.com	800-247-3737	Club Premier 800-711-2271
Air Canada	www.aircanada.com	888-247-2262	Aeroplan 800-361-5373
Air France	www.airfrance.com	800-237-2747	Frequence Plus 800-232-2557
Air Jamaica	www.airjamaica.com	800-523-5585	7th Heaven*
Air New Zealand	www.airnz.com	800-262-1234	Airpoints*
Alitalia	www.alitalia.com	800-223-5730	Mille Miglia*
Aloha Airlines	www.alohaairlines.com	800-367-5250	Aloha Pass 800-367-5250
ANA (All Nippon)	www.ana.co.jp	800-235-9262	ANA Mileage Club*
British Airways	www.british-airways.com	800-247-9297	Executive Club 800-955-2748
British Midland	www.flybmi.com	800-788-0555	Diamond Club*
Cathay Pacific	www.cathayusa.com	800-233-2742	AAdvantage (American Airlines) 800-882-8880

China Airlines	www.china-airlines.com	800-227-5118	Dynasty Program*
El Al Israel Airlines	www.elal.com	800-223-6700	Matmid 212-852-0604
Finnair	www.finnair.com	800-950-5000 800-950-4768	Finnair Plus 800-950-3387
Garuda Indonesia	www.garudausa.com	800-3-GARUDA (42-7832)	*
Icelandair	www.icelandair.com	800-223-5500	Iceland Frequent Flyer Club*
Japan Airlines (JAL)	www.jal.co.jp (Click on "English" in the left corner.)	800-525-3663	Mileage Bank 800-JAL-MILE (525-6453)
Malaysia Airlines	www.malaysia-airlines.com/enrich	800-552-9264	Enrich www.malaysiaairlines.com/enrich
KLM (Royal Dutch Airlines)	www.klm.nl	800-374-7747	Flying Dutchman 31-20-430-93-20
Korean Air	www.koreanair.com	800-438-5000	Sky Pass 800-525-4480
Lufthansa	www.lufthansa.com	800-645-3880	Miles and More*
Mexicana	www.mexicana.com	800-531-7921	Frecuenta 800-531-7901
Olympic	www.olympic-airways.gr	800-223-1226	Icarus*
Qantas	www.qantas.com	800-227-4500	Qantas Frequent Flyer 800-227-4220
SAS	www.sas.se	800-221-2350	Euro Bonus 800-437-5807
Singapore	www.singaporeair.com	800-742-3333	Kris Flyer*
South African Airways	www.flysaa.com	800-722-9645	Voyager*
Thai Airways International	www.thaiair.com	800-426-5204	Royal Orchid Plus*
Turkish Airlines	www.turkishairlines.com	800-974-8875	Miles and Miles*
Varig	www.varig.com	800-468-2744	Smiles*
Virgin Atlantic	www.virgin-atlantic.com	800-862-8621	Freeway 800-365-9500

*No program/not available to U.S. residents.

APPENDIX C

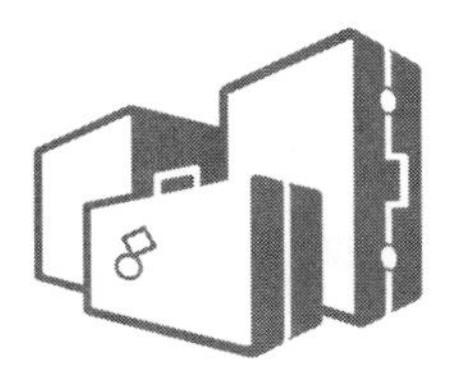

North America Low-Cost Airlines

Airline	Web Site	Reservation Phone #	Frequent Flyer Plan Name & Phone #
AirTran	www.airtran.com	800-247-8726	A Plus Rewards 888-327-5878
America West	www.americawest.com	800-235-9292	Flight Funds 800-247-5691
ATA (America Trans Air)	www.ata.com	800-435-9282	ATA Travel Awards
Frontier Airlines	www.flyfrontier.com www.frontierairlines.com	800-432-1359	Early Returns 866-263-2759
JetBlue Airlines	www.jetblue.com	800-538-2583	True Blue 800-538-2583, ext. True
Song (Delta's Low-Cost Airline)	www.flysong.com	800-FLY-SONG	800-323-2323 (Delta's Sky Miles)
Southwest Airlines	www.southwest.com	800-435-9792	Rapid Rewards 800-445-5764
Spirit	www.spiritair.com	800-772-7117	None
Sun Country Airlines	www.suncountry.com	800-Fly 'N' Sun (800-359-6786)	None
Tango (Canada)	www.flytango.com/en/index	800-315-1390	800-361-5373 (Air Canada's Aeroplan)
Ted (United's Low-Cost Airline)	www.flyted.com	800-241-6522	800-421-4655 (United's Mileage Plus)
Zip (Canada)	www.4321zip.com/en/	866-432-1947	800-361-5373 (Air Canada's Aeroplan)

APPENDIX D

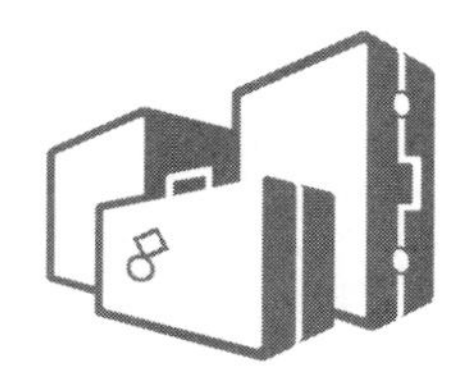

European Low-Cost Airlines

Airline	Web Site	Reservation Phone #
Basiq Air	www.basiqair.com	31-20-406-0-406
Bmibaby (value affiliate for major airline British Midland)	www.bmibaby.com	44-870-264-2299
EasyJet	www.easyjet.com	44-870-600-0000
Ryanair	www.ryanair.com	353-1-609-7800
Spanair	www.spanair.com/es/	888-545-5757
Virgin Express	www.virginexpress.com	32-2-752-0505

APPENDIX E

Hotel Chains

1. **Accor**—Sofitel, Novotel, Motel 6, Red Roof, Formula 1, Ibis
2. **Best Western**—Best Western
3. **Carlson**—Country Inns, Park Plaza and Park Inns, Radisson Hotels, Regent International
4. **Cendant**—Days Inn, Ramada, Knights Inn, AmeriHost, Howard Johnson, Super 8, Travelodge
5. **Choice**—Comfort Inns, Comfort Suites, Econo Lodge, Quality Inns, Clarion, Rodeway, Sleep Inn, Mainstay Suites
6. **Hilton**—Hilton, Embassy Suites, Doubletree, Hampton Inn, Conrad, Homewood Suites, Hilton Garden Inn, Hilton Grand Vacations Club, Homewood Suites by Hilton, Scandic Hotels
7. **Hyatt**—Grand Hyatt, Hyatt Regency, Park Hyatt. (Earn Hyatt Gold Passport points for stays at Hawthorne Suites)
8. **Marriott International**—Marriott Hotels, Renaissance, Ritz Carlton, Residence Inn, Courtyard by Marriott, Fairfield Inn, TownePlace Suites, SpringHill Suites
9. **Radisson**—Radisson, Park Plaza, Park Inn, Country Inns and Suites
10. **Six Continents**—Holiday Inn, Holiday Inn Select, Crowne Plaza, Inter-Continental, Staybridge Suites
11. **Starwood**—Sheraton, Westin, W Hotels, St. Regis, Luxury Collection, Four Points by Sheraton

APPENDIX F

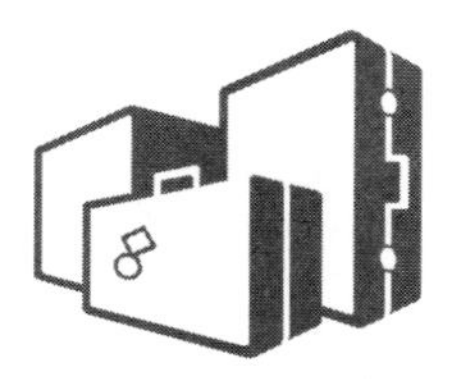

Hotels

Hotel	Web Site	Reservation Phone #	Frequent Stay Plan Name & Phone #
Fairmont	www.fairmont.com	800-527-4727	President's Club 800-553-3658
Four Seasons	www.fourseasons.com	800-332-3442	No Program
Hilton	www.hilton.com	800-HILTONS (445-8667)	Hilton HHonors 972-788-0878
Hyatt	www.hyatt.com	800-233-1234	Gold Passport 800-544-9288
Intercontinental	www.ichotels.com	800-327-0200	Priority Club 888-211-9874
Loews Hotels	www.loewshotels.com	800-LOEWS-11 (56397)	Loews First 800-563-9712
Marriott	www.marriott.com	800-228-9290	Marriott Rewards 800-249-0800
Omni Hotels	www.omnihotels.com	800-THE-OMNI (843-6664)	1-800-FOR-OMNI (367-6664)
Radisson	www.radisson.com	800-333-3333	Gold Points Rewards 800-508-9000
Ritz Carlton	www.ritzcarlton.com	800-241-3333	No Program
Starwood Hotels	www.starwood.com	888-625-5144	Starwood Preferred Guest 888-625-4988
Wyndham	www.wyndham.com	800-996-3426	Wyndham by Request 888-994-2227 (Wyndham does not offer points toward free stays, but does offer special amenities to members during their stay)

APPENDIX G

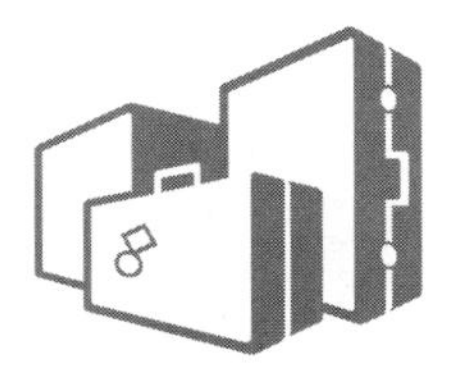

Hotel Consolidators

Company	Web Site	Phone #	Destinations
1800usahotels.com	www.1800usahotels.com	800-872-4683	United States
Express Hotel Reservations	www.express-res.com	800-356-1123	Select U.S cities
Hotel Conxions	www.hotelconxions.com	800-522-9991	United States and London, England
Hotel Locators	www.hotellocators.com	800-423-7846	Worldwide
Hotel Locators.com	www.hotellocators.com	800-576-0003	United States
Hotels Online.com	www.hotelsonline.com	800-383-2270	Worldwide
Hotel Reservations Services	www.hotelquest.com	925-473-2230	Worldwide
Hotres.com	www.hotres.com	N/A (Only contact is online)	United States
Hot Rooms	www.hotrooms.com	800-Hotel-00 (468-3500)	Chicago
Hotels.com	www.hotels.com	800-2-HOTELS (468357)	Worldwide
Quikbook	www.quikbook.com	800-221-3531	Worldwide
Reservations Service	www.reservation-services.com	800-950-0232	Select U.S cities
Resort Reservations Network	www.rezrez.com	604-904-9300	North America
San Francisco Reservations	www.hotelres.com	800-677-1550	San Francisco and Bay Area
Travel Accommodations	www.hotel-accommodations.com	888-254-0637	Worldwide
Washington, D.C. Accommodations	www.wdcahotels.com	800-554-2220	Washington, D.C.
Worldres.com	www.worldres.com	650-372-1700	Worldwide

APPENDIX H

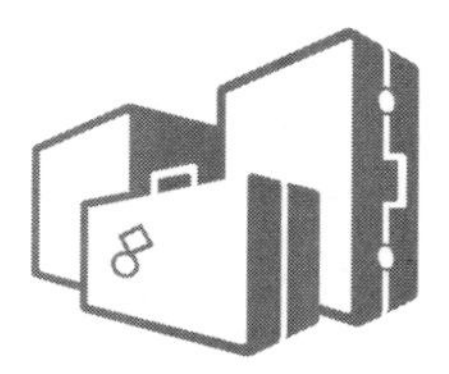

Car Rental Agencies

Rental Company	Area	Phone #	Web Site
Alamo	Domestic	800-GO-ALAMO (462-5266)	www.goalamo.com
	International	800-522-9696	www.freeways.com
Auto Europe	Europe	888-223-5555	www.autoeurope.com
Avis	Domestic	800-331-1212	www.avis.com
	Canada	800-879-2847	
	International	800-331-1084	
Budget	Domestic	800-527-0700	www.budgetrentacar.com
	International	800-472-3325	
Dollar	Domestic	800-800-4000	www.dollarcar.com
	International	800-800-6000	
Enterprise	Worldwide	800-325-8007	www.enterprise.com
Europebycar	Europe	800-223-1516	www.europebycar.com
Hertz	Domestic	800-654-3131	www.hertz.com
	Canada	800-263-0600	
	International	800-654-3001	
Kemwel	Europe	800-678-0678 877-820-0668	www.kemwel.com
National	Domestic	800-328-4567	www.nationalcar.com/index.html
	International	800-227-3876	
Thrifty	Worldwide	800-367-2277 800-847-4389	www.thrifty.com

APPENDIX I

Credit Cards

Airline Credit Cards

For Web sites, go to search engine and type in an airline name, and then "credit card apply online."

Airline	Bank	Phone #
Alaska	Bank of America	888-345-2632
America West	Bank of America	800-928-2933
American	Citibank	800-359-4444
British Airways	First USA	866-255-3428
Continental	Chase	800-261-4667
Delta Sky Miles	American Express	800-SKYMILES (759-64537)
Midwest	Juniper	866-693-6453
Northwest	US Bank	800-360-2900
Southwest	First USA	800-SWA-VISA (792-8472)
United	First USA	888-536-6202
US Airways	Bank of America	800-335-4337

Hotel Credit Cards

For Web sites, go to search engine and type in "hotel" and "credit card apply online."

Hotel	Bank	Phone #
Hilton HHONORS	American Express	877-621-2639
Hilton HHONORS (Visa card)	Citibank	800-252-3776
Marriott	Bank One	800-776-5214
Intercontinenal/Crown Plaza/ Holiday Inn (Priority One)	Bank One	800-234-9063
Starwood	American Express	877-621-2639

Specialty Credit Cards

For Web sites, go to search engine and type in the bank name and "card apply online."

Bank	Phone #
American Express	877-621-2639
American Express Business	800-SUCCESS (782-2377)
Diners	888-92DINERS (346377)

Index